Sally
Graham

Gidon Lippman is head of the Fashion Department at Harrow School of Art and formerly lectured at the Royal College of Art.

Dorothy Erskine lectures at Harrow School of Art and has worked extensively in fashion journalism in London and South Africa.

Both authors have had wide experience as designers in the fashion industry.

FASHION DRAWINGS:
Alan Couldridge

TECHNICAL DIAGRAMS:
Linda Jones

GIDON LIPPMAN
DOROTHY ERSKINE

Sew It Yourself

HOW TO MAKE YOUR OWN FASHION CLASSICS

A SPECTRUM BOOK

PRENTICE-HALL, INC., Englewood Cliffs, New Jersey 07632

Library of Congress Cataloging in Publication Data

Lippman, Gidon.
    SEW IT YOURSELF.

    (A Spectrum Book)
    Edition of 1974 published under title: Dressmaking
made simple.
    Includes index.
    1. Dressmaking. 2. Sewing. I. Erskine, Dorothy.
II. Title.
TT515.L49 1977   646.4'3'04   76–26931
ISBN 0-13-807305-8
ISBN 0-13-807297-3 pbk.

10 9 8 7 6 5 4 3 2 1

PRENTICE-HALL INTERNATIONAL, INC., London
PRENTICE-HALL OF AUSTRALIA PTY., LTD., Sydney
PRENTICE-HALL OF CANADA, LTD., Toronto
PRENTICE-HALL OF INDIA PRIVATE, LIMITED, New Delhi
PRENTICE-HALL OF JAPAN, INC., Tokyo
PRENTICE-HALL OF SOUTHEAST ASIA PTE., LTD., Singapore
WHITEHALL BOOKS LIMITED, Wellington, New Zealand

Foreword

There is today an enormous interest in making things: using one's hands, reverting to artisanship. Proof of this is apparent in the variety of do-it-yourself books and magazines now available.

However, for the serious student of professional clothes construction it is rare to find authoritative and up-to-date books that will guide one through every aspect of producing well-cut, well-made professional garments. Whether you are a young student studying to make fashion your career or simply wish to make your own clothes for economic reasons, I am certain that this book will guide and prepare you in a very sound and logical way.

The authors have had enormous experience, both in the fashion industry and in the teaching of students destined to become names in that industry. For these reasons it will be clear that this book is one in which you can have complete confidence. But it is your diligence to practice what the book preaches that will make your efforts successful, *your* sustained interest and perseverance. As with all skills, constant practice will make perfect, whether learning to play a musical instrument or making a piece of furniture—so it is with producing clothes.

The information and knowledge that abound in this book cover an enormous range, even to the choice of fabrics and indeed the relative behavior of fibers, both manufactured and natural.

Recent decades have brought forth rapid and constant change within the fashion industry in design and technique. Despite the use of highly sophisticated machinery, basic principles remain and are usually elegantly simple. Once learned, they enable one to proceed with inventiveness and freedom. Indeed, these words are synonymous with good fashion, as are innovation and individuality. This book will provide those basic principles and will admirably serve students beginning training as designers or technicians, as well as those simply wishing to perfect their methods of producing well-made clothes for themselves.

JOANNE BROGDEN

Professor of Fashion
Royal College of Art

Preface

In a world of mass production, making your own clothes, if you have the knowledge and skill, is immensely enjoyable and rewarding.

The beginner all too often becomes frustrated, because of the temptation to be overambitious as, for instance, choosing a fabric that is difficult to handle or a too intricate or complicated pattern. This book shows how to sew the *simple* way.

Introduction. A planned, progressive sequence in the choice of design, pattern, and material.

Making Six Simple Garments. Explains how to put together six basic garments, using simple techniques.

Further and Advanced Techniques. Contains the additional and the more advanced techniques for anyone wishing to extend their expertise and knowledge of the subject.

Included in the book is a comprehensive Glossary of dressmaking and fashion terms, fabric descriptions, and textile terms, which could provide a ready source of reference and interest. Measurements in this book are first given in metric units, followed by the traditional equivalents in parentheses.

It is a book suitable for all beginners. The general reader either attending recreational classes or working alone will find that it is a helpful introduction and that it adds to the pleasure and satisfaction of producing her own work. Students will find it particularly valuable, since it maintains a balance between theory and practice. Lecturers in schools and colleges will also find it a useful book for teaching and demonstration purposes.

The numerous diagrams, charts, illustrations, and stage-by-stage instructions will achieve results in a relatively short time. This is important, since if garments are to be crisp, new, and professional, the work must be carried out without excessive handling and worrying over. We believe that dressmaking is part of fashion and that with experience the craft of construction can ultimately be combined with the art and design of human decoration. One is complementary to the other.

We offer a word of advice to anyone setting out on this venture. Making it simple is the essence of success. Confine yourself to using fabrics that handle easily (as suggested in Chapter Three) and begin with our basic garments. Moreover, in order to accumulate experience, try "variations on a theme"—that is, use the same basic shape and construction of a garment a few times and make the changes with different design details or decorations, selecting similar fabrics that have a common "feel." This experience will be invaluable in providing a sound background to the subject and so make progress to more difficult garments less discouraging.

However varied the reasons for dressmaking may be, we hope this book will fulfill its aim by making a contribution to the enjoyment of life for many people.

We offer our sincere appreciation and grateful thanks to our editor, Margaret Anderson, for her invaluable help in the presentation of this book (British edition). We are also indebted to our reader, Mr. F. Stillman, CMG (Hons.), ACI, CTI, ASIA, Chief Examiner, City and Guilds of London Institute, for useful comments and advice. Our thanks are due to Fritz Gegauf, Ltd., manufacturers of the Bernina sewing machine, for their cooperation and assistance. Special thanks go to Pat O'Gorman for giving so much of her time in typing the manuscript.

GIDON LIPPMAN
DOROTHY ERSKINE

Contents

INTRODUCTION

Choosing the Design

INTRODUCTION TO DESIGN

There are progressive sequences in making clothes. Before you start work the choice of design, pattern, material, and their suitability to your figure, coloring, and purpose must be considered. The first step is to choose the design.

The Importance of Design

People wear clothes for a variety of reasons: naturally for protection and warmth, but personal satisfaction is always important, as is the need for group identification and admiration. The season and time of day makes a difference; and work, social activities, and leisure are all vital factors in the way people want to dress.

Women today have far more freedom in the way they dress, since the old dogmas about which design suited a certain shape have been abolished and rules on where, when, and how to wear stripes, checks, horizontal, diagonal, or vertical lines have become outmoded. The result is that more time and effort must be spent on actually choosing a design. Great care is necessary before making the final decision and adequate attention must be paid to all details. This is especially true when people are making their own garments, since they do not, of course, have the finished product in front of them. Though the rigid rules have disappeared, the sheer number of possible choices can be overwhelming. With a few guiding principles to help you make the right personal choice, you will avoid the more obvious pitfalls.

COLOR AND FABRIC

When choosing clothes, everyone is attracted to certain elements of a dress design, the term used to describe the numerous ingredients of a total look. The use of color; the type and quality of fabric, its texture and pattern; and the shape, cut, and fit of a garment are all part of the creative art of dressmaking and contribute to the final result. However, in the process of clothes selection, the first decisive factors are usually the choice of color and fabric. We find both exciting and often cannot resist purchasing materials for the enjoyment of handling and feeling them. We love colors and think about the potentially beautiful effect they will create in the finished garment—consequently, fabrics are frequently hoarded! A drawer full of dress lengths that have never been used for the purpose they were intended, is all too familiar.

The authors hope that the following pages will go some way toward solving that problem. In this book we offer suggestions on what type of fabric to choose and guidance on how to cut and make up these fabrics.

Color Defined

Color is defined as the sensation produced by rays of light on the eye. A particular color is determined by the frequency of the light. Artists divide colors into (1) primary (blue, red, yellow) and (2) secondary, a mixture of two primary colors—for example, blue and yellow mixed make green. Colors with tones close to each other are harmonious, or contrasting if the tones are apart. There are warm and cold colors. Used separately, or with other colors, they have a vital influence on the effect of a garment design—color impact can be powerful and is often striking when differences combine. There are, of course, fashions in colors and colors, or a combination of them, at times thought of as peculiar (such as black in summer) or even vulgar (orange with red) are at other times considered visually pleasing and desirable.

Changes in attitudes toward our surroundings are the result of many events and influences in our society, which is much the better for them. Our lives are enriched by variety, which stimulates and excites our critical faculties.

The Feel for Fabrics

Modern textile technology supplies a multitude of manufactured fibers, for fabrics with great versatility, side by side with those made from natural fibers. "Easy-care" clothes are undoubtedly an asset. But because the range of manufactured fibers is now so vast that only the experts know with a degree of accuracy the exact composition of fiber content in any given simulated fabric, no attempt is made here to describe or discuss the intricacies of textile technology (but see pages 55–56 for more information).

We need to know certain things about fabrics which affect the making of garments. Will a particular material lend itself to soft folds? Will it hang well? Can it be cut on the cross-grain? Will it pleat? Will it stretch, or can it be washed? In short, the behavior of the fabric determines the choice of a design, for each fabric has certain characteristics, constructed by the technologist to provide a determined performance. It is most important that the nature of the material is fully understood, so as to exploit it to the fullest advantage.

To understand the nature of fabrics and their characteristics, and to learn what they are best suited for, refer to Chapter Fifteen, which describes a wide range of fabrics and their performances. We confine ourselves to suggesting only a few fabrics, for the first attempts at dressmaking, in Chapter Three.

Selection from both the wide spectrum of colors and the extensive range of present-day textiles available depends in the first instance, on individual preferences and taste. Everyone has a favorite color and likes to wear it, taking into account and complementing such things as hair and skin coloring—people also have favorite fabrics. Since the choice is wide, why not put it to good advantage by using imagination and enjoy a little experimentation?

Window Shopping

Inspiration for these new ideas can come from various sources and window shopping, when opportunity allows, is one of them. Iris Ashley, journalist and an authority on fashion, once described window displays as the *dreams of fashion*. See these displays as often as possible, since fashion colors and fabrics on their own, in the garments displayed in windows, or inside shops and stores, will tell a story. Colors, textures, and types of fabric will stand out as being seasonal and will be identical on most fabric counters and in many ready-to-wear clothes. Newspapers and their supplements, magazines, and advertisements are other sources for ideas. All these sources complement each other and form part of a coordinated fashion picture.

PLANNING AHEAD

Facing the challenge of dressmaking will seem less of an ordeal if the importance of planning ahead is not underestimated—indeed it cannot be stressed often enough. But, then, the act of planning is itself an inherent part of the pleasure of making clothes.

Let us try to understand what initial planning involves and how to solve some of the problems that will be encountered.

Admittedly with the change of fashion development during the past years—from a situation where a mere handful of designers dictated which fashion was "in" from season to season, to the time where the guidelines and directions come from so many more origins—choice and selection of fabrics and designs may well appear to be more confusing. International influences, changing at an ever-growing rate, can easily present perplexing advice.

Before making any firm decisions on design selections, the following hints will be of value.

The Scrap Bag

Collect fabric cuttings/samples, the larger the better, from any and every available source; keep them in a "scrap bag" and have easy access to it. These samples will initially assist you in gaining knowledge and understanding of the various types of fabrics. The "feel" of any fabric suggests its probable behavior in wear, its comfort and performance.

Note the construction of fabrics by carrying out the following tests. Try to detect if material is woven, knitted, or of bonded type. Feel the weight and compare one with another and get to know the differences between them—ignoring specific fiber contents, does it feel like cotton, linen, silk, or wool, irrespective of it being natural or manufactured. Hold a cutting in your hand, crush it, open your hand, see if it creases and, if so, does it recover? Does it feel soft or hard? Try to stretch it. Pull it and see if there is much, little, or no give at all. These tests will help to develop your knowledge of fabric behavior. Study cuttings for texture and pattern; if the sample is large enough you will be able to see the repeat of a printed, woven, or knitted design (large repeat patterns in any shape or form affect cutting at a later stage).

Observe colors. Take cuttings and "play" with them for color combinations. Move your cuttings around and mix colors—see which blend and which contrast. This will sharpen your color sense invaluably.

The Scrapbook

Cut out photographs and drawings of interesting designs from newspapers and magazines and build up a small library, perhaps in the form of a scrapbook or notebook. See how parts of garments can be interchanged—for example, put the top of one with the skirt of another. The results of these simple tests will help you in learning how to select the most suitable fabric for any chosen design. This will increase your excitement, the urge to pick up scissors and needle will become stronger, and you will approach sewing with greater confidence. Remember to build up to it gradually and, above all, remember that the essence of good design is simplicity. Resist the temptation to use decorations excessively; if in doubt leave off rather than pile on.

You will soon understand current fashion and learn to discriminate and to combine it with your individual preferences. The ultimate choice need not be either way-out fashion, difficult to carry off for all but a few, or a style devoid of any fashion influences, which turns enjoyable clothes into dull clothing. How much better that the choice of garments should be based on an attitude of mind and not purely on fixed ideas about age or status.

Working Facilities

Finally, give some thought to working facilities. For those people fortunate enough to have a separate workroom at their disposal, dressmaking may seem more pleasant and progress faster. However, the absence of a separate room does not mean that you cannot manage. A hard-top table is most important for cutting out and, if at all possible, arrange to have this and all other tools and equipment in one area. Place the sewing machine close to the ironing board and iron (you should always press as you go). Moving some distance from one to the other is tiring and time consuming.

Keep all tools in a workbox for easy access. Prevent the mislaying of vital sewing aids by keeping a tape measure around your neck and a pin cushion on your wrist.

Most important of all, ensure that the lighting is good. Bad or insufficient light can be disastrous and you will tire very quickly from eyestrain. This will lead to a host of mistakes and constant ripping out is not only a bore, but makes for overhandling of garments which then look tatty and far less successful.

Last but not least, the working area must be clean, for some stains are stubborn and may withstand all removal efforts.

CHANGING FASHIONS

The basic fact about clothes is that arms go in sleeves, coats fasten, skirts start at the waist (wherever they may end), and dresses cover the body from shoulder to hem. Designers can indulge in the wildest flights of fancy, or dip into past decades for inspiration, but one thing remains constant—clothes are still cut out and constructed more or less as they have been for centuries. After the toga, worn alike by Roman men and women, the development of shape in clothes led to cutting, fitting, and sewing together the different parts.

So today, coats, jackets and dresses sit on the shoulders, with balance, and fit from shoulder and bust. All are shaped and joined with darts and seams. Similar rules apply to skirts—whether flared, pleated, straight, long, or short, they must fit around the waist area. Trouser legs vary greatly with the prevailing fashion mood, but they still have to fit well over the seat and sit well at the waist.

Even the most far-out shapes in fashion have a basic method of construction, which is totally unaffected by apparent style changes. Look closely and you will observe that fashion does not change quite so rapidly as reports seem to show. Careful analysis reveals that trends can appear many years before they are taken up on a wholesale basis. Often the timing is wrong and the public eye misses the message. An avant-garde French designer produced a range of thirties- and forties-styled coats a good ten years before they hit the wider fashion scene. The

A   B   C

Fig. 1.   Blazer (a), tailored jacket (b), and cardigan-style jacket (c).

A   B

Fig. 2.   *Shirtwaist dress (a) and belted topcoat (b).*

Fig. 3   Polo-neck sweater (a), V-neck sweater (b), and cardigan (c).

A

B

Fig. 4   *Burberry-style trenchcoats.*

A   B   C

Fig. 5   Circular skirt (a), pleated skirt (b), and culottes (c).

Fig. 6. *Pajama-style evening pants* (a), *tailored slacks* (b), *and jeans* (c).

change is always more gradual than it appears. The function of clothes, as well as the method of putting them together, however, does not change. It is the shape and outline that alter according to the fashion mood of the time.

CLASSICS

Keeping function and method in mind, one is led naturally to the classics. The very word indicates a clean, smooth, undated line and comprises a set of basic designs which can vary their shape enough to fit in with the current fashion look.

The twentieth century has produced some remarkable classics, from ideas that date from way back, were later refined, and have been worn continuously, in some form or other, for the past sixty years.

The shirtwaist dress, the Burberry style trenchcoat, slacks, tailored suits, skirts and sweaters had been seen earlier, but were accepted generally during World War I. Necessity and practicability were two excellent reasons for this acceptance.

Next, leading French designers promoted them as resort wear for the rich in the postwar years. Finally, when the skirts narrowed and shortened and the lines were simplified to a new elegance, they filtered through to the general public. (It is interesting to note that two or three great film stars of the thirties who are still very much with us, classics themselves, were famous for their raincoats, slacks, and the generally sporty image that evolved with them.)

The classics were given a "utility" look for World War II, when the fashion was for shorter, squarer, and more military-looking clothes. Fuller and longer once again, they survived through the wilder excesses of the "New Look" in the late forties and early fifties.

The shirtwaist, in fact, made up in the most luxurious fabrics, gave a new dimension to these classic ideas. It is still here today as living proof that good design fits in with any period and is totally adaptable to any situation.

SUITABILITY TO FIGURE

Are you short, tall, fat, thin, average, square-shouldered, round-shouldered, bulging, or drooping? Do you know what shape you are? Eating and standing the right way help greatly to improve your figure, but figures do vary individually. An accurate record of measurements and an honest appraisal in the mirror can help you assess your figure type. So can a candid photograph!

Choosing a design suitable for you or for someone else can be a

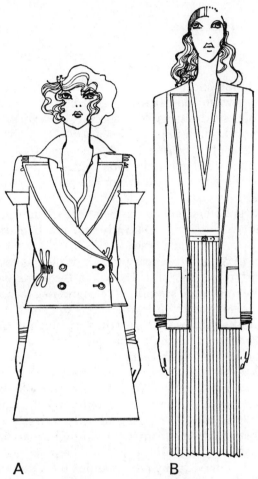

A   B

Fig. 7.   Bad designs for a short figure (a) and a tall figure (b).

stimulating exercise. As suggested earlier in this chapter, give a little thought to the current shapes of clothes, fashion lines, color, and fabrics, and learn to know which are most flattering to your particular figure. Keep in mind the following simple points. Generally speaking, vertical shapes, but not necessarily design lines, make you look taller, whereas horizontal lines make you look broader. Straight lines are harder but they can be strong design lines, although a curved line is more graceful.

A waist-length jacket looks younger than a hip-length one, but can you afford to be horizontally sliced across the middle? You can keep the short look by simply dropping the jacket length a matter of 5–8 cm (2–3 in). It can be fitted or straight, depending on the current fashion, but

A   B

Fig. 8.   Lines from Fig. 7 reversed.

remember that the longer the jacket the heavier it looks, especially at the lower hip length. Necklines, sleeve lines, waistlines, and hemlines all act as dividers. Remember that the length of these can usually be varied enough to suit you without altering the basic fashion line of the design.

Skirts slightly flared toward the hem are good for all shapes, but especially for those with heavier hips. Pleated skirts are always attractive, but for large sizes pleats should be stitched at hip level, or sewn in groups of two or three. Straight skirts are not as apt to flatter, unless the wearer is slim and the skirt length a good balance for the person's height. Gathered skirts are a downright danger on anyone with an average-plus waistline and plus hips! Circular skirts also tend to increase the appearance of the hip size, but are flattering when the fullness starts at or just below hip level.

Keep dramatic collars for dramatic occasions. If you like the idea of a cape effect, try it out first to see if you look like a mushroom as opposed to a model.

The burning question of length will always be with us. Let common sense rule here. Only the ancient Egyptians solved this one—they hardly changed the length or style of their garments for 3000 years, which could indicate a stable and happy people. Find the length that suits you best and, in spite of fashion changes, vary it no more than 2.5 cm (1 in) up or down. You may end up with your own classic.

2
Taking Measurements

METRIC AND TRADITIONAL MEASUREMENTS

The units of traditional measurement are the inch and the yard. The units of metric measurement are:

Millimeter (mm.)
Centimeter (cm.) = 10 millimeters
Meter (m.) = 100 centimeters

The following is a conversion and comparison chart, with metric measurements rounded up to the nearest 0.5 cm (a metric conversion chart for fabric buying is given on page 308).

INCHES TO NEAREST CENTIMETERS

Inch	Cm	Inch	Cm
⅛	0.3	19	48.5
¼	0.6	20	51.0
⅜	1.0	21	53.5
½	1.3	22	56.0
⅝	1.5	23	58.5
¾	2.0	24	61.0
⅞	2.2	25	63.5
1	2.5	26	66.0
1¼	3.2	27	68.5
1½	3.8	28	71.0
1¾	4.5	29	73.5
2	5.0	30	76.0
2½	6.5	31	79.0
3	7.5	32	81.5
3½	9.0	33	84.0
4	10.0	34	86.5
4½	11.5	35	89.0
5	12.5	36	91.5
5½	14.0	37	94.0
6	15.0	38	96.5
7	18.0	39	109.0
8	20.5	40	101.5
9	23.0	41	104.0
10	25.5	42	106.5
11	28.0	43	109.0
12	30.5	44	112.0
13	33.0	45	114.5
14	35.5	46	117.0
15	38.0	47	119.5
16	40.5	48	122.0
17	43.0	49	124.5
18	46.0	50	127.0

HOW TO TAKE BODY MEASUREMENTS

When garments do not fit well, the reason is usually that incorrect body measurements have been taken. Well-fitted garments require, initially, the correct use of the tape measure. When taken accurately at the main parts of the body, measurements can easily be compared with the flat pattern, checked, and adjusted if necessary. Commercial patterns are available in a large variety of sizes, to suit most figure types. Therefore, alterations to patterns from your own body measurements should be minimal; this will make fittings later on easier and more successful. In order to avoid discrepancies, be sure to take your measurements with precision. Here is how to do it.

Start by wearing the foundation garments you feel happiest in—the ones that will most likely be worn with the planned garment. Wear them throughout all the fitting stages, because when measuring the body or fitting your clothes, changing from one type of foundation garment to another can lead to enormous differences in measurements. Tie a narrow belt, cord, or string around your waist. This marks the natural position, where it is smallest. Stand in front of a full-length mirror. For full-length dresses or pants wear the type of shoes you normally like best, to give an accurate reading for length.

A plea at this stage: do not use excessive zeal and measure too tightly. It may well be psychologically tempting to do so, but breathing in and holding breath is cheating and ultimately only accentuates any feature meant to be played down. There are better ways of hiding figure faults.

It is also worthwhile to be fully aware of the contours and bone structure of the body and how its limbs work, although a wealth of anatomical knowledge is not essential. By seeing and feeling your body you become aware perhaps as never before, for we take it for granted that limbs articulate in a certain manner. The lower arm bends forward from the elbow, but cannot do the reverse. Legs bend backward from below the kneecap, but not forward. Sitting down is obviously vastly different from standing up.

Clothes must accommodate our requirements for movement and comply with the demands of our physical actions. Garments too tightly fitted may not only look aesthetically wrong but also restrict essential normal movements of the body and feel most uncomfortable. Tight fit, desired by some women, can still be realized if applied in the correct

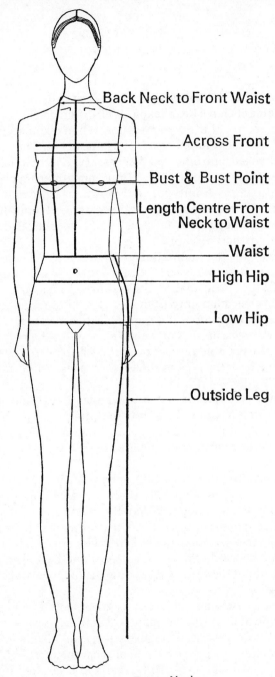

Back Neck to Front Waist

Across Front

Bust & Bust Point

Length Centre Front
Neck to Waist

Waist

High Hip

Low Hip

Outside Leg

Fig. 9. *Front of body.*

form, but the type of fabric to be used must also be taken into account. Where one material gives to pressure of body and limbs, as for example a knitted jersey, others do not. Yet the opposite, not measuring tautly enough, produces equally undesirable results.

Readers may ask if it is necessary to measure all the parts of the body listed on pages 22–26. Indeed, if no help is available from someone else, measuring some of them would prove a very difficult task, but to obtain maximum accuracy it is obvious that assistance is highly desirable. Should this not be possible, measure only those listed in **bold type.** Commercial patterns are often confined to a minimum number of measurements: these are adequate for purchasing your current size, but garments may require more attention at fittings. The additional measurements mentioned, if available (taking some from old garments made of firm, nonstretch material may help), can be checked against patterns. Adjustments can be made, if necessary, before proceeding to cut out the fabric and you are then prepared for fittings with fewer problems to face.

Figures 9–12 illustrate the positioning of the tape measure on and around the front of the body.

Measure the girth on the main parts of the body by holding the tape horizontally, keeping it straight and taut, and measure the following (once your statistics have been taken, keep them in a safe place, preferably in the form of a chart as suggested on page 30):

1. **Bust.** Place the tape over the fullest part of the bust and around the body. Do not let it slip down at the back.
2. **Waist.** A belt, cord, or string, tied around the waist, finds its normal position, where it is smallest. Measure around the waist.
3. **Hips.** Measure:

   a. High hips at 7.5–10 cm (3–4 in) below the waist.
   b. Low hips at 18–20.5 cm (7–8 in) below the waist.
   c. From the hips, and with both feet together, slide the tape over the thighs. When these are prominent, take the measurement at the widest part.

4. **Back waist length** (center back neck to waist). Measure from nape of neck to center back of natural waist.
5. **Front waist length.** Measure:

   a. From nape of neck at center back, pass around the side of neck at shoulder to the most prominent point of the bust.
   b. Over bust to waist. (Note both (a) and (b) measurements.)
   c. Base at front neck (hollow between the collarbones) to center from waist.

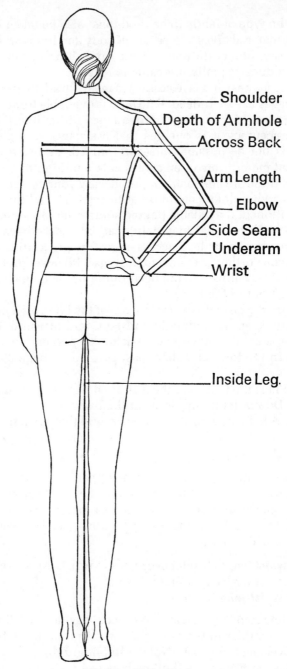

Shoulder
Depth of Armhole
Across Back
Arm Length
Elbow
Side Seam
Underarm
Wrist

Inside Leg.

Fig. 10.   *Back of body.*

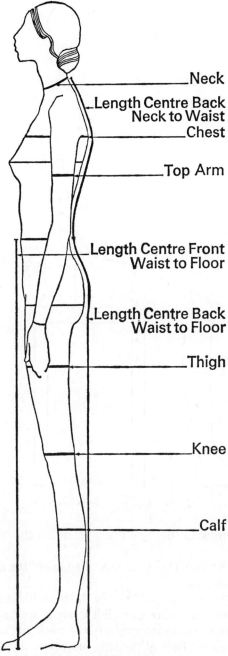

Neck

Length Centre Back
Neck to Waist

Chest

Top Arm

Length Centre Front
Waist to Floor

Length Centre Back
Waist to Floor

Thigh

Knee

Calf

Fig. 11. *Side of body.*

25

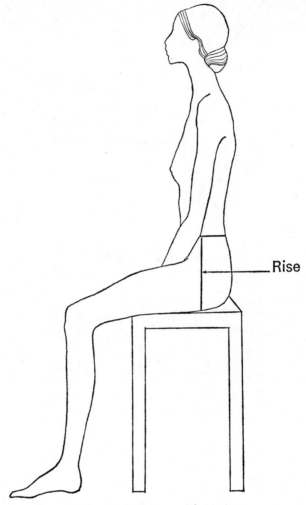

Fig. 12.   *Waist to crotch (rise).*

6. **Chest.** Measure with the tape directly, under the arms, all around the body.
7. **Across front.** At 9 cm (3½ in) below the base of the front neck, from left to right armhole.
8. Across back. At 12.5 cm (5 in) below the prominent bone at the base of the back neck, measure from left to right armhole.
9. **Neck.** Measure the circumference of the neck just above the base.
10. **Shoulder.** From the base at the side of neck to the shoulder bone.
11. **Bodice side seam** (depth of armhole). Measure from about 2.5 cm (1 in) under the armpit to the waist at your side. (The measurement between the top of the side seam at the armpit and the end of the

shoulder seam, at the shoulder bone, equals the depth of the armhole and the height of the sleeve crown.)

12. Full length (waist to floor). Measure:

    a. Front waist to floor.
    b. Side waist to floor.
    c. Center back waist to floor.

13. Arms. Measure:

    a. Fullest part of the **upper arm** in a bent position.
    b. **Around wrist.**
    c. With the arm bent, place the tape at the end of the shoulder at
       the shoulder bone, measure to elbow.
    d. From elbow to wrist, in the direction of the little finger. (Note
       (c) and (d) measurements.)
    e. Underarm length from about 2.5 cm (1 in) below the armpit.

14. Legs (for trousers). Measure:

    a. Around the **thigh.**
    b. Around the **knee.**
    c. Around the **calf.**
    d. The outside leg length.
    e. The **"rise"**—from crotch to waist. Sit on a hard chair or stool,
       measure from the waist at the side of the body to the top of the
       chair seat.
    f. The inside leg length. This can be found by deducting the rise
       from the outside leg measurement.

Add the date and size when known to the above statistics; any future
changes in the shape of your body should be compared with your
previous chart of measurements and recorded. In this way future adjustments to patterns, if changes occur, are easier to make and so are time
saving. Avoid frequent remeasuring of all parts of the body, with the
possibility of different readings—by only remeasuring those parts that
have obviously changed, greater accuracy is assured and success in
perfect fit maintained.

BUYING A PATTERN

Paper patterns are sold by most leading stores and sewing shops.
The pattern catalogues are divided into sections with designs grouped
under various styles of garments and figure types. These *figure types* do

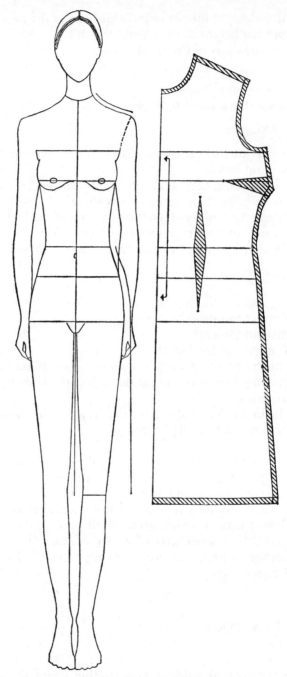

Fig. 13.   Front of body and front pattern.

Fig. 14. Back of body and back pattern.

MEASUREMENT CHART

	Cm	/	In
1. **Bust**	_____	/	_____
2. **Waist**	_____	/	_____
3. **Hips**			
a. High	_____	/	_____
b. Low	_____	/	_____
c. Prominent	_____	/	_____
4. **Back waist length**	_____	/	_____
5. **Front waist length**			
a. Center back neck to bust point	_____	/	_____
b. Bust to waist	_____	/	_____
c. Base of front neck to center front waist	_____	/	_____
d. Front waist length: (a) and (b) combined	_____	/	_____
6. **Chest**	_____	/	_____
7. **Across front**	_____	/	_____
8. Across back	_____	/	_____
9. **Neck**	_____	/	_____
10. **Shoulder**	_____	/	_____
11. **Bodice side seam**	_____	/	_____
12. Full length (waist to floor)			
a. Front	_____	/	_____
b. Side	_____	/	_____
c. Back	_____	/	_____
13. Arms			
a. **Top**	_____	/	_____
b. **Wrist**	_____	/	_____
c. Outside length to elbow	_____	/	_____
d. Outside length from elbow to wrist	_____	/	_____
e. Underarm length	_____	/	_____
f. Full outside length: (c) and (d) combined	_____	/	_____
14. Legs			
a. **Thigh**	_____	/	_____
b. **Knee**	_____	/	_____
c. **Calf**	_____	/	_____
d. Outside leg length	_____	/	_____
e. **Rise**	_____	/	_____
f. Inside leg length: deduct (e) from (d)	_____	/	_____
Height	_____	/	_____
Size	_____		
Figure Type (see below)	_____		
Date	_____		

not always refer to age groups. For example, although a "junior" belongs to a young girl, it is just as possible for a woman of 40 to have the same measurements and proportions. All the major pattern companies work on similar lines with their catalogues divided into sections depending on garment and figure types. In turn, each of these figure types are made in various sizes and it is most important, once your measurements have been determined, to find your correct size by comparing them with the standard body measurements given. This will eliminate much pattern and garment alteration.

PATTERN MEASUREMENTS

Some confusion may arise as soon as a comparison between your body measurements and the pattern measurements is made. Having bought the "correct" size, it may come as a surprise to find that the pattern exceeds your body measurements, but remember that when you measured your body you made no allowance for body movement, as previously discussed. A given amount of *ease* is incorporated into every pattern and these allowances in measurements, over and above those of the body, vary considerably. As already mentioned, the amount will depend on the type of fabric used and taking its give and stretch into account. For example, about 7.5 cm (3 in) on the bust, 2.5 cm (1 in) at the waist, and 5 cm (2 in) on the hips is allowed on "misses" patterns, with much less allowed for knit fabrics.

Silhouette

At the same time the silhouette of every design determines the extra allowance so that a pattern for a fitted garment has less, a semi-fitted has a little more ease and allowances are further increased for a loose-fitting garment. Because this is calculated for all parts of the garment and worked out proportionately, it is wise when buying the first pattern not to settle for a smaller size than recommended.

Sizing

Major commercial pattern companies have a uniform sizing system (not to be confused with wholesale sizes) and their patterns should not be at odds with each other in matters of size denominations. But, if in doubt, it is safer to opt for a slightly larger pattern rather than one that is too small. Taking in seams at the fitting stage is a good deal easier than letting them out and there is, of course, a limit to how much you can let out seams. In due course your experience will allow for better discrimination between the variety of patterns available and you will settle for the one nearest to your figure.

There is still another aspect of ease which must be understood. While your size based on body measurement is constant for all types of clothes, pattern measurements must increase for every garment worn over another. A jacket, worn over a blouse and skirt, must allow for this. A coat worn over a suit must be large enough to fit over it comfortably. As the layers increase, so does the amount of ease and this in no way detracts from the principle of shape on any type of garment. A coat can be small or large, fitted, fully flared, or boxy in shape or look, but its size denomination remains the same.

Personal Choice

Choose the pattern with the bust size nearest your own for dresses, coats, and blouses—this will give a better fit around the neckline, shoulder, and armhole, the difficult fitting areas. Buy pants and skirt patterns according to waist size and adjust the hip measurement if necessary. If your hip size is much larger in proportion to your waist, then the pattern should be bought to hip size. With combination patterns—coat, top, trousers, and skirt—choose the bust size and adjust the waist and hip if necessary. When measurements fall between two sizes, choose the smaller sizing if you are small-boned, the larger if you are large-boned.

Look for designs that have few seams, darts, or details such as pockets, collars, or buttonholes. Suitable fabrics are also suggested for each design and it is essential to check on these, because wrong fabrics would alter the design shape. On the back of the pattern envelope there is a description of the garment as well as a back view. It is most important to read this, since an easy-looking flared skirt with unpressed pleats may have concealed pockets, making it a more complicated pattern to work on for the first attempt.

The number of pattern pieces is also given and comparing it with similar designs can help you to find the simplest design to make up. A list of notions needed (zippers, thread, etc.) is also given. Combination patterns with skirts, pants, tops, or jackets and coats in one pattern envelope are the best value. Children's patterns follow similar lines with special sizings for toddlers and children, including chubbier ones.

Fashion Measurement

Professionally, there is yet another way of measuring known as *fashion measurement*: this quite simply refers to the ever-present question of the length of the skirt, the depth of the neckline, and the width of the shoulder in prevailing fashion trends.

It means, in practice, the gentle art of keeping the design in balance while shortening, narrowing, or lengthening. It is not, therefore, feasible to lop 20 cm (8 in) off the hem and trust you have a new short length, or add 30 cm (1 ft) and expect the result to be current fashion.

In high fashion, measurements are often carried to extremes to make way for change. The skirt is brought down to midcalf, for example, in order to get everyone used to the idea that the mini has had its day, or the shoulders are widened to pave the way again for a padded look.

ADJUSTING PATTERN TO FIGURE

The variety of fashion designs and the diversity of design adaptations are too numerous to count, but adjustments to patterns to fit the individual figure are common to most.

Having taken a closer look at yourself, you will have gained a better appreciation of the complex structure of your body. The pattern can now be seen in relation to its contours and the reasons for seams and darts to accommodate your shape will seem less mysterious. Good patterns are positive statements of design and fit. They are constructed to comply with the human anatomy and the splendid articulation it is capable of. But we must realize and take note of the fact that no two people are exactly alike, whether in build of body, appearance, or any other form whatsoever. So some adjustments of patterns to allow for individual differences in basic figure types are inevitable. On the whole though, these should only be of a relatively minor nature and mainly consist of small additions to, or subtractions from girth and/or length measurements.

There is one rule, however, that must be obeyed: alterations to one part of a pattern invariably affect another and so *lengthening or shortening any given seamline must be accompanied by doing the same to any other, which ultimately holds two separate parts together.* To give just one example, an addition to length of front shoulder requires an equal increase to back shoulder seam. Where facings and linings are affected by alterations to main parts of the pattern, do make sure that here, too, identical adjustments are made. Although really an elementary principle, this is often ignored or overlooked.

Irrespective of any type of design other than one consisting of one piece of fabric (not very often found), no single part of a garment is of any use on its own unless sewn to another at some position, and all of them must be cut to fit together perfectly. At the same time, a pattern for a design consisting of numerous parts need not be frightening to any reader. After all, every garment when finally assembled has reverted from x number of oddly shaped, separate pieces to one whole complete recognizable form, with clearly definable lines such as center front, center back, and sides throughout the whole of a garment.

Anticipating Chapter Five, in which we suggest six basic garments, four of these will be used to illustrate likely adjustments on patterns (the same adjustment methods can apply equally to the two remaining garments):

1. Skirt.
2. Sleeveless shift dress.
3. Jacket with sleeves.
4. Slacks.

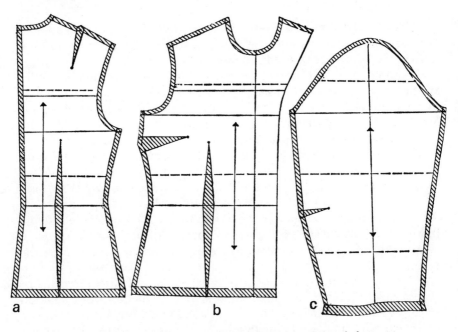

Fig. 15.   Seam allowances for jacket back (a), front (b), and sleeve (c).

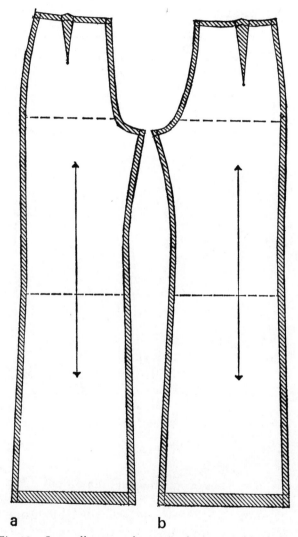

a   b

Fig. 16. Seam allowances for trouser front (a) and back (b).

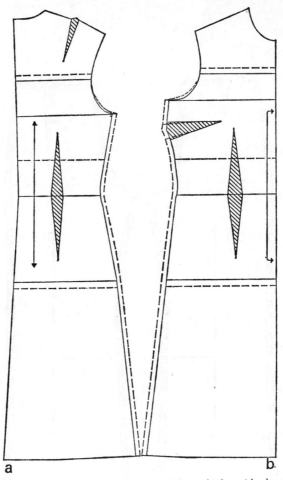

Fig. 17.   *Increasing side seams of dress back* (a) *and front* (b) *for wider bust, waist, and hips.*

When the pattern has been removed from the envelope, smooth out any creases with a warm, dry iron. The accompanying instruction sheet repeats front and back views of the garment(s), alongside the pattern view. Each piece of pattern is distinctively marked for easy identification. Place body pattern pieces on a table with the side seams facing each other; the back on the left-hand side, front on the right-hand side; collar near the neckline; cuff near the sleeve; and facings close to where they going to be sewn. Remember that you are looking at half of the back or front piece (each to be cut twice).

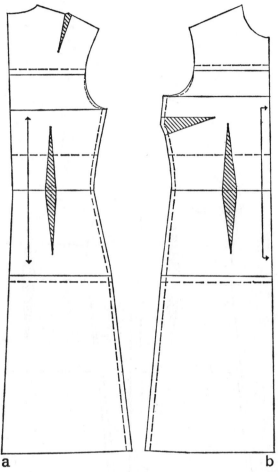

Fig. 18.   *Decreasing side seams of dress back (a) and front (b) for narrower bust, waist, and hips.*

Compare the *bust, waist,* and *hip* measurements of the pattern with your own by measuring from center back to side seam and from side seam to center front at the appropriate place. Make certain that seam allowances, pleats, darts, overlaps, and buttonhole allowances are not included. Double this measurement and you can now ascertain the exact amount of ease allowed on the pattern. These are usually quite generous and it is left to your discretion to decide if, by comparing your body measurements to those stated on the pattern envelope, increases or

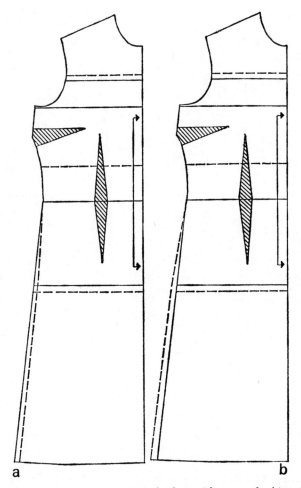

Fig. 19. *Decreasing* (a) *and increasing* (b) *dress side seams for hip width only.*

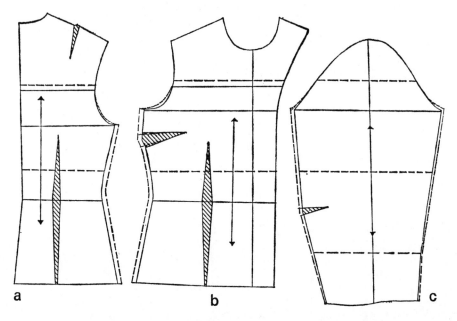

Fig. 20.   Increasing side seams of jacket back (a), front (b), and sleeve (c) for wider bust, waist, and hips.

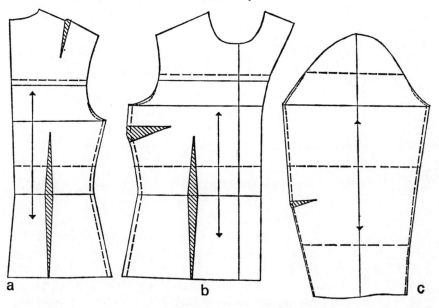

Fig. 21.   Decreasing side seams of jacket back (a), front (b), and sleeve (c) for narrower bust, waist, and hips.

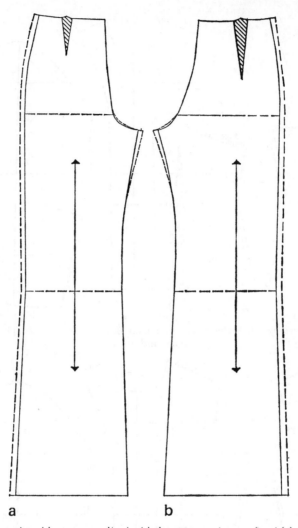

Fig. 22. *Increasing side seams and/or inside leg seam on trouser front (a) and back (b).*

a   b

decreases are needed. Carry out the same comparison for all other measurements listed on your chart by measuring the appropriate parts of the rest of the pattern. Because the majority of these are not stated on the envelope and you cannot determine the ease allowances, your common sense will help in making decisions about likely additions or subtractions. (In most cases no more than half the allowance is added/reduced at the side seams.)

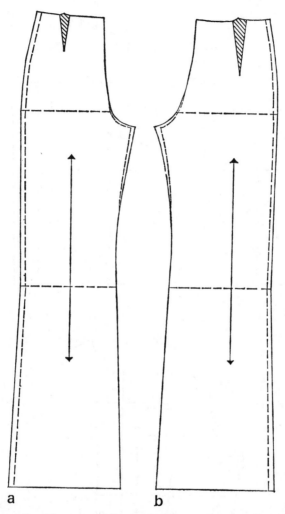

Fig. 23. *Decreasing side seams and/or inside leg seam on trouser front (a) and back (b).*

Increase or decrease width by splitting the total amount equally over the four side seams—for example, 2.5 cm (1 in)=6mm (¼in)—or half of the total for across front, across back, sleeves, and cuff measurements. Write down the amount to be added/reduced on the pattern, nearest to where it is to take place. Increases are made by taping new clean paper to appropriate parts of the pattern, making the addition, and re-marking new sewing and cutting lines. For decreases, measure off the amount to be lost and re-mark as before.

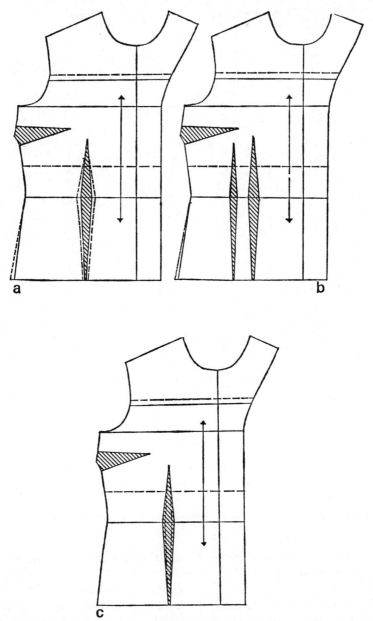

Fig. 24. Increasing depth of dart of jacket front for smaller waist/more prominent bust (a); adding second dart to spread greater increase more evenly (b); decreasing dart for larger waist (c).

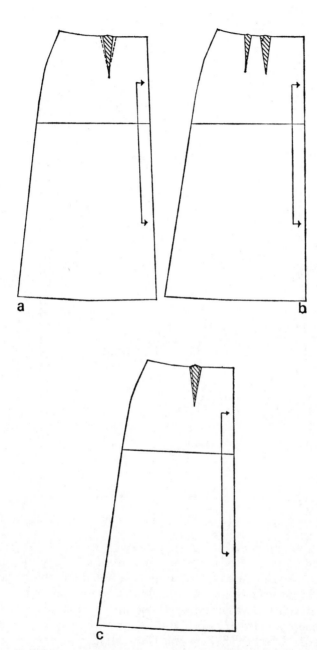

Fig. 25.   Increasing dart on skirt for smaller waist/more prominent hips (a); adding second
dart to spread greater increase more evenly (b); decreasing dart for larger waist (c).

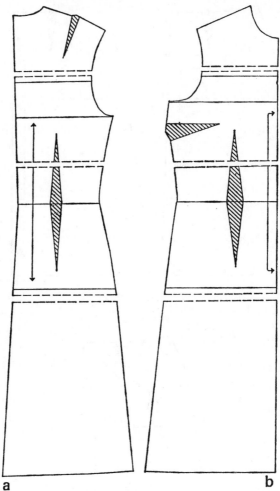

a   **b**

Fig. 26.   Lengthening dress back (a) and front (b) on bodice and/or skirt.

When adjustments are necessary on only the bust, waist, or hips, good use can also be made of darts as an additional aid toward good fit. Darts are used to create shape, to control fullness for a smooth fit. Hence to *shape* material from a prominent bust and/or hips to a small waist requires a deep waist dart, while the reverse (large waist, small bust and/or hips) needs only a shallow one. Generally, when deviations from a standard set of measurements occur, adjust to individual measurements by increasing or decreasing the size (depth and length) of waist darts, or add a second dart for decreases.

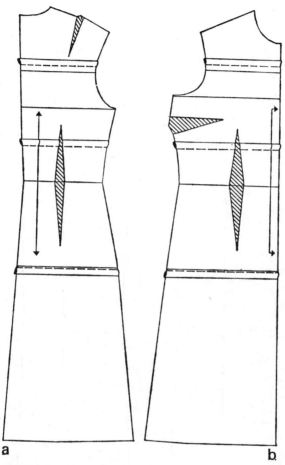

Fig. 27. Shortening dress back (a) and front (b) on bodice and/or skirt.

Patterns are usually marked with special lines at the places most suitable for lengthening or shortening: by cutting into to open, or folding to close, the desired amount can be adjusted. The alternative of adding to, or chopping off at hems will most likely distort the balance and proportion of the design (as previously mentioned on page 00) and will also have detrimental effects on the fit of garments. Some alterations carried out "inside" the areas of pattern pieces, rather than at outside cutting lines, are close to the professional method of grading which, if done accurately, makes some ready-to-wear garments so perfect in fit.

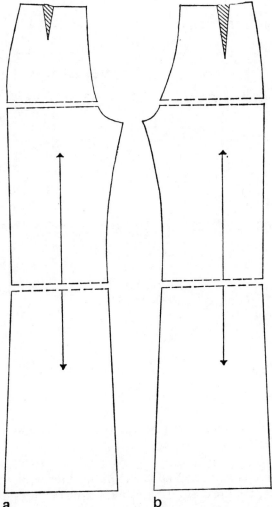

Fig. 28. *Lengthening trouser front (a) and back (b) from waist to crotch and/or crotch to hem.*

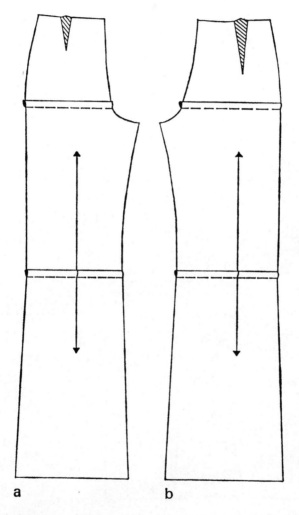

a   b

Fig. 29. Shortening trouser front (a) and back (b) from waist to crotch and/or crotch to hem.

Fig. 30. Split the difference to find the new crotch line.

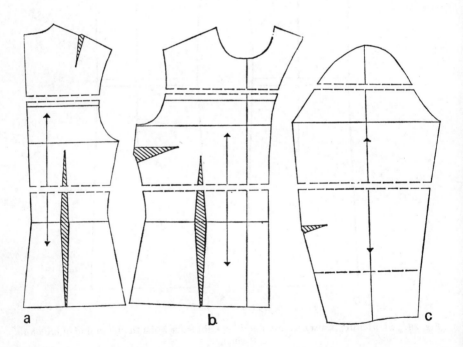

Fig. 31. Lengthening the jacket back (a), front (b), and/or sleeve (c).

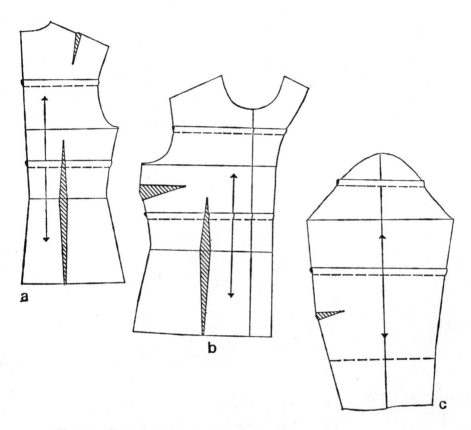

Fig. 32. *Shortening the jacket back* (a), *front* (b), *and/or sleeve* (c).

On many designs, the spaces between a group of buttonholes and buttons may be affected by lengthening or shortening. Re-mark to ensure that spaces are equidistant again.

But above all else, remember to carry out *equal adjustments* wherever two pieces join to become one. This includes, for example, the increase or reduction in length from the base of the armhole to the shoulder seam. Alteration to this area affects the height of the sleeve cap, so raise or lower it correspondingly, as shown in Fig. 31(b).

Measure all curved lines with tape in an upright, rather than flat position. This way *accurate* readings can be taken. A flat tape moved along a curve increases the true amount between two given points.

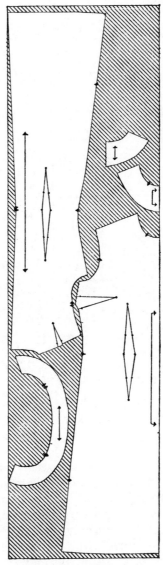

Fig. 33. Layout of dress pattern on narrow fabric.

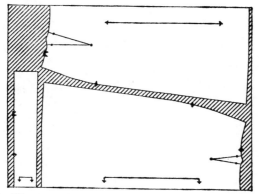

Fig. 34. Layout of skirt pattern on wide fabric.

PREPARING PATTERN FOR LAYOUT ON FABRIC

Once again, make sure that all creases on the pattern have been ironed out. Count all the pieces and check that none have gotten lost. Look out for instructions stating the number of each pattern piece to be cut. If you use a fabric with a right and wrong side, make absolutely certain that the two halves of all parts are paired—finding two left sleeves after cutting out is not going to please you very much. Study grain markings on all pieces and never ignore them.

One of the instructions may read *Place on fold*—be sure to do so, for, if you do not, this particular part of the garment is useless, because no seam allowance has been added and there are now two half-pieces where there should have been one whole piece.

Be sure to recognize specific markings for cutting lines, stitching lines, notches, seam allowances, and marks denoting center front and back, darts, buttonholes, and pocket and button positions. Finally, cut off all surplus paper on the pattern, leaving clean lines for cutting. You may indeed feel anxious and impatient to get on with the cutting of your fabric, but minutes spent in good preparation of the pattern may save hours of frustrated sewing.

3
Fabrics

TYPES OF FABRICS

With so many different fabrics available, choice can be quite bewildering. This chapter provides some basic facts on the main categories of fabrics, and a selection is made from these of the most suitable for simpler construction.

There are five main categories of fibers: cotton, linen, silk, wool, and manufactured fibers. Cotton and linen from vegetable fibers, and silk and wool from animal fibers, are known as "natural." Manufactured fibers are made, as the name implies, from a wide variety of chemicals and raw materials.

GOOD AND BAD POINTS

Naturally to the Natural Fibers First

Cotton, from the seed pod of the cotton plant, is very absorbent, durable, lightweight, strong (and even stronger when wet): it combines comfort with washability and smoothness. No bad points here, though it has a slight tendency to crease and is not warm enough in winter for some people. The good points, apart from those already mentioned, are that it is easy to work with, presses beautifully, and does not stretch or distort when handled.

It blends with manufactured fibers to give even greater crease-resistance, drip-dry qualities, and finishes. Among the many weights and types are poplin, sailcloth, denim, gingham, cotton gabardine, piqué, seersucker, organdy, chintz, velveteen, and corduroy.

Linen, from the flax plant, is another durable and absorbent fiber, with a lustrous finish. It is very hard-wearing but, unless it has a special finish, creases easily and frays, making it rather difficult for beginners to use. Blended with manufactured fibers it contributes absorbency, texture, and strength and can be made crease-resistant. Dress linen, synthetic and linen blends, household textiles, and upholstery fabrics are among the best-known linens.

Silk, spun from the cocoon of the silkworm, could well be labeled exquisite. It is lustrous, very strong, durable, and springy though very fine and delicate to handle. It has the added virtue of being warm in cold weather and cool in very hot climates. A fairly experienced hand is needed to work with it—it needs very special care. A wide variety of weights include brocade, chiffon, crêpe, foulard (tie-silk), georgette, jersey, lace, organza, satin, shantung, velvet, and faille.

Wool, coming from the warm and woolly sheep, has a fiber that is springy, durable, with good insulation and absorption. It is crease- and flame-resistant. This warm and comfortable product makes up very well and is shrinkable, so it is excellent for tailoring where shape can be achieved with pressing. Some finishes on wool need special attention: when there is a surface texture, care must be taken so that it does not shine or mark, as described on page 60. Some of the many types of woolen fabrics include felt, flannel, gabardine, jersey, melton, velour, serge, tweed, barathea, and crêpe.

Manufactured Fibers

Manufactured fibers form two main groups, *cellulose* and *synthetic*. The first group includes rayon, acetate, and triacetate. Although they are processed from wood pulp, a natural base, it is through chemistry that they are obtained. The term "synthetics" is used loosely for all manufactured fibers, but in fact it refers only to those chemically created—nylon, polyester, and acrylic fibers, among many others. They certainly have many easy-care qualities such as being drip-dry, washable, and crease-resistant but, on the other hand, they do not handle as well as natural fabrics and can be harder to use. When they are blended with naturals, a happier compromise is reached with the best qualities of the manufactured ones and the texture and handle of the natural fabrics. The better known from the manufactured groups, including some blends, are nylon, orlon, acrilan, dynel, rayon, courtelle, tricel, polyester, and vinyl.

THE FABRIC FOR THE GARMENT

Beginners, Please

Now that you have an idea of the tremendous variety of fabrics available and an outline of their qualities, the choice can be simplified. We recommend the best of these for ease in construction, looks, and in gaining experience in handling fabric perhaps for the first time. From the cotton group choose denim, sailcloth, cotton gabardine, or medium-to heavyweight poplin and, if patterned, a small print only is advisable. They are easy to stitch, press well, will not distort or stretch in handling and so retain their shape. Because they do not fray too easily, ragged seams and hems are avoided. Look for crease-resistant finishes and minimum-care labels.

Wool, plain worsted flannel, closely woven tweed, or similar plain wool cloth all are easy to use. Because these are softer fabrics, some may need shrinking, although most are preshrunk (more about this on page 59). The fabrics hang particularly well and plain grey flannel is an all-time classic; it looks expensive too. Tweed needs no further introduction, but remember it must be closely woven such as "Donegal" or "Herringbone," both of which are patterned weaves.

Jersey—the medium- to heavier-weight double knit type—has the

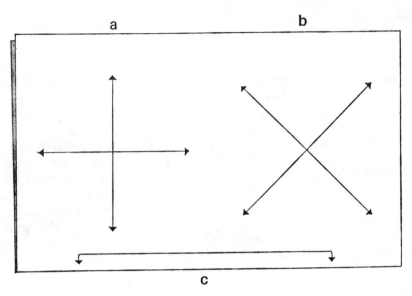

Fig. 35.   Straight grain (a); bias grain (b); fold of fabric (c).

same qualities as woven wool but is stretchier because it is a knitted fabric. Even so, it sews as easily as the others and is certainly one of the most comfortable materials to wear.

With all of these a good finish is easy to achieve, and there are no headaches over initial preparation, which is so much more encouraging than a desperate fight with some springy velvet or saggy crêpe!

SOME FABRIC TERMS

You will need to be well acquainted with some descriptions of fabrics and terms; these will crop up regularly on pattern envelopes and in the instructions. The essential ones for beginners in particular, because they can affect fabric choice and construction, will be explained here, and a more comprehensive list is given in Chapter Fifteen.

Grain

Clothes cut correctly on the grain hang well and retain their shape, but what is "grain"? Woven fabric has two sets of threads running at right angles to each other. The *warp* is the lengthwise grain, running

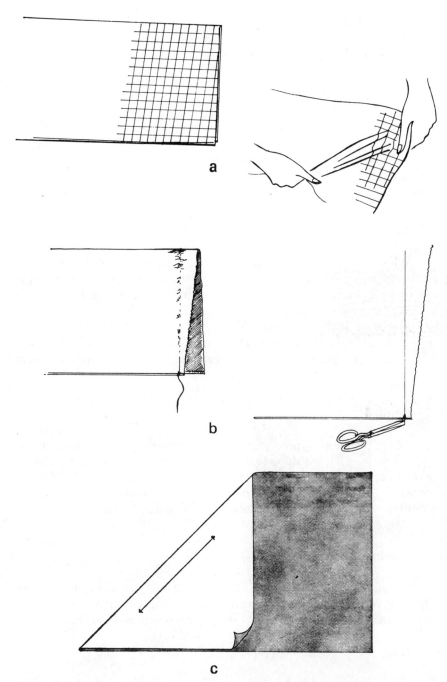

Fig. 36. For distortion in weave, pull fabric diagonally (on bias) to straighten (a); for uneven/torn edge, pull thread crosswise, then cut along line (b); fold fabric triangle to find true bias grain (c).

vertically along the fabric and the *selvage* is the finished edge lengthwise. The *weft* is the crosswise thread, running horizontally from selvage to selvage and called the crosswise grain.

Bias

The diagonal of the fabric is sometimes referred to confusingly as the "bias". The true bias is found when the fabric is folded in a triangle so that the crosswise threads go in the same direction as the lengthwise threads; where they meet, at the folded edge of the triangle, is the *bias*—here there is maximum stretch to the fabric.

Off-grain

When the lengthwise and crosswise threads are not at true right angles to each other or if there is a curve in the weave, the material is referred to as being off-grain. This can be checked by seeing if the ends of the fabric have been cut or torn evenly. If they have not, make a tiny cut in the selvage at the end, and pull a crosswise (weft) thread. Even if it does not come out completely it will mark the grain with a line, which can be used as a guide for cutting, otherwise the garment will not hang well.

Bonded

When two fabrics have been sealed to become a single fabric, this is called *bonding*. This is done for several reasons: woven and knit fabrics, or laces, are bonded to tricot knit or taffeta for self-lining; coating fabrics are bonded to interlining for warmth and shape retention; and two fibers are often bonded together to make one reversible fabric.

Laminated

Lamination is another term for a fabric that is joined to a backing of synthetic foam to provide insulation and warmth with little weight; this also allows the fabric to keep its shape and be crease-resistant.

Nap

Some hairy or downy fibers are brought to the surface and then brushed or pressed flat to give a soft effect or sheen. This napping on woolens such as broadcloth, fleece, and doeskin (so called because of its suedelike finish) reflects a different light in each direction, so all garment sections must be cut with this nap running in the same direction. These fabrics are among those prone to watermarking, dealt with on page 60.

Pile

Pile fabrics are woven with an extra set of looped yarns raised on the surface and clipped to stand up and form the rich surfaces of velvet, velour, and velveteen. Corduroy velvet has fine to wide ribs or "wales," or can be patterned and textured in many ways. The same cutting problems exist for these as for the napped fabrics and for the same reasons, although there are some velvets produced that can be cut in both directions. Deep-pile fabrics are very thick and usually made from manufactured fibers to simulate fur.

These napped and pile fabrics are not suitable for beginners to work on, but they need explanation because they often appear in the pattern description and, if the terms are not understood, can cause confusion.

PRE-CUTTING PREPARATION OF FABRIC

Shrinking

This applies mainly to woolen goods, although it is wise to remember that cottons, too, often need preshrinking. Shrinking is the contraction of fabric after washing or dry-cleaning, or when fabric has not been fully shrunk by the manufacturer. Most fabrics are pre-shrunk, but this still allows for a 3 percent reduction. To make a test, cut a small section of the material and trace its shape for accurate measurement. Then soak the material scrap in water, dry with a hot iron, and measure against the tracing to see if there has been any reduction in size.

If further shrinking is necessary, try to make an ironing space as wide as possible to lay the fabric on—a kitchen table covered with an old clean piece of blanket or sheet is ideal. Lay the fabric right side down and thoroughly dampen a clean absorbent cloth (a linen tea towel, or a piece of sheeting) and place it over the fabric. With a hot iron gently press, without sliding the iron as you would normally do, so that the heat goes right through without pushing or distorting the fabric. Continue pressing until all the fabric has been completely covered; a light press to dry off the top cloth should then be adequate.

Fabric Defects

Look out for defects when buying fabrics. These may have occurred during weaving or knitting by the manufacturer and should be marked with strings, threads, tape, etc. on selvages for easy identification. Shops will make an allowance on the length in compensation, but you can insist on a faultless length if you consider this allowance to be insufficient.

Sometimes creases are found in fabric lengths in the shops. There is a possibility that they may have been made at the production stage, and will be nearly impossible to remove. Rare enough perhaps, but if this has happened and had not been noticeable in the store, the material should be returned to the manufacturer. For normal creasing, pressing under a damp cloth should be sufficient. On jersey fabrics, however, the fold is not always removable, in which case the pattern should be laid on the fabric so as to avoid the fold line.

Watermarks

These occur on fabrics with a surface as in blazer cloth, some flannels, fine wool such as doeskin, and on pure silks. The marks may have been caused by sprinkled water or uneven pressing with a damp cloth, which leaves patches or spots when the fabric is dry. Apart from the fact that some of these should not have been damp-pressed anyway, or at least should have been done on the wrong side under a cloth, the remedy is to steam or press all the fabric again under an evenly damp cloth. Do not put pressure on the iron; the idea is to steam the surface gently to revive the flattened or marked patches. The entire surface must be redone otherwise a new set of marks may appear.

LABELING FOR CONSUMER PROTECTION

With all these dreadful warnings, it would appear that choosing a fabric, which might or might not need special care, depends on guesswork but, of course, carefully labeling giving a description of the fiber content is required by law in this country. The labeling on care of fabrics also protects the consumer and the retailer. These labels state whether or not the fabric is washable, crease-resistant, dry-cleanable, noniron, and so on, so that its suitability for a particular design or easy handling can be evaluated (for details see pages 316 and 333–41).

FINISH

This is a treatment applied to a fabric to add to its serviceability, to make its appearance more attractive as well as making it more pleasant to handle. Finishes are applied to all fabrics, special finishes being added to counteract any undesirable features in a fiber.

Special finishes available include those that make fabrics colorfast, crease/wrinkle-resistant, drip-dry, durable press, mildew-resistant, stain- and spot-resistant, shrinkage controlled, wash and wear, washable, waterproof, and water-repellent/resistant.

CHOOSING A FABRIC FOR LINING

The purpose of a lining is to give body to a garment and help it keep its shape. Its main purpose is to finish the inside, enclosing all the raw edges. Loosely woven and stretchy fabrics will retain their shape more readily and linings are essential in straight skirts to prevent bagginess. This type of lining is not meant to give shape to the garment—that is the purpose of the interfacing or backing.

The lining should be firm, yet soft and pliable. Today there are many manufactured materials (such as polyesters and polyester blends) that can be used as linings for virtually every kind of fabric. Needless to say, a lining material should be chosen according to the kind of cloth that will be used for the garment. A heavy woolen will require a different lining than will a slinky jersey, for example. Weight, washability, weave, and ease of handling must be considered.

A comprehensive list of fabrics, with notes on the care and handling of the more difficult ones, will be found in Chapter Fifteen, with the more advanced dressmaking techniques (Chapter Fourteen) and the glossary of sewing and fabric terms (pages 333–41) will supply further information.

Fig. 37.   Small-print cotton top (a); flannel pants suit (b); herringbone tweed jacket (c); plain cotton sundress and jump suit (d); patterned wool jacket (e); jersey battle jacket and skirt with leather trim (f).

Fig. 38.   Flannel jacket with fur collar (a); dogtooth wool jacket (b); cotton gabardine suits
(c); herringbone tweed jacket (d); cotton jacket, bra, and trousers (e); jersey jacket with
knitted collar (f).

4
Hand Tools
and Equipment

Apart from investing in a good sewing machine, if you do not own one already, most hand tools and items of equipment for dressmaking are not very expensive and are easily obtainable. Because some are more essen-

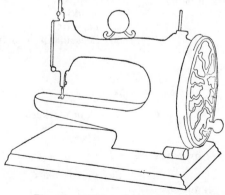

Fig. 39.   1870-model sewing machine.

tial than others, they are listed in two groups, (1) the most necessary ones and (2) those which are desirable, followed (on page 67) by a more detailed guide.

Essential for   **Desirable for**

Machine Stitching

 1. Sewing machine   32. Silicone aerosol spray
 2. Bobbin case
 3. Bobbins
 4. Machine needles
 5. Machine oil
 6. Brush
 7. Screwdriver

Pressing

 8. Iron   33. Tailor's ham
 9. Ironing board   34. Tailor's pressing block
10. Sleeve board   35. Velvet board
11. Damp rag/pressing cloth

Cutting and Handsewing

12. Cutting shears   36. Electric cutting shears
13. Tape measure   37. Cutting table/board
14. Meter/yardstick   38. Pinking shears
15. Steel pins   39. Pin cushion
16. Tailor's chalk   40. Wax chalk
17. Ruler   41. T-square
18. Tracing wheel   42. French curves
19. Paper scissors   43. Stiletto
20. Pattern weights   44. Felt-tip pens
21. Pencils   45. Magnet
22. Eraser   46. Seam ripper
23. Plain, white, or tissue paper   47. Clippers
24. Transparent tape   48. Bodkin
25. Sewing needles   49. Fashion templates
26. Small scissors   50. Dressmaking tracing paper
27. Thimble

Fitting

28. Dress form   51. Hem marker

Garment Care and Protection

29. Clothes brush   52. Plastic bags
30. Cleaning fluid—alcohol or
    aerosal stain remover
31. Coat hangers

ESSENTIAL EQUIPMENT

1. Sewing machine

Brand names and makes of sewing machines are numerous, but the basic principle of sewing is common to all. Modern precision-built machines are refined for better performance; they are faster and require less effort. Some domestic types are built with specific emphasis on taking a variety of attachments for decorative stitches, buttonholes, overcasting, embroidery, etc. (See page 76.)

2. Bobbin case

This is a small round case, fitting underneath the plate, which holds the bobbin wound with sewing thread. This thread connects and "locks"

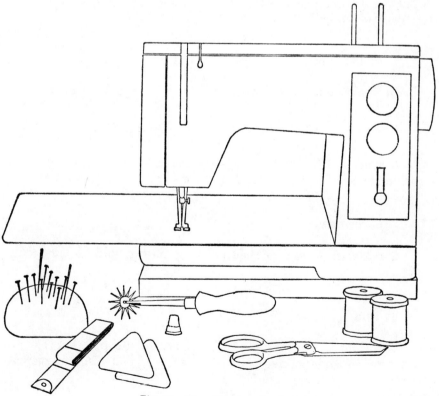

Fig. 40.   Some basic equipment.

with the top thread passed through the needle. At least one spare is advisable. On some machines the bobbin case is a fixture and spares are unnecessary.

3. Bobbins

Usually made of metal, bobbins are also available in transparent materials for easy identification of colored threads. Keeping a reasonable number at hand, saves constant rewinding of the same or other colored threads used.

4. Machine needles

There are various sizes of needles. No. 9 is a very fine needle for sheer tricot, satin tricot, net, and fine lace; No. 11 is for lightweight fabrics such as sheer crêpe, dimity, lawn, silk, and chiffon; No. 14 is suitable for broadcloth, flannel, jerseys, cotton percales, and synthetics; No. 16 is used for thicker wools, corduroy and coatings; No. 18, rarely used, is for very thick wools. Today ballpoint needles are also available for knit and stretch fabrics.

5. Machine oils

Ordinary domestic oil in a suitable tube or can is adequate.

6. Brush

A small brush for cleaning areas above the plate and below the bobbin is essential. An old toothbrush or small paintbrush works well.

7. Screwdriver

Check what sizes you need to fit the screws holding the needle, plate, etc.

8. Iron

Use a medium-weight iron with heat control. Keep the base clean at all times, but when stained clean with steel wool pad or silicone aerosal spray (see §32.)

9. Ironing board

The normal domestic type is adequate—ideal when its height is adjustable. It must be free from wrinkles and creases on the underlay and cover, and should be firm and stable when in use.

10. Sleeve board

Some are attachable to ironing boards, otherwise use a heavy type to prevent movement along the board. It is essential for all tubular-shaped garments.

11. Damp rag/pressing cloth

A plain white piece of cotton, approximately 1 m × 46 cm (39 × 18 in) is sufficient for cottons and similar fabrics, and soft canvas is best for wool. A pressing cloth can be obtained pretreated, otherwise soak it in plain water overnight to extract any dressing on the fabric, or it will stick to the iron. Machine-finish all raw edges.

12. Cutting shears

The best shears are 25–30 cm long (10–12 in) with two sizes of handle; one small for the thumb and one large for the fingers. Cut out with long, clean strokes and do not use these shears for anything but fabric (paper cutting will blunt them). Avoid dropping them for, if you do, they may need resetting. If they are made of quality steel they will last a lifetime.

13. Tape measure

Use a traditional or metric tape measure. Buy a good quality, non-stretch measure, preferably with solid metal ends.

14. Meter/yardstick

Use a traditional and/or metric yardstick. This is usually obtainable in wood or metal and must be smooth for marking long lines on patterns.

Use for leveling hemlines at fittings, unless a T-square (41) is available or a hem marker is preferred (51).

15. Steel pins

Be sure to use dressmaker steel pins with sharp points, because other pins bend easily. Sizes start at 2.5 cm–4.5 cm (1 in–1¾ in). Short pins are best for use on paper and thin fabrics and longer ones for heavier and thicker materials.

16. Tailor's chalk

Use white tailor's chalk for marking out the pattern and the alterations at fitting stages. Test the chalk mark on a sample of fabric first to make certain it can easily be removed. When white chalk does not show up well on a fabric do not use colored chalk, because it smudges and leaves permanent marks. A hard pencil, lightly applied on the wrong side of the fabric, is better than colored chalk.

17. Ruler

Use metric and/or traditional rulers, 30 cm (12 in) minimum, for marking short, straight lines on patterns and garments.

18. Tracing wheel

Use for transferring marks from one part of pattern to another, from pattern to fabric or the reverse, and from fabric to fabric. The type with a wooden handle and sharp spikes is recommended, because blunt, cheap ones require heavy pressure and leave marks difficult to see. If the table used is precious and you do not want it damaged, place a piece of cardboard between the table and tracing area, since the wheel leaves permanent marks.

19. Paper scissors

Use fairly large scissors—paperhanger's scissors are ideal.

20. Pattern weights

Any small, heavy, flat objects that are lying around are suitable, or they can be bought in specialist shops. Use for weighing down patterns when adjusting, tracing, or marking on fabric.

21. Pencils

Use medium to hard, black, and colored pencils for easy identification of the adjustments/alterations on patterns. When drawing curved lines, let the pencil follow the movement of the wrist.

22. Eraser

This can be any size or shape, but it must be clean.

23. Plain, white, or tissue paper

Use fine white, clean pattern or tissue paper for pattern adjustments.

24. Transparent tape

Additions to paper pattern with plain white or tissue paper are best held with transparent tape for permanency, because pins fall out easily and damage the original pattern. Tape is also useful for removing dust, etc., from garments.

25. Sewing needles

Needles are usually available in ten sizes from 10—short and thin, to 1—long and thick (average size 7–8 for general sewing, slightly larger for basting). Within this range, sizes of needle eyes also vary from very small to large. The thickness of fabric and thread determine the size of needle. Unless the fabric is particularly delicate, avoid using very short needles, because they are just a trifle difficult to work with, unless you are accustomed to using them.

26. Small scissors

These should be about 12.5 cm (5 in) long, with sharp, pointed ends for buttonholes. Use them for cutting off ends of threads, etc.—small surgical scissors are ideal.

27. Thimble

The closed type is commonly used. Look for one with a magnetic head to catch stray pins. The tailor's open thimble is also available, but using it requires practice.

28. Dress form

A large variety of makes and types are available in shops and stores: stands are made of cardboard or wire and some are adjustable to accommodate varying figure types and to comply with a multitude of different body measurements. This is certainly an advantage, but on all of these forms you are restricted to only pinning the garment. If you contemplate trying your hand at making a muslin copy (toile) of a design, or even if you do not, consider investing in a type of form normally used by professionals, which is available in specialist shops. On these the base is covered with strong canvas with slight padding underneath to take pins. It is adjustable in height and rests on either a flat metal base or a tripod with castors. Some have collapsible shoulders, which is an asset when you are trying to get tight garments over it, but do not sacrifice a good shape for the sake of having a collapsible type. Choose the form nearest to your own measurements and if necessary slightly smaller (it can be padded out) rather than larger.

29. Clothes brush

A clean brush is necessary for removal of dust and loose threads. For a pile fabric use transparent tape, because dust, etc. will stick to it and a brush will only spread it around.

30. Cleaning fluid—alcohol or aerosal stain remover

There are many commonly used types on the market. The fluid must be applied with a clean piece of cloth and always test first on a sample piece.

Accidents may happen. If you prick your finger with a needle or pin and bleed, and this soils your fabric, remove the bloodstain in the following way. Cut off a length of white sewing cotton from the reel, roll it into a small ball, moisten, and dab the stain with it. Renew the cotton ball as often as necessary.

31. Coat hangers

Keep garments being made on hangers at all times. If garments with shoulder seams have not been joined, pin them together. Keep skirts and trousers on hangers with bars. Bundling garments up in any stage of sewing produces unnecessary creases and loss of shape.

DESIRABLE EQUIPMENT

32. Silicone aerosol spray

This is used to maintain smooth surfaces on the machine, iron, and scissors. It is not an alternative to oil for the moving parts of the machine.

33. Tailor's ham

Shaped parts of garments—i.e., those having curved seams or darts—should not be pressed on a flat surface: to maintain shape, place the shaped area over a tailor's ham and then press.

34. Tailor's pressing block

A smooth block of wood with a flat base, used for penetration and evaporation of steam as soon as the pressing cloth has been removed from the first pressed section of the garment. "Pat" with the block and leave it on the section for a short time.

35. Velvet board

Velvet, not the easiest of fabrics to handle, cannot be pressed in the ordinary way. Wire needle boards made of stainless steel come in strips wide enough for pressing seams; shaped to lay on sleeve boards; or as large boards to be used on parts of garment other than seams or small areas. These are relatively expensive and not absolutely essential: steaming velvet is often preferable to pressing.

36. Electric cutting shears

Small battery-operated scissors can make cutting easier on the more difficult and thicker fabrics.

37. Cutting table/board

The table should be high enough to work comfortably on in a standing position. A wooden surface is best, but remember that a tracing wheel leaves marks so, if necessary, protect the table by placing a board on top. Cardboard is very suitable and can be purchased in any required size.

38. Pinking shears

Use in place of machine finishing or overcasting edges on the seams of lighter-weight fabrics; the zig-zag edge reduces fraying of seams. The medium size, around 18 cm (7 in), is recommended.

39. Pin cushion

The wrist type is best and can easily be made by putting layers of soft pieces of material inside an outer cover, which is stitched together by hand. Then attach elastic to the two lower sides so that it fits snugly around your wrist.

40. Wax chalk

Use as white tailor's chalk (see 16). The wax melts under a hot iron and is, therefore, removed automatically. Is not suitable for many fabrics, so test first on a sample.

41. T-square

A large T-square is very useful for leveling hemlines and is essential for pattern lines at right angles. A transparent one is best.

42. French curves

These help in marking curved lines on pattern or garments—for example, necklines and armholes. Use either a transparent plastic type or one made of rubber which bends to any desired shape.

43. Stiletto

This is a wooden handle with a sharp, pointed end, which is used to punch holes on patterns for darts, pocket positions, etc.

44. Felt-tip pens

These work especially well on muslin for modeling on the dress form, but are also used for marking all types of lines on paper patterns. Use black and colored *thin* ones, so one line can be distinguished from another.

45. Magnet

Pins in boxes often get knocked over and so a magnet saves time (and temper) in clearing them up.

46. Seam ripper

Ripping out stitches is a faster method then using scissors.

47. Clippers

These are an alternative to small scissors.

48. Bodkin

This is a needle with a large eye and without a point. It is used to draw tape/elastic through narrow channels.

49. Fashion templates

Templates of this kind are prepared outline drawings of the human body, ready for the introduction of design lines—available in specialist shops.

50. Dressmaking tracing paper

Tracing paper is an aid for marking with the tracing wheel, from paper to paper, paper to fabric, or fabric to fabric. Great care is needed to ensure that markings are transferred to the wrong side of fabric. It is most suitable for use on smooth medium-weight fabrics such as cotton or rayon.

51. Hem marker

Two main types are available for leveling hemlines: (a) the pin type and (b) powder or tailor's chalk. In most cases, a meter/yardstick or a T-square is adequate.

52. Plastic bags

Garments made over a period of time collect dust, so protect them at all times by keeping them under a cover.

CARE AND USE OF THE SEWING MACHINE

The variety of sewing machines available and in use makes it impossible to cover all types and to discuss in detail every aspect of care and maintenance here.

As far as all newly or recently acquired machines are concerned, the manuals supplied give full instructions for care and maintenance. For the benefit of owners of both new and older types of sewing machines, and particularly for those without manuals, this section deals with basic information on the general use of sewing machines.

When using a portable sewing machine, do not place it too close to the edge of your table. Allow sufficient space for your left elbow to rest on the table, so that your arm is well-supported. Sit exactly in front of the needle, leaning your body slightly forward.

Make sure that the motor is correctly connected for safety.

Always use the correct needle size and type suitable for the fabric. Never use a blunt, bent, or hooked needle. Inspect the needle regularly. Some synthetic fabrics can blunt a needle during the course of sewing a single garment. You can easily detect a blunt needle by moving your fingernail against the point, when the machine is not in use.

Insert the needle either according to the manual supplied, which is normally with the groove facing you, or on some machines, to the left side. Push the needle up as high as it will go before securing it with the needle clamp screw. Loosen the screw for the needle insertion by a half-turn only.

Always use suitable thread size and type, and the same thickness for top and in bobbin. The combined thickness of top and bottom thread should never exceed the thickness of the fabric being sewn.

Threading the Machine

Thread the needle with the presser foot in a raised position, otherwise there is too much pressure on the thread tension disc. Turn the handwheel, at the right side of the machine, toward you to bring the needle to its highest position.

To bring up the bottom thread, hold the needle thread loosely, turn the handwheel to lower the needle into the needle hole of the plate, and bring the needle up. Pull the needle thread slightly, and the bobbin thread will come up at the same time. Pass both threads under and to the back of the presser foot.

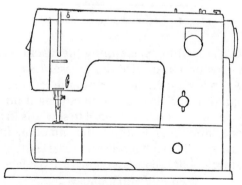

Fig. 41. Current-model sewing machine.

Sewing

Begin sewing by placing the fabric under the raised presser foot and needle. Line up the needle exactly on the seamline, but just a fraction below the cut edge of the fabric. Lower the foot, place your fingers on the thread ends, and turn the handwheel until the needle is pinned to the fabric. By starting to sew tith the needle already in the fabric, the moving parts of the machine are set at positions that cause least initial load on the motor. This releases the pressure on the first stitch, avoids the possibility of the thread breaking, and also ensures that the fabric will not be pushed out of position by the lowered presser foot. Stitch for about 1 cm (⅜ in) and reverse stitch. Then using even pressure with the fingers on the right hand, guide the fabric slowly and evenly through the front of the presser foot without pushing or pulling the fabric, but holding it gently at the side and toward the back with the fingers (not the flat) of the left hand. Do not watch the needle, but keep an eye on the presser foot.

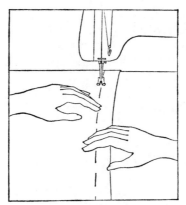

Fig. 42.   Correct hand position.

At the end of a seamline, on stopping the machine, take the needle up to its highest position and raise the presser foot to release the top thread tension. Always remove the fabric to the rear of the machine and leave at least 5 cm (2 in) of thread before cutting it off.

To turn a sharp corner, do not attempt to sew this in one continuous movement. Instead, stop the machine at the end of the first sewing line, with the needle lowered into the fabric on the last stitch, and so pinning the needle to the fabric. Lift the presser foot, turn the fabric to the second sewing line, lower the foot and carry on sewing.

Tension

Normally the tension should not need altering if it has been accurately set at the beginning, except when you want special sewing effects such as topstitching, when you need to use thicker buttonhole twist or silk thread.

Incorrect tension causes uneven stitches or "looping" in either top or bottom thread. If looping occurs on the underside of the fabric, the top tension is faulty, if at the top of the fabric the bottom tension will need adjusting. Most tension problems are caused by

1. An incorrectly inserted or damaged needle.
2. The use of incorrect thread on the fabric.
3. A wrongly set tension mark on the machine.
4. Incorrect bobbin tension. Test this by removing the bobbin case. With the full bobbin left inside, hold the thread end and suspend the entire case. It should descend slowly and evenly when the end of the thread is shaken gently. If it falls too quickly or does not move at all, the tension spring will need adjusting by a slight turn of the small screw in the bobbin case. Turn it clockwise to tighten or counterclockwise to loosen. Hold the bobbin case over a tray or table in case the screw comes out, so that it can easily be found.

Cleaning and oiling

Keep the machine clean at all times. Fluff and pieces of thread collect around the bobbin area and plate. Brush out, and oil the working parts lightly and frequently before, rather than after, use. One or two drops of oil put into the points provided (and usually marked) are sufficient. Too much oil will stain the machine and the fabric.

Accidental oil stains can be removed from most fabrics if you cover the stained area with French chalk (powdered) or tailor's chalk (scraped with a knife or blade); allow the particles of chalk to settle on the affected area. Leave the chalk to soak up the oil. This may take some hours and is best done overnight.

Breaking of Thread

Constant breaking of thread or seam irregularities may be caused by

1. Thread tension being set too tightly.
2. Damaged, incorrect size needle, or wrong insertion of needle.
3. Faulty (knotted/weak) thread.
4. Fluff or pieces of thread around bobbin area and/or plate.

ATTACHMENTS

The wide range of attachments available is equal to the variety of sewing machines. Many of these are designed for advanced sewing processes. Among the many and most useful ones supplied with most well known makes are: (1) *general-purpose foot* and (2) the *zipper foot.*

1. *The general-purpose foot* is designed to allow the needle to sew in a variety of widths for decorative stitching and the finishing of seam edges. The needle is set according to the width required. With the needle set in the center position, this foot is also used for straight stitching.

2. *The zipper foot* has two "cut-outs" to allow the needle to stitch to the left and right sides of the normal center. The zipper is sewn in from

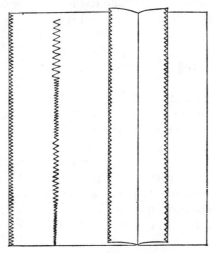

Fig. 43.   Zigzag stitches.

Fig. 44. *Zipper foot (a) and general-purpose foot (b),*

one end of each side with the position once set to the left and once set to the right side.

This attachment is also ideal for piping edges on garments or cording inserted into seams, when the ordinary presser foot does not lend itself to accurate stitching over and close to raised surfaces on the fabric.

MAKING SIX SIMPLE GARMENTS

5
Six Basic
Garments

COORDINATING

One of the effects of changing attitudes in recent years has been the popularity of fashion coordinates and separates, with the opportunity to mix and match style and color. For this reason and for simplicity, we are introducing six basic garments equally suitable for adults and children. Readers can try these with confidence, and later go on to many more advanced designs. All six garments have common features in design and construction procedures, which are built up progressively.

Similar shapes are used (as shown in Figs. 45–48, on pages 86–89 for

1. Skirt. Semi-flared, to any decided length.
2. Slacks. Semi-flared, waist or hip-hugger style.

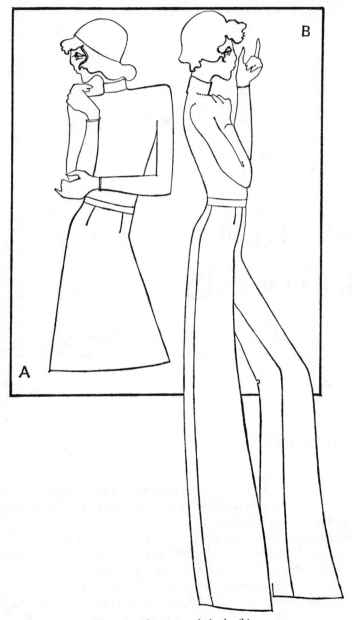

Fig. 45. *Skirt (a) and slacks (b).*

Fig. 46.   Semi-fitted dress.

3. Semi-fitted dress. With or without sleeves, semi-flared.
4. Jacket.   ⎫ Semi-fitted, semi-flared, edge-to-edge cardigan
5. Lightweight coat. ⎬ style, single- or double-breasted or wrapover.
6. Top/shirt. With or without sleeves, semi-fitted.

Illustrations of interchanging these garments to form an extensive wardrobe are given in Figs. 49–53. Other permutations are possible and can be increased by mixing fabrics and/or color.

As the illustrations show, only five decorations are used at this stage:

1. Plain patch pocket.
2. Patch pocket with flap.
3. Collars: (a) shirt and (b) collar with facing.
4. Buttonholes.
5. Topstitching.

It is suggested that these five decorations also be used in varying positions on different garments later on. They are intended as practice, so you can learn correct proportions.

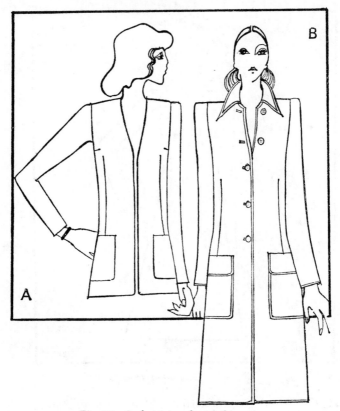

Fig. 47. Jacket (a) and coat (b).

PLANNING

By now you should have organized the tools and equipment needed for dressmaking. You have become familiar with terms generally used, or at any rate can refer to them in the Glossary. Measurements have been taken and pattern size is known. Now planning becomes crucial.

Within the range of our six basic designs (see pages 86–89) we recommend that readers make a plan for a basic wardrobe. For what use and when are the garments to be worn? To arrive at a final decision it is necessary to ask the following questions. Apart from the reasons described on pages 3–4, for what purpose is the skirt, dress, or jacket to be used? Perhaps a summer holiday, so an interchangeable set of separates in denim would be ideal; or a winter weekend when slacks, coat, and skirt in flannel would be suitable; or the complete set of garments in

Fig. 48.   Top (a) and shirt (b).

jersey for the year round. Depending on the fabric and design chosen, with adaptations the possibilities are endless.

Eventually everyone will determine their own individual reasons for making clothes, which will express their personality and in which they feel good and know they look attractive. At the same time these clothes will cater to the concept of being "in fashion," bearing in mind that even the ambition to look dressed in a casual way only succeeds if deliberately preplanned.

Study the large range of commercial patterns available and follow the suggestions we offer. Select a skirt as near as possible to the shape shown in Fig. 45(a); do likewise for the other designs. We shall describe all processes involved in making this garment and repeat instructions for the other five in the order set out, leaving out those details already covered, progressively in designs one to six.

We suggest that readers select only a few fabrics, which will be suitable for the six, before moving on to more advanced ideas in dress-making and working with a greater variety of materials. (Chapters Fifteen and Sixteen contain a more detailed discussion on fabrics, linings and interfacings, threads, and notions. They also cover a wider range of designs and their relationship to fabrics.)

Fig. 49. *Skirt and shirt (a) and slacks and shirt (b).*

Fig. 50.   Sleeveless, semi-fitted dress over shirt and slacks.

Fig. 51.   Jacket over semi-fitted dress and shirt (a) and jacket over shirt and slacks (b).

Fig. 52. *Coat over jacket with skirt and shirt (a) and coat over shirt and slacks (b).*

Fig. 53. *Coat over semi-fitted/dress with top/shirt (a) and coat over jacket and slacks with shirt (b).*

The following fabrics, as mentioned on pages 55–56, are ideal for our purposes. We list them again:

Woven wool
    Plain worsted flannel
    Plain closely woven tweed (or similar fabric)

Woven cotton (small prints, if patterned)
    Medium to heavyweight poplin
    Sailcloth
    Gabardine
    Denim

These fabrics are not difficult to handle, because the firm and close weave structure prevents undue stretching and retains shape. Large patterns should be avoided at this stage, because they require matching and make sewing more difficult.

Knitted wool
    Medium to heavy doubleknit jersey

In the case of wool jersey, some stretch and give takes place; a knitted fabric is meant to give, but it is still firm enough compared to loose-structure fabric. Although allowances over and above body measurements are smaller (as explained on page 31), jersey has a beautiful handle and feel. Its characteristics are most suitable for many designs and it is extremely versatile.

Having decided on the fabric and bought the required amount, select a matching lining if possible for the wool fabrics—plain lightweight polyester blend is ideal. Our patterns will look better if they are lined, because this helps them to retain their shape longer and they will also feel better in use.

A list of notions for each garment will precede sewing instructions. These must be at hand before you begin cutting out and constructing.

6
The First Design: The Skirt

In order to eliminate unnecessary repetition, the processes for each section will be listed in groups and individually described, when appropriate, at the beginning of each design. These processes will follow through all the other designs, with new ones added where applicable. For example, processes for seams, darts, hems, etc. for the skirt will be used throughout as basic methods and are good for all fabrics. Simultaneously, the handsewing and other processes on practice pieces, as suggested, will help you to gain experience in handling fabrics.

THE BASIC SKIRT

The basic skirt is semi-flared, with two side seams and one center back seam, with a zipper opening set on the waistband. The method of putting the zipper into the back seam is the same as for putting it into a side seam.

Now that the pattern has been chosen, its measurements are checked (and adjusted if necessary), the fabric has been bought, and the tools are ready.

Fig. 54.   Basic skirt.

Notions

The following notions are required:

1. White/contrast colored basting thread.

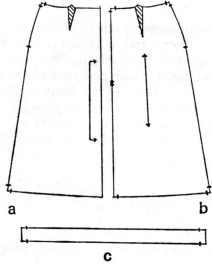

Fig. 55.   Basic pattern shape: front (a); back (b); waistband (c).

2. The fabric you select will determine the weight and type of thread
   you use. If a perfect match is difficult to obtain, choose a slightly
   darker color—this will work in well and is a better match than
   lighter colors.
3. Skirt-weight zipper 20.5 cm (8 in) in length.
4. Iron-on interfacing for the waistband (see interfacings on page 000).
5. Skirt hooks and eyes for the waistband, size 2.

BASIC HAND STITCHES

The five basic hand stitches (in order of use) are as follows:

▶ *Tailor Tacking*
▶ *Basting*

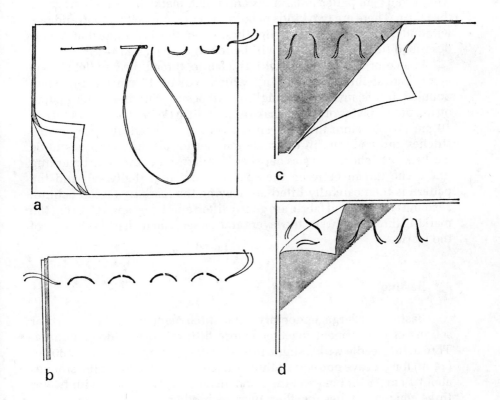

Fig. 56.   Tailor tacking.

▶ *Overcasting*
▶ *Blindstitch (Invisible stitch)*
▶ *Slipstitch*

Practice Piece

For a beginner, hand stitches, machine-stitching, and any new process should be worked out on a sample piece of fabric before the garment is put together. This will save much time and unnecessary handling of the garment, as well as giving confidence and accuracy. A piece of fabric—the same weight and texture as the one you will be using, 25 cm (approximately 10 in square)—cut in half will be ideal.

Tailor Tacking

The first stitch needed is the marking stitch, called tailor tacking, which transfers pattern markings and notch marks from the pattern to the fabric. There are two kinds of tailor tacking, one with a loop and one without. Because the latter is slightly simpler, this is the one that will be described (the other method will be found on pages 214–15).

In a color that contrasts with the fabric, thread the needle. Use no more than about 90 cm (36 in), which will be 45 cm (18 in) when doubled. If it is any longer, tangling will occur. With the pattern paper on top of two layers of fabric, make a stitch 1 cm (⅜ in), leaving a space of 10 cm (4 in) before the next stitch. Do not pull tightly between the stitches and continue in the same manner for all the long lines to be marked, with shorter spaces between, for darts and other short marking lines. The thread between the spaces is cut first (halfway), and the pattern is then carefully lifted off, leaving the marking thread behind. Next the two layers of fabric are gently lifted apart, just enough to cut the marking threads between the layers and, so separated, mark both sides of the fabric.

Basting

Basting is a large, temporary hand stitch made to hold two parts or sctions of the garment together before fitting and machine-stitching. Thread the needle with a single thread of contrasting color, about 60 cm (24 in) long. Leave one end slightly longer and knot it. Make the stitches about 1 cm (⅜ in) long and the same distance apart. Finish with two or three smaller stitches together, over each other.

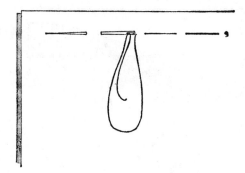

Fig. 57.   Basting stitch.

Overcasting

This is a small, close, slanting stitch which prevents raw edges from fraying. Use the same thread as for machine stitching and hand finishing. Hand overcasting is an alternative to machine zigzagging.

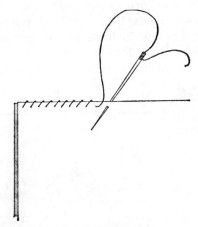

Fig. 58.   Overcasting.

Blindstitch (Invisible Stitch)

This is so called because it is practically invisible on the right side of hems. First the hem is basted up on a basting line about 2 cm (¾ in) from the raw edge. The edge is then turned back fractionally and a very small stitch is taken on the hem allowance, with the next stitch made approximately 1 cm (⅜ in) further along. Only one or two threads should be picked up, on the garment side. Do not pull tightly between stitches, just firmly enough to hold the two layers together.

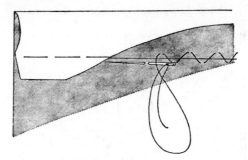

Fig. 59. Blindstitch.

Slipstitch

The slipstitch is another stitch that holds two layers of fabric together, with one thread of material picked up on each side alternately.
This is used for hems and waistbands with a turned-in folded edge. It is
used here on the skirt to turn in the waistband on the inside, for the
lining hem, and for sewing the lining to the zipper tape. Pick up a single
thread of the material below the folded edge, then slip the needle in the
fold for about 6 mm (¼ in). Pick up another single thread below the
folded edge where the needle comes out and repeat for the rest of the
hem.

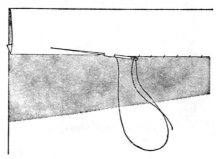

Fig. 60.   Slipstitch.

MACHINE STITCHES

The regulation tension on a sewing machine is set for 5–6 stitches
per cm (⅜ in).

Practice Piece

On sample pieces (two halves), having marked and basted a seam, place the beginning of the seam under the presser foot of the machine, with the needle lined up exactly on the seamline, but just a fraction below the cut edge. Lower the foot, stitch for about 1 cm (⅜ in), and then reverse stitch. Using even pressure, guide the fabric slowly and evenly through in front of the presser foot. Do not push or pull the fabric, but hold it gently at the side and toward the back with one hand, guiding it through the front with the other hand. This will ensure a straight seamline. Do not watch the needle, but keep an eye on the foot; this is a better way to keep the machine-stitching on the sewing line.

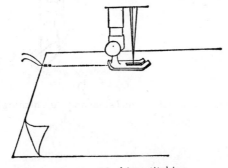

Fig. 61. Machine stitching.

Mark and baste a small dart on the peice of fabric. Sew from the wide end to the point of dart, tapering off to make the last stitches exactly on the folded line. Leave the thread ends long enough to tie in a knot—and don't pull them; this would pucker the end of the dart.

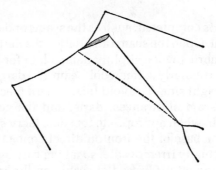

Fig. 62. Stitch dart.

Staystitch

A line of machine-stitching on the curved or bias cutting lines of garments, between the cut edge and sewing lines and close to the latter, prevents stretching when working on fabrics. It is used, in this instance, at the seam of an armhole.

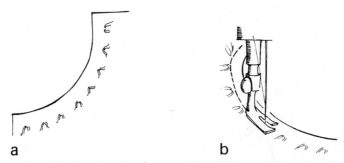

Fig. 63. *Marking thread (tailor's tacks) (a) and staystitching (b).*

PRESSING

Press as You Go

As one process is completed, such as the seams or darts, underpressing is most essential. Open the seams and flatten the darts by pressing on the wrong side of fabric (over a slightly damp cloth for woolen fabrics). On some fabrics, particularly softer wool, seam and dart impressions are apt to show on the right side. To avoid this, place a piece of thin narrow card between the seam allowances, darts, and the garment. Using a damp (or a dry cloth, when appropriate for some fabrics) prevents shine marks caused by the base of the iron on direct contact with the fabric. Shine marks are virtually irremovable, so taking care by using a cloth at all times is worth the effort. Press flat seams on the ironing or sleeve board and shaped parts over the tailor's ham.

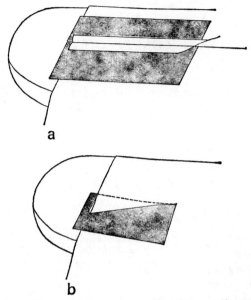

a

b

Fig. 64.   Place thin card between garment and seam allowances or dart.

Heat

Set the iron at the recommended heat control and test on a sample piece to find out just how much heat and dampening the fabric needs. You may find that slightly more or less heat is needed than the manufacturer suggests.

Pressure

Pressing is not ironing, so use some pressure to allow heat and steam to penetrate. A combination of pressure on the iron and sliding it with a continuous lifting movement is the professional way. On removal of the damp cloth, allow the steam to dry before moving the pressed section of skirt. "Patting" it with the flat back of a brush or tailor's block hastens this process.

Iron Marks

The base of the iron will gradually stain. If these stains are not removed, the iron will stick and leave marks on the pressing cloth and these marks will easily transfer to the fabric (see page 68).

PROCESSES IN ORDER OF CONSTRUCTION

The list set out below is an outline of the processes involved in constructing a skirt; following it there is a description of each stage:

Initial processes (see pages 107–9)
    Fabric and pattern preparation: layout of fabric
    Laying out and pinning pattern to fabric
    Cutting out fabric, lining, and interfacing
    Marking
    Applying interfacing

First steps to first fitting (see pages 109–10)
    Staystitching
    Pinning cut-out pieces and darts
    Basting darts, seams, and zipper
    Basting waistband and hem

First fitting for shape and alteration (see pages 110–14)

Final assembling and completion (see pages 114–17)
    Stitching and pressing darts and seams
    Inserting zipper
    Attaching lining to waist seam
    Waistband

Second fitting (see page 117)
    Adjustments and final stitching

Finishing (see pages 117–18)
    Seams
    Waistband
    Lining
    Hem

Final pressing (see page 118)

INITIAL PROCESSES

Fabric and Pattern Preparation: Layout of Fabric

With your fabric checked for shrinkage and correct grain, fold it as described in the cutting layout accompanying the pattern instructions.

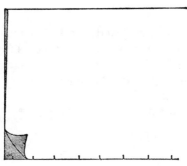

Fig. 65. Snip into selvage.

Generally, if it is not already folded, you should fold it in half along the lengthwise grain with right sides facing, one selvage on top of the other. If these selvages are tight and pucker, release tension by snipping into them at regular intervals; this will allow the fabric to lie flat. Ensure that the fold is always on the grain.

Laying Out and Pinning Pattern to Fabric

Lay the pattern pieces on the fabric according to the layout, as shown on the pattern envelope. Place the pieces that lie on the folded edge first. Check very carefully that the straight grain lines on the pattern pieces correspond to the straight grain of the fabric. Place weights on the pattern pieces to hold them in position and pin paper to fabric, making sure that neither pattern nor fabric are pulled or distorted.

Cutting Out Fabric, Lining, and Interfacing

Fabric. Cut with long, even strokes, using shorter strokes for curved edges. Cut notches outward, not into the seam, otherwise there could be problems if seams must be let out.

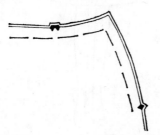

Fig. 66. Cut out around notches.

Lining.   If the skirt is to be lined, the lining is cut from the skirt pattern, with no alteration except that it is cut shorter—i.e., at the finished skirt hemline—and the waistband is not required. Apart from this, cutting is the same as for skirt in fabric.

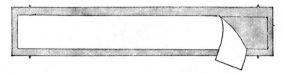

Fig. 67.   Waistband and interfacing.

Interfacing.   Cut the interfacing for the waistband without seam allowances.

Marking

Before removing the pattern from the fabric, all sewing and fitting lines must be marked with tailor tacking. On the skirt these lines are the side seams, darts, waist, hem, zipper opening, center back seam, and waistband. After removing the pattern, additional basting lines to mark the center front, and crosswise grain at hips, will be a help for the first fitting.

Fig. 68.   Basting marks for center front and crosswise grain.

Applying Interfacing

Interfacing, not to be confused with lining, gives body, strengthens and stiffens a part of a garment—in this case the waistband. The iron-on type is easiest to apply. Match grade to weight of fabric and stiffness required (see pages 317–18). Follow directions that come with the interfacing to be used. Press under a dry cloth, using pressure only, and *do not* slide or push the iron, which would wrinkle or twist the fabric and interfacing. Press so that the entire surface is thoroughly covered and allow the heat to penetrate and fuse interlining to fabric. Do not handle the interfaced part for a few minutes, until it has cooled.

FIRST STEPS TO FIRST FITTING

Always work with clean hands and protect the garment from getting grubby during the construction process. Light-colored fabrics, especially white ones, should be kept (semi-wrapped) in an old, clean sheet or similar cover.

Keep all cut-out parts not being worked on in a neat pile. Work on one part or section at a time, to avoid confusion.

Staystitching

Staystitch the waistline and hip curve seams.

Pinning Cut-Out Pieces and Darts

Matching sewing line basting, fold and pin darts, which should taper to a point. Pin the side seams next, matching the notches. Baste and prepare the lining in the same way.

Basting Darts, Seams, and Zipper

Baste darts and seams and lay the zipper right side up inside the opening of the center back seam (or left side seam) with the top of the tape ends at the waist cutting edge. Pin the right-hand seam allowance with the folded edge next to the zipper teeth. Tack 3 mm (⅛ in) from this edge. Turn back and pin the left side seam allowance to where it just barely covers the right edge of the opening. Baste this lapping side 1 cm (⅜ in) from the folded edge.

Basting Waistband and Hem

Waistband.   Before attending to the waistband, pin and baste lining to the inside waist, with seams of lining facing seam of skirt. Pin the waistband, right sides together, to skirt waist, matching notches and darts, and baste firmly.

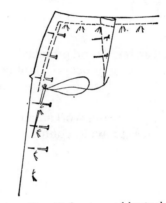

Fig. 69.   *Staystitch, pin, and baste darts and seams.*

Hem.   Pin back the hem allowance and baste 2 cm (¾ in) from cutting edge.

FIRST FITTING FOR SHAPE AND ALTERATIONS

Drastic alterations should not be necessary if care has been taken in carrying out all processes so far. Good fit is based on the following main aims:

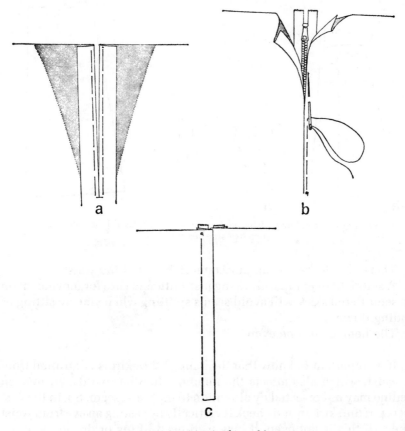

Fig. 70. Zipper opening (a); pin (b) and baste (c) zipper.

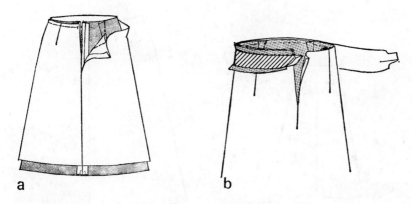

Fig. 71. Baste lining to waist (a) and waistband to skirt waist (b).

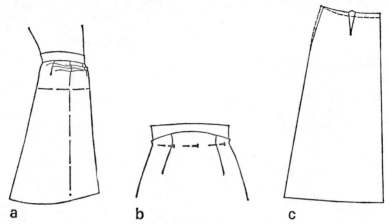

Fig. 72. For tightness below waistband (a), pin out wrinkles (b), cut off surplus, and increase side seam (c).

a. There should be a snug but comfortable fit at the waist.

b. A smoth fit over hips, allowing just sufficient ease for movement on this semi-flared skirt, will avoid seams splitting when you are sitting or bending down.

c. The hem should be even.

It is important to know that the hang of the skirt is controlled from the waist, which also affects the hemline. In other words, an uneven hemline may be corrected by alteration to the waist seam. So, in the first place, put the skirt on and check it vertically by casting an eye from waist to hem. If this is not even, it may well need lifting or dropping at the waist. Firm fabrics retain their shape and should not droop.

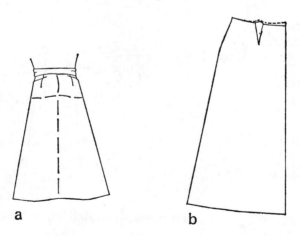

Fig. 73. For riding up in front (a), raise pattern at waist (b).

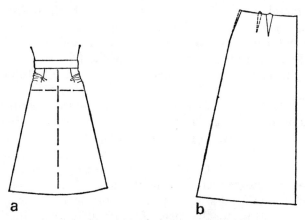

Fig. 74. For tightness at side front (a), add second dart (b).

As soon as you have taken a look at the skirt, return to the waist and start fitting from top to bottom. Bear in mind that the varying thicknesses of fabrics may make a difference to girth measurements. The skirt made in a cotton fabric will require slightly smaller measurements for waist and hips and the reverse applies to thicker fabrics. If the skirt fitting is carried out without wearing a blouse, remember to allow room for it.

If your skirt feels slightly too tight but does not show any wrinkles, or is a fraction too loose, release both side seams and rejoin for extra width, or pin out excess for a snug and comfortable fit.

Horizontal wrinkles below the waistband mean that the skirt is too tight. These are pinned out and eventually the amount to be lost is passed upwards and the surplus is cut off at the waist seam. This alteration may be combined with additions to the side seams, by letting

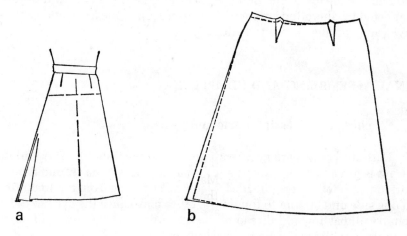

Fig. 75. For uneven flare at side (a), lift waist and take in flare (b).

them out. Remember to split increases (or decreases) at side seams evenly over all seams at both the left and right side.

Riding up at the front is caused by a large abdomen, or at the back, by a large seat. Raise at the front/back waist of the pattern at center for additional length and taper the waist seam allowance to the original width at the sides.

Prominent hip bones may cause tightness at the sides of the front. If so, open the side seam at the waist and a section of the waistband, and release part of the dart, using the gained amount toward a second dart. Leave a space of 3.8 cm (1½ in) from the first one and pin out the second approximately 2–2.5 cm (¾–1 in) deep, in slanting direction to the most prominent part of the hip bone. Add the small amount lost by the additional dart to the front side seam and re-pin seam and waistband. The principle relating to the use of darts discussed in Chapter Two—"Adjusting Pattern to Figure" (pages 33–50)—still holds true. A proportionally small waist and prominant hips equals a deep waist dart(s) or the reverse.

An uneven flare at the sides is caused either by fabric that has been cut off-grain (see pages 56–58) or by uneven hips. In both cases lift the waist to shorten the side seam or drop at the waist to lengthen the side seams.

Finally, attend to the hemline, ensuring that it is level, with the aid of a yardstick, T-square, or hem marker; measure from floor level up to the required length—then mark it accordingly. Once the hem is level, a decision to lengthen or shorten the skirt is a simple procedure.

When you have taken the skirt off, re-mark any alterations where pinned with a contrasting color, single thread, on both sides of the pins and transfer the alterations to the pattern. Remove lining, waistband, and unbaste the lower end of the zipper (if in the side seam). If the waist is affected by alterations, remove the zipper, open the hem, and rebaste new seams on the skirt and lining.

FINAL ASSEMBLING AND COMPLETION

Stitching and Pressing Darts and Seams

Darts and seams are now ready for machine-stitching. This should always begin at the top (waist) and finish at points of darts, and hem of skirt, on both left and right sides. Machine-stitching from top to bottom on one side and bottom to top on the other may cause the skirt to twist. Remove all basting and thread marks and underpress seams and darts; press darts with the fold edge toward center.

Do likewise with the lining, but leave a gap (for the zipper) unstitched. Raw edges on thin fabrics not hand overcast can be machine-finished if you turn seams back just under 6 mm (¼ in) and topstitch them from the wrong side; or you can zigzag them.

Inserting Zipper

If the zipper has been removed from side seam because of alterations, baste it and stitch it to the skirt, using the zipper foot attachment. Open the zipper before sewing it in, stitch well down on one side of the teeth, move the zipper tab out of the way of the presser foot, and repeat the same procedure on the other side.

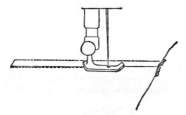

Fig. 76. Stitch zipper with zipper foot.

Attaching Lining to Waist Seam

Before attaching the lining to the skirt, turn up the hem about 2 cm (¾ in) and press back a narrow turning of about 6 mm (¼ in) to prevent fraying. Baste back the hem and slipstitch. After pressing, attach lining to the inside waistline of the skirt, wrong side of the lining to the wrong side of the skirt (seams of both facing) matching darts, seams, and notches. Baste firmly in position.

Waistband

Before basting the waistband to the skirt, which may have needed altering to fit a smaller or larger waist, finish the ends, which will eventually lap to fasten. The waistband is folded in half, right sides together. Each end is then machine stitched across and up to the mark on the seam allowance, which joins the band to the skirt (see Fig. 77).

Next cut the corners off the seam allowances to reduce bulk and to make neat corners when they have been turned right side out. Make a small cut at the ends of the stitching almost to the stitching line at the mark where it finishes. Then pull the ends through to the right side—the corners can be made sharper, if you gently pull them with a needle. Press the ends, and press one seam allowance in along the waistband at the same time. This will save time later, when this edge will be sewn to the inside lining of the skirt. Rebaste the waistband to the skirt (after any necessary alterations have been made), unpressed right side of the waistband to right side of the skirt. Machine stitch on the basted line. Do

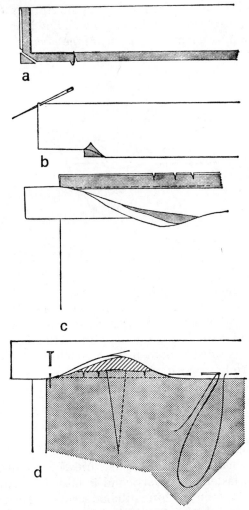

Fig. 77.   Stitch ends of waistband and cut off corners (a); pull ends right side out (b); baste unpressed right side of waistband to right side of skirt (c); baste inside waistband to inside waist seam (d).

not press waist seam open. Both seams should face upward, into the band, but the seam allowance may have to be cut back or clipped on slightly curved parts. This keeps the band from puckering. Turn the band to the inside skirt, laying pressed-in edge to the machine line, and baste down.

SECOND FITTING

Adjustments and Final Stitching

With the hem basted back, slip on the skirt once more for a final fitting. It is now unlikely that alterations will be called for, but there may be a need for small adjustments. Taking in or letting out small amounts can still be easily carried out. Check the length of the skirt for final proportion.

FINISHING

Seams

Overcast all remaining raw edges, either by hand or machine.

Waistband

Slipstitch the waistband over lining to the waistline seam. If you wish, cut and make loops for hangers from tape or ribbon, and sew to the inside waist at side seams. Sew two hooks to one end of the waistband

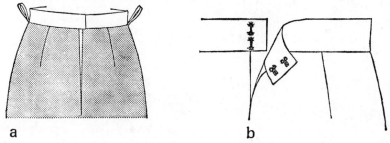

a   b

Fig. 78. Sew loops to waist at sides (a); sew on hooks and eyes (b).

and two eyes to the opposite end. The hooks are sewn to the inside of the overlap, with tightish overstitching, and with a few stitches underneath the hook itself; this will keep it flat. The eyes are sewn to the right side of the underlap, again securely through the loops.

Lining

The lining is sewn to the zipper tapes with small slipstitches on each side of the zipper.

A few long stitches to form a bar can be sewn at the hem of the lining at the seams, to join it to the skirt hem. This keeps the lining from dragging up inside the skirt.

Hem

Baste 1 cm (⅜ in) from the cut edge, then blindstitch.

FINAL PRESSING

Final or "top" pressing will give your skirt a crisp, finished look. Good underpressing has taken care of most of this process. All that remains is to press out any remaining creases and to cover parts such as the waistband, zipper, and hem, which need a little extra attention. Remember to press over a pressing cloth, straight parts on the ironing board and shaped ones over a tailor's ham.

7
The Second Design: Slacks

MAKING THE SLACKS

The actual sewing processes for making slacks are the same as for the skirt. The difference between the two is in the fitting and alterations to garment and pattern. Referring back to Chapter Two—"How to Take Measurements" (pages 23–27) and "Adjusting Pattern to Figure" (pages 33–35)—will also help you to achieve a perfect fit.

One major point is to make sure that the leg sections are clearly marked "front" and "back" on the cut-out fabric, and the right side of the material is marked, when this is not obvious. Front and back trouser legs look very similar and when separated can easily be confused, resulting in a left front put to a right back, or even two front leg sections sewn together.

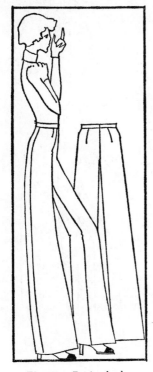

Fig. 79.   Basic slacks.

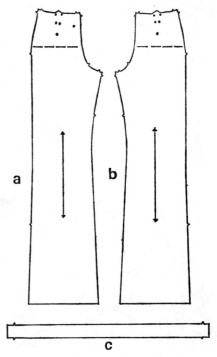

Fig. 80.   Basic pattern shape: front (a),
back leg (b), and waistband (c).

Notions

The same type of notions are used as for the skirt:

1. White/contrast colored basting thread.
2. Sewing thread.
3. Skirt-weight zipper 20.5 cm (8 in) in length.
4. Iron-on interfacing for the waistband.
5. Hooks and eyes for the waistband, size 2.

INITIAL PROCESSES

After the pattern has been taken off, with seams and darts marked, apply interfacing to waistband, then staystitch the waist curve, crotch, top section of inside legs, and curved hip seams. Pin and baste darts.

Additional basting lines, placed horizontally at hip level, representing the straight crosswise grain, will be a help for the first fitting.

Next take the left front and left back leg sections, pin and baste the outside leg seam first, right sides facing. Then pin and baste the inside leg seam. Do likewise with the right sections.

Fig. 81.   Waistband and interfacing.

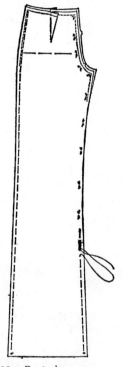

Fig. 82.   Staystitching, marking thread, and basted dart.

Fig. 83.   Baste leg seams.

On completion of both legs, turn them through to right side, match notches and the inside leg seams at the crotch, and pin the legs together in this position. Then pin and baste from the center back waist to the crotch and to the opening mark on the center front for zipper insertion or, if this is at the side, through to the front waist. The crotch seam is always stitched last, in the manner described, otherwise a good fit here will not be achieved.

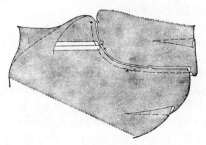

Fig. 84.   Join legs together at crotch seam.

Then

a. Pin and baste the zipper, using same method described for the skirt.
b. Pin and baste the waistband to waist seam, right sides together.
c. Pin and baste leg hem allowances.

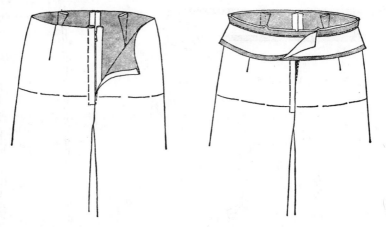

Fig. 85. Baste zipper.   Fig. 86. Baste waistband to waist seam.

FITTING AND ALTERATIONS

At the first fitting aim for

a. A snug, but comfortable fit at the waist.
b. A smooth fit over hips and seat, as tight as you like, but allowing
   sufficient ease for movement and no dragging wrinkles at crotch
   seam.
c. Legs and side seams hanging plumb straight.

Wear the shoes that will go with your slacks, for without them the
right length cannot be decided.

You will need assistance with this fitting.

Fitting the waist and hip area is very similar to that done in making
the skirt. In both cases your individual body contours and the way you
stand, which are unique to you, will determine the alterations needed.

As you did for the skirt, adjust the side seams by taking in or letting
out, for slight tightness or if fit is a fraction too loose, provided that no
wrinkles show on any area of the trousers. Tightness below the waistband, which makes the trousers ride up, is due to a large abdomen, seat,
prominent hip bones, or uneven hips. Alterations are carried out as
described on page 123, but—with the existence of an additional seam

which joins the center front, through the crotch and to the center back —fitting slacks demands a little more attention.

Inside leg and crotch seam alterations will be necessary for the following faults.

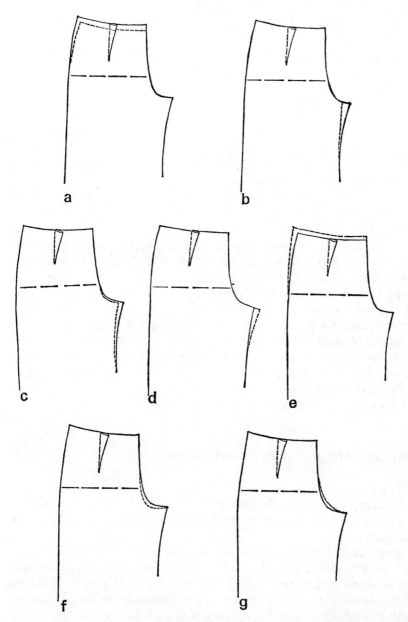

Fig. 87.   Lower waist seam and tighten waist (a); take in inside leg seam (b); with inside leg seam taken in, lower crotch curve slightly (c); let out inside leg seam (d); raise waist seam and loosen waist (e); take in (f); let out crotch seam (g). (Broken lines represent alterations.)

A low crotch: lower and tighten waist seam, but only if *no bagginess shows* at the inside leg, just below the crotch. If it is baggy here take in the seam as shown in Fig. 87 (b). This alteration will automatically eliminate both bagginess and shorten the rise, so that raising the waist for a higher crotch is not always necessary.

If the crotch is not too low and the inside leg is taken in, the crotch curve will need to be slightly lowered.

A high crotch, if combined with tightness at the inside leg, will have to be let out.

A high crotch: lower and loosen the waist.

Wrinkles showing at the lower end of the center front/back seam either side of the center of the crotch can also be removed by taking in or letting out the crotch seam curve as shown in Fig. 87 (f) and (g). Faults at either front or back are rectified by alterations to the affected legs only.

Keep an eye on the horizontal basting marks throughout your fitting and ensure that it is not distorted by alterations.

Aim for a clean, wrinkle-free fit from waist to crotch, with particular emphasis on the center seam.

Both legs should now fall free and straight. Have the length fixed so that the hems at the center of the front legs just rest on the insteps of your shoes. The best way to obtain the correct leg crease is to find the center of the right front leg at the bottom of the hem (above the center of the instep), hold it with your first finger and thumb, and then pin it into a fold. Further pins are then placed gradually toward the top of the leg in spaces of about 9 cm (3½ in), in line with the grain. Replace pins if the first attempt to achieve a straight fold fails and until it has been pinned at right angles to the hip grain mark. Do not try to pin the other trouser leg. You will find this crease when pressing, as described on page 126.

To increase/decrease the width at the hem, let out or pin in equal amounts at both inside and outside leg seams.

FINAL ASSEMBLING AND COMPLETION

On completion of the fitting, mark carefully where alterations are to be made, in the same manner as for the skirt, and transfer the alterations to the pattern.

Baste the leg crease where pinned, and remove pins.

Even if no alterations need to be made before stitching, remove the waistband and zipper, and open the crotch seam and hems. To make the next step easier still, it is preferable to open the inside leg seam. This way machine stitching and underpressing of side seams and darts now (the latter pressed toward the center, facing each other) will be more effi-

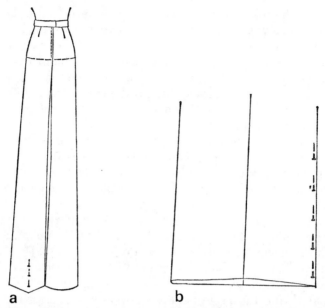

Fig. 88.   Pin crease above instep (a) and continue pinning crease (b).

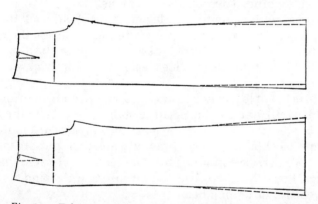

Fig. 89.   Take in, or let out equal amounts on both leg seams.

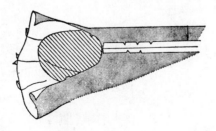

Fig. 90.   Press seam on sleeve board.

cient. Then the inside leg seams are stitched, from top to bottom, and underpressed. If you cannot slide the legs over the ironing board, use the sleeve board instead.

Finish the side and inside leg seams with hand overcasting or zigzagging on woolens, or machine-finish on cottons.

Rebaste the crotch seam, following the pre-fitting method. For this you will need a machine setting of about 8 stitches to 1 cm (⅜ in) or 20 stitches per in.

Ease the fabric carefully around the crotch curve, then machine-stitch again over the same line to reinforce this seam.

Clip seam allowance on the curved, lower part of crotch every 2 cm (¾ in), or cut back to 1 cm (⅜ in). Press seam open on a sleeve board or tailor's ham.

Reset the zipper and machine stitch as skirt zipper. Stitch final waistband ends as shown on page 116 and pin, baste, and machine-stitch the waistband to the waist seam of the trousers.

Rebaste hem allowances, slip the trousers on for a second fitting, and check the right leg crease and length of legs before final pressing.

Finally, after fitting, finish the waistband with slipstitch to waistband seam, sew on hooks and eyes. Finish raw edges of hems by overcasting or zigzagging. Then blindstitch hems.

Final pressing is done for one leg at a time. Fold back the left leg toward the top of the trousers, as shown in Fig. 91. Press the right leg, lightly at first, on the basted front crease; remove the basting thread.

Smooth fabric from the front leg crease toward the back and press in this position.

Turn over to left leg, match inside leg seams of both legs from hem to crotch, which will give you the position of the crease. With the right leg folded back, press the left one in the position you have just found. Front and back creases should now be in identical positions on both legs. Place both legs together, check, and press once more on each side of the outside legs. Press the upper section of trousers, waistband, and zipper on a sleeveboard or tailor's ham.

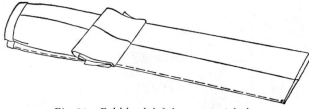

Fig. 91.   Fold back left leg, press right leg.

8
The Third Design: The Semi-fitted Dress

THE BASIC DRESS

The dress (sometimes called a tunic) is semi-fitted, semi-flared, with faced neckline, a zipper in the center back seam and set-in sleeves, or a sleeveless version with facing.

All stitches, seams and darts, zipper insertions, hem, and optional lining are carried out using the same methods as for the skirt and slacks.

New Processes

The two new processes are:

a. The faced neckline (and armhole).
b. The set-in sleeve.

Notions

The following notions are required:

1. White/contrast colored basting thread.
2. Two reels of sewing thread.
3. Dress-weight zipper, 56 cm (22 in) in length.
4. Lining (not including sleeves) optional.
5. Iron-on interfacing for neck.
6. Hook and eye for back neck opening, size 1.

Fig. 92.   Basic semi-fitted dress.

INITIAL PROCESSES

Having followed through similar working plans on the skirt and trousers should make you feel confident about basic construction methods—e.g., staystitching, sewing seams and darts. Now practice stitching a curve on two layers of fabric and turn the fabric to the right side to see that the finished edge had a good shape and lies flat.

If the garment is to be lined, cut the lining to the same shape as the dress, but shorter (as for the skirt, see page 108) and without sleeves.

Cut the interfacing, using the neck facing pattern, but without seam allowances.

After marking, staystitch neck, armhole, and hip curves, because these are liable to stretch. Apply the interfacing to the neck of garment,

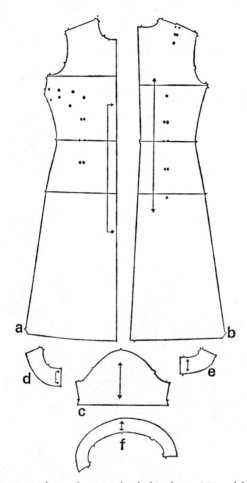

Fig. 93. Basic pattern shape: front (a), back (b), sleeve (c), and facings (d, e, f).

cut edge of interfacing placed to sewing lines of neck and shoulders.

Single-thread basting lines placed vertically at the center front from the neck to the hem, through the center of sleeves, and horizontally across bust and hips, will be of great help at the fitting stage.

First, pin and baste all darts, then the center back seam below the zipper opening. Pin and baste the zipper—leaving a small gap 6 mm (¼ in) from the neck sewing line to the first zipper teeth—followed by the shoulder seams, side seams, underarm seam, and lastly the hem.

Do likewise with the lining, leaving upper part of the center back seam open for the zipper. With the wrong side of lining to wrong side of dress, pin and baste lining to neck and armholes of the dress.

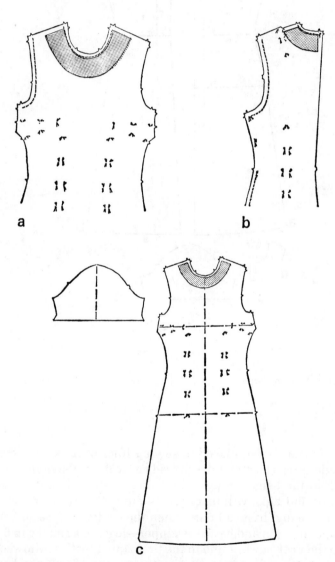

Fig. 94. Mark, staystitch, and interface fabric (a, b); simple basting marks for center front, bust, hips, and center sleeve (c).

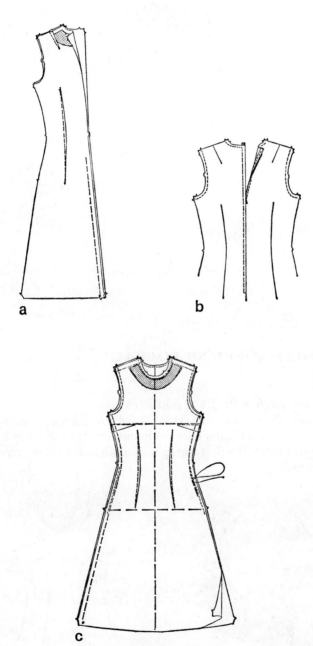

Fig. 95.   Baste darts and center back seam (a); baste zipper (b); baste shoulder and side
seams (c).

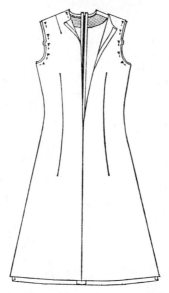

Fig. 96. Pin and baste lining to inside dress.

THE FACED NECKLINE (AND ARMHOLE)

Next, the facings for front and back neck are joined, right sides together, at the shoulder seams. This is basted to the neckline, right sides together, matching shoulder seams. Do not turn the facing to the inside of the neck until after the first fitting in case alteration to the shape of the neck is needed.

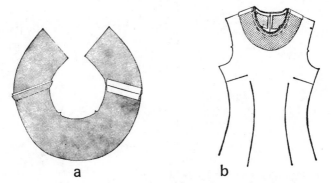

a   b

Fig. 97. Join facings (a) and baste facing to neckline (b).

On a sleeveless dress join the armhole facings, matched to notches, and baste them to the armholes in the same manner as with the neck facings.

THE SET-IN SLEEVE

The top of the sleeve, called the *cap*, is always larger than the armhole and must be eased in to allow for, and fit, the top of the arm and shoulder bone. Therefore, the sleeves need a gathering thread from the notch at one side to the notch on the other. This can be done with the largest stitch on the sewing machine. Fastened securely on one side, this thread is then drawn up to reduce the length of the cap to the circumference of the armhole and fastened on the other side. Spread the fullness evenly and avoid puckers or pleats. Sleeves made in woolen fabrics are comparatively easy to fit into armholes, whereas special care is needed for cotton. Placing gathered sleeve caps over the rounded end of a sleeveboard and pressing them before attaching them to armholes is an additional help.

With hems of both sleeves basted up, you can now fit them into each armhole. (Be sure to fit the left sleeve to the left armhole and right to right armhole.)

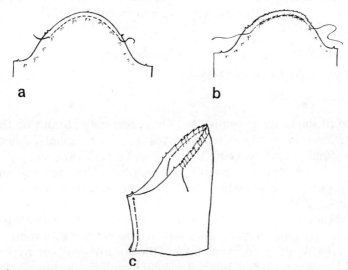

Fig. 98.   Sleeve cap with gathering thread (a); gathering thread drawn up (b); gathered sleeve cap and basted underarm seam (c).

With both sleeve and dress right side out, place and pin the top of the underarm seam to the base of the armhole at the side seam.

Turn the dress to the inside, place and pin the sides of the sleeve cap to the sides of the armhole seams, matching notches. Take great care to see that they do match, because a lot of sleeves have been set in backwards because notches were absent or ignored!

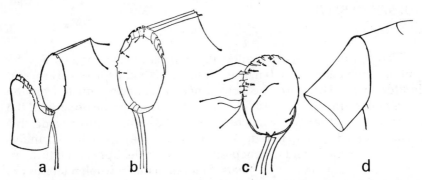

Fig. 99.   Pin underarm of sleeve to bodice side seam (a); pin sleeve to armhole on inside (b); hold back top of sleeve over hand (c); smooth, finished sleeve cap (d).

With pins holding the sleeve to armhole, pin the top of the cap to the shoulder seam. Now hold the sleeve to the armhole at the top sides and the bottom, and pin (at right angles to seams) and baste throughout. Remember to ease in where the cap is gathered and avoid pleats or puckers. As an additional aid, the fullness can be spread and more easily distributed by holding the sleeve as shown in Fig. 99(c).

FITTING AND ALTERATIONS

To fit the tunic or semi-fitted dress, remember to put on the same foundation garments you wore for taking measurements. Put on your most suitable shoes, make up to look your best, and arrange your hair to leave the neck easily accessible for the fitting. Give yourself and your assistant ample time, so that the fitting can be carried out in a relaxed manner.

Inasmuch as the hang of the skirt is controlled from the waist, the fit of the semi-fitted dress is determined first by the shoulders. Correct balance between the front and back of the dress depends on how well the shoulder seam is placed, no matter what length the design of the skirt. A hemline shorter at the front than at the back, or the reverse, may well require alteration to the shoulder seams, rather than lengthening at the hem. So apply the same rule as for the previous two garments and first scrutinize from top to bottom. Make a mental note of any obvious faults before getting on with the actual fitting. Success will come with patience.

Aim to have this garment free from wrinkles, without pull or strain on any parts in one direction or another. Bust and hips should fit well, but not so tightly as to restrict movement. Working from top to bottom as before, make it your objective to achieve:

a. A well-shaped, comfortable neckline to lie smoothly on the base of the neck, neither binding nor too loose and gaping.
b. Straight shoulder lines, of the correct length from the base of the neck at the sides, to the shoulder bones.
c. Sleeves falling free, parallel to your body, comfortable below the armpits—without unnecessary and unsightly bagginess. (Arms should be able to move freely, with adequate fabric across the front and the back of the bodice, between armholes on both sides.)
d. A smooth-fitting bustline, with darts placed in the correct positions.
e. The waistline as tight as possible, but without strain caused by overfitting.
f. A smooth fit over hips allowing sufficient ease (as for the skirt—see pages 112–13).
g. Center back seam and side seams, as well as the center front seam, to fall straight—ensuring that both left and right sides of the garment are even and do not show more flare on one side than the other. (Your basted grain lines will be a guide.)
h. A level hemline, given by good balance between the front and the back of the dress.

Remember, too, that your body is not only different from anyone else's but also that one side varies from the other. The pattern that you have used cannot allow for this fact, but the fitting process can.

Fig. 100. Mark lower neckline.

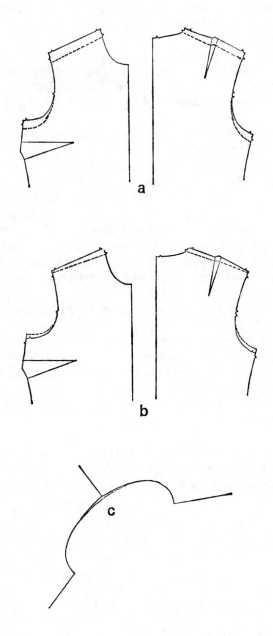

Fig. 101. Alteration marking lines for lifted shoulder and lower armhole (a); raised
armhole and let-out shoulder (b); keep rounded armhole shape (c).

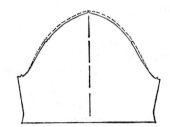

Fig. 102.   Let out sleeve seam at cap.

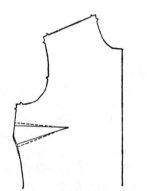
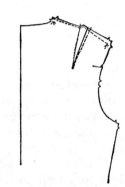

Fig. 103.   Take in underarm bust dart.   Fig. 104.   Take in shoulder dart.

To rectify faults, in sequence from (a) to (h), the following alterations are called for:

a. A too-high neckline can be lowered by pinning, as shown in Fig.
100. A too-low neckline can be raised by reducing the seam allowance;
also, see if taking in the shoulder seams at the neck will help.

b. Excess fabric because of sloping shoulders, take in the shoulder
seams and lower the armholes, as shown in Fig. 101(a).
Tightness across the bust may only need the releasing and letting
overcome by letting out shouldr seams and raising the armholes. This
alteration may only be necessary for one side. Your shoulder bone
structure also affects the length of the shoulder seam. Lengthen or
shorten it to see that the sleeve cap fits to the end of the bone. Make sure
that the top of the armhole at the shoulder seams retains a rounded shape
after alterations.

c. Caps that are too short and so are dragging the sleeves up, need
lengthening. Prominent shoulder bones may be the cause. In this event
(as with all shoulder seam and armhole alterations) remove the sleeves
and reset them, after letting out the sleeve seam at the cap.

Strain across the front or the back of the bodice between the armholes, which causes tightness at sleeves, can be remedied by letting out the armhole seam where it is tight.

Excess fabric, horizontally between shoulders and bust at the front armholes, is corrected by opening the shoulder seam and lifting the front shoulder only—from shoulder bone to nothing at the neck—or, if close to the bust, by increasing the depth of the underarm bust dart by the amount of excess visible, and by as much as the front side seam can be lengthened upwards, to rematch the back side seam. At the back armholes lift the back shoulder seam only and increase the depth of the shoulderblade dart, by as much as the back shoulder seam can be lengthened, to rematch the front.

d. The bust is one of the most important areas for a well-fitting garment, but neither your bust measurement nor your pattern give an accurate indication of the actual size of the bust and its shape.

The reading obtained on measuring includes the bone structure and contours of your back, resulting in a total circumference measurement. This does not automatically imply that the bust is of a particular shape. So alterations to darts for the correct control of fullness, creating shape for the bust, may well be necessary.

The underarm bust darts, and those from waist to bust, should be placed in the direction of the most prominent points of the bust and to within 2.5 cm (1 in) of it.

If your shoulder-to-bust-point measurement has been taken accurately and checked with the pattern, and if you wore the same foundation garments when measuring your body as you are now for the fitting, the darts should be in their correct positions. But check just the same and adjust them if necessary.

Tightness across the bust may only need the releasing and letting out of the side seams, but alterations here affect the circumference of the sleeve cap, as shown in Fig. 105. The underarm seams will have to be adjusted accordingly.

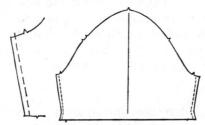

Fig. 105.   Adjust underarm seam.

If after that wrinkles still show, the depth of the underarm darts should be increased and the loss of length on the front side seam made good, by as much as the seam allowance at the base of the armhole can be reduced.

e and f. Side and center back seams at the waist and hips can be adjusted by taking in or letting out small amounts, as previously described for the skirt on page 113. Equally, and in addition, waist darts can be increased or decreased. But beware of overfitting, which will result in unsightly wrinkles—those which look like soft folds, deep in the center but shallow at the ends (best observed on trousers between the knee and crotch when the leg is lifted with the knee bent) mean tightness, wherever they are. The direction in which these wrinkles show indicates the area from which the tightness originates. Releasing seams at the point(s) mentioned will eliminate this type of fault.

g. Keep an eye on the basted grain lines during the fitting. As long as the horizontal ones remain at right angles to the vertical, distortion will have been avoided.

h. An uneven hemline, caused by lack of balance between the front and the back section of the dress, is often affected by your stance; this is put right by pinning out the surplus length and then re-marking and re-cutting the shoulders and neckline by the amount to be lost after the fitting, as shown in Fig. 106.

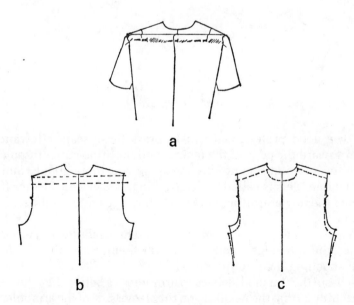

Fig. 106.   Pin out surplus length evenly (a); mark the amount to be taken out (b); remark shoulder, neck, and armhole (c). (The front can be altered in the same way.)

Before you remove your dress for re-marking the fabric and pattern, do a final test. Move around, sit, bend down, and lift your arms. If the garment not only looks right but has become part of you, it has passed the test with flying colors.

FINAL ASSEMBLING AND COMPLETION

When all the necessary alterations have been marked, remove the lining, facing, sleeves, and zipper. Transfer the alterations to the garment and pattern. As with the previous garments, all darts and seams on the garment and the lining are machine-stitched and underpressed, but leave the facings for joining to the neck, and sleeves to armholes until later. Seam allowances are finished with overcasting, or machine-finishing. The lining hem can also be finished at this stage.

With the garment stitched, the zipper reset, and the hem basted for a second fitting, pin and rebaste the lining to the armholes and neck, wrong sides facing. Now machine-stitch facings to neck (and armhole if sleeveless). Clip or cut back seam allowances to allow the facings to lie flat, when they are turned to the wrong side.

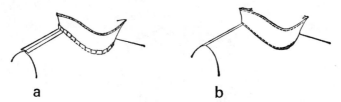

a   b

Fig. 107.   Stitch facing to neck and clip seam (a); understitch neck seam (b).

For a good professional finish, press these seam allowances together, toward the edge of the facing, and machine-stitch through both seam allowances and facing, close to the sewing line—about 3 mm (⅛ in) from the line. This is called understitching; it keeps the facings flat and prevents them from rolling back and showing on the right side of the garment.

With the underarm seam machine-stitched, rebaste the sleeve hems, overcast the raw edges, and blindstitch them. Press the sleeves well before attaching them to the dress.

Rebaste the finished sleeves to armholes as before. Lay the dress on the machine so that the needle is on the sleeve side of the armhole. Stitch carefully on the basted line, avoiding pleats or puckers on the sleeve cap as before. After machine-stitching, and checking on the right arm, trim the seam allowances to 1 cm (⅜ in), stitch a second row close to the raw edges, and overcast them.

With the dress inside out, press sleeve and armhole seams together toward the sleeves on the rounded end of the sleeve board. Press gently and do not push the iron too much, because this causes stretching and loss of shape. The seam allowances on the neck facings at the center back are turned in and basted to the zipper tape. (Leave enough space between the facing and zipper teeth to allow the zipper tab to run freely.)

Sew the outside edges of the facings to the shoulder seams of the lining at each side (armhole facings if sleeveless to the shoulder and side seams).

Slip the dress on for second fitting and make final adjustments if necessary.

Finally, finish off the hem as described on page 101. (Catch lining hem to dress hem with a few hand stitches, to prevent the lining from riding up.)

Sew a hook and eye to the top of neck above the zipper to take the strain here.

Sew the center back of the facings and lining to the zipper tapes with slipstitches.

Fig. 108.   Catch facing and lining to zipper tape.

Remove all remaining marking and basting threads.

Final pressing should now only consist of touching up, especially at the neckline, zipper, and hem. Do not press these areas too heavily, otherwise impressions of the facings, etc. will show on the right side of the garment. Press sleeve caps over the rounded end of a sleeve board or a small tailor's ham. The straight, flat skirt sections are best pressed over the ironing board on the wrong side of the garment, and all shaped areas over a tailor's ham—but do not press any part without a pressing cloth.

Careless pressing will flatten and destroy, whereas careful pressing will mould, retain, and improve the shape as built in by darts and seams.

Slight puckering may disappear if the seams are held taut when pressing, but do not stretch them and cause loss of shape.

9
The Fourth Design: The Jacket

THE JACKET

The basic jacket is semi-fitted, semi-flared, edge-to-edge cardigan style, with faced fronts, set-in sleeves, and patch pockets.

New Processes

The new processes in this are:

a. The felling stitch.
b. The patch pocket.
c. The jacket facings.
d. Insertion of shoulder pads (optional).
e. Hand-finished lining (optional).

Fig. 109.   Basic jacket.

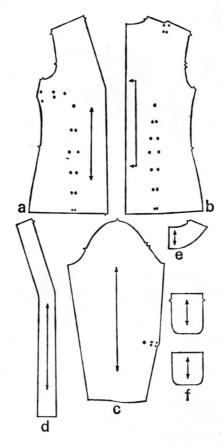

Fig. 110.   Basic pattern shapes: front (a), back (b), sleeve (c), facings (d, e), and pockets (f).

Notions

The following notions are required:

1. Basting thread cotton and sewing thread.
2. Lining (optional).
3. Interfacing for fronts, pockets, and back neck.
4. Shoulder pads (optional).

THE FELLING STITCH

This is a small hemming stitch used for hand finishing where machine-stitching is not possible, or where it would show to disadvantage. It is used mainly to sew in linings to clothes.

A fractional amount of garment fabric is taken for the first stitch, then an equally small amount in the hem turning. Stitches are close together and made on the very edge of the hem turning and immediately below the hem, and should not show on the right side. In the case of linings this is easy, because the stitches are only taken through the lining material and the facing.

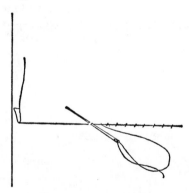

Fig. 111. Felling stitch.

INITIAL PROCESSES

If you decide to line the garment but no pattern is supplied, cut it to the same shape as the jacket, but shorter and without facings (as for the dress and skirt).

Interfacings for the back neck and front facings and the pockets are cut without seam allowances.

On completion of marking—including the position of pockets and single-thread basting for the grain at the bust, hips, center, back and center of sleeves—staystitch the neckline and continue down the fronts

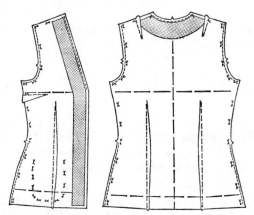

Fig. 112.   Staystitch, mark, and baste darts; attach iron-on interfacing.

to the hem. (This is very important, because these must not stretch.) Staystitch armholes and hip curve as before. Apply the interfacing to the wrong side of the garment (see Fig. 112). Next, pin and baste darts.

THE PATCH POCKET

The patch pocket is an all-purpose pocket, suitable for cotton or woolen fabrics.

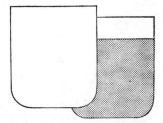

Fig. 113.   Patch pocket.

The pockets are made up and basted to the jacket fronts before the side and shoulder seams are joined: this is easier and more accurate than placing and attaching them after the seams have been joined.

A *practice pocket* in a similar or the same fabric should be made first of all to gain experience in sewing corners and to achieve a uniform shape. Detailing on garments is most important and meant to be good—a careless, inaccurate finish on only one corner can ruin the effect of an otherwise well-finished garment.

The pocket is cut with its own facing, so the lined part will not show (see Fig. 114(a)).

The lining is cut to the same width as the pocket, but shorter, to meet the self-facing when folded back (see Fig. 114(b)). The edges of the facing and top of the lining need additions of seam allowances.

Interfacing, cut and applied as shown in Fig. 114(c) eliminates unnecessary bulk in turnings. First mark and staystitch the pocket and then apply the interfacing to the wrong side of the pocket, exactly to the marking lines.

Stitch the pocket lining to the top of the pocket facing (right sides facing) leaving a gap in the center of the seam of at least 6.5 cm (2½ in).

Fold over the pocket lining, right sides facing, so that all the edges meet (see Fig. 114(d)). Baste in this position and machine-stitch all the way around the sides and lower edge. Use the edge of the interfacing and staystitching as a guide.

Trim the seam allowances and top corners, and notch the curved lower edges to ensure a neat, even shape on the curves when they are turned through to the right side.

Pull the pocket to its right side through the gap left in the seam between the lining and the facing. Use a needle and gently pull out the top corners, to give them a sharp shape (see Fig. 114(f)). Smooth the curves at the bottom end, making sure that the lining does not "roll," so that it shows on the right side. Sew up the gap in the seam (see Fig. 114(g)).

Baste the pocket all the way around, underpress, remove basting, and press again, to ensure that no impression of basting is left (see Fig. 114(h)).

When the two pockets have been completed, they are ready for pinning and basting to marking lines on the jacket fronts—before the side and shoulder seams are joined. Leave the pockets basted only for the fitting, before attaching them permanently, in case alterations are made to the length of the jacket or the side seams, which would affect their placement (see Fig. 114(i)).

Proceed to pin and baste side, shoulder, and underarm seams. Put a gathering thread in each sleeve cap, draw up, and spread the fullness evenly. Press on a sleeveboard.

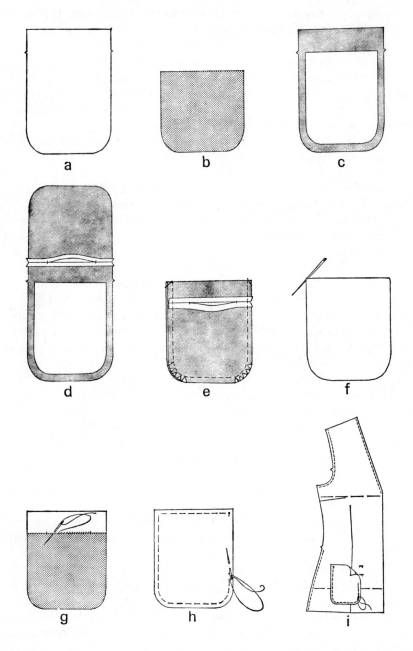

Fig. 114. Pocket and facing cut in one piece (a); lining (b); apply interfacing to wrong side of pocket (c); leave gap open (d); stitch seam and clip corners (e); pull out corners after turning pocket right side out (f); sew gap together (g); baste pocket all the way around (h); baste pocket to jacket (i).

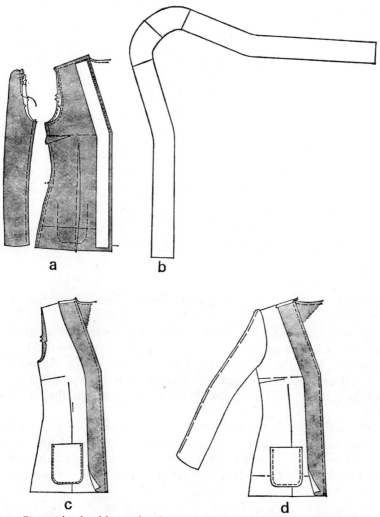

Fig. 115.   *Baste side, shoulder, and underarm seams* (a); *join facings at shoulder* (b); *baste facing to jacket* (c); *set in sleeves* (d).

THE JACKET FACINGS

Join facings at the shoulder seam, right sides facing. (For an unlined version, machine-finish the outer edges of the facing to avoid overhandling at later stages.) Pin and baste at the front/back neck facing to the

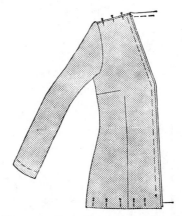

Fig. 116.   Baste lining to inside jacket.

jacket, right sides facing, and set in the sleeves identically to that method described, for the dress, on page 134.

If a lining is used, join the sections together in the same order as the jacket. Baste the hems of the jacket and sleeves. With the jacket turned inside out, place the wrong side of lining to the wrong side of jacket.

Pin the shoulder seams of both together to hold in position. Pin and baste the raw edges of the lining to the neck, front, and the shoulder of jacket.

Pin and baste the hems, but allow the lining to be slightly longer from the shoulder to hem at the front and back, and also from the cap to hem of the sleeves. A too-tight lining will drag up the garment when it is turned back to the right side. You are now ready for the first fitting.

FITTING AND ALTERATIONS

There are only a few differences in fitting the jacket to those shown in the previous designs. The aims for a good fit were listed on page 135 and the correction of faults has been described.

If you plan to wear a heavier blouse, shirt or jumper, or even a skirt or slacks with your jacket, they must be worn for the fitting.

INSERTION OF SHOULDER PADS (OPTIONAL)

To achieve a more "tailored" look, you may want to use shoulder pads. Place the center of these to the shoulder seams, with the wide side into the sleeve heads (Fig. 117) and pin into position before alterations to the shoulder area.

Fig. 117.   Pin shoulder pad in place.

When standing still, the front opening should be edge to edge as designed and not show gaps below the V of the neckline.

A commonly found fault is to have the fronts falling away to expose a widening gap at the lower part of jacket, toward the hemline. If this does occur, one way of fixing it is to lift the front shoulder seams (to nothing at shoulder bone) until the center front edges meet (Fig. 118).

This alteration *may* cause tightness at the hip side seams, and the front will need to be released at the lower jacket side seams.

Make sure that the basted grain lines are not distorted and that the bust and hip lines remain at right angles to the center back and front edges.

Shortening or lengthening the jacket is likely to affect the positioning of pockets, so raise or lower them accordingly.

Check for a level hemline and make sure that the lining does not cause strain to any parts of the garment.

Fig. 118.   *Lift front shoulder seam and let out side seam.*

FINAL ASSEMBLING AND COMPLETION

In preparation for a second try-on, mark alterations, remove the lining, and open the seams. Re-mark, re-cut, and transfer any alterations to the fabric and pattern. Machine-stitch the darts and underpress. Stitch the pockets to the final position on the jacket fronts either by

a. Machine-stitching on right side, close to the pocket edges. Back-stitch securely at the top corners (Fig. 119(a)); or
b. Handsewing with very small stitches—just taking in the edges of the pockets and one or two threads of the jacket fabric.

Now join the shoulder and side seams, and also the facings, to the back neck and front edges.

Press the seams open, but with facing seams together toward the front edges. Then understitch the facings. Turn, baste, and press them to the inside. Pin, baste, and sew in the sleeves and press on sleeveboard, as for the dress (see page 141).

Place shoulder pads with the pointed end to the center of shoulder seam, and the wide edge level with the edge of the armhole seam

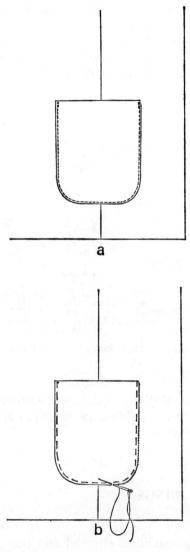

Fig. 119. *Pocket machine-stitched* (a) *and hand-stitched* (b).

allowance, or even a fraction beyond. Pin in this position and handsew (with a firm but not-too-tight basting stitch) the armhole seam allowance to the shoulder pads as shown in Fig. 120(b). Turn the pointed end back by about 1 cm (⅜ in) and catch the pads to the shoulder seam with a few loose stitches.

Blindstitch hems on the sleeves and jacket (check that hem allowances are even in width) and then the facings to the inside jacket, with loose stitches to avoid sewing impressions on the right side. Finish the bottom of the facings over the jacket hem, slightly short on the finished edge with the felling stitch, making sure that facing is not sewn tight lengthwise. Remove all basting marks (see Fig. 120(c)).

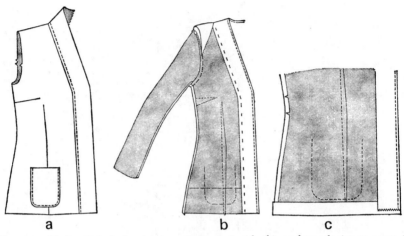

Fig. 120. *Understitch facing (a), turn facing to inside (b), and sew facing to seam (c).*

Press the jacket well all over, before re-inserting the lining. You may like to slip on the garment at this stage, before completion, in case there are any minor adjustments.

HAND-FINISHED LININGS

With the lining machined-stitched and pressed, turn the jacket inside out and put the wrong side of the lining to the wrong side of jacket, preferably on a dress form.

Pin to, and hold back, the lining at the shoulder seams. Sew the inside lining, shoulder seam allowances to the jacket shoulder seam allowances, with loose stitches. Start from the front neck edge, pass over the shoulder pads (or through to the end of the seam allowances if no pads have been used) and fasten off securely.

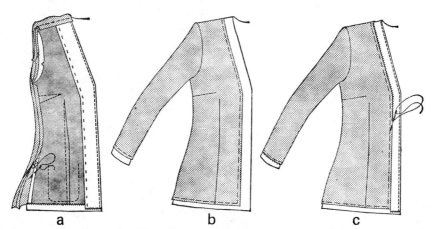

Fig. 121. *Sew lining shoulder seam to jacket shoulder seam (a), baste lining to inside jacket (b), and fellstitch lining (c).*

Match up the side seams and attach the lining to the jacket at the seam allowances in the same way. Securing the lining in this manner prevents it from twisting when the jacket is worn.

Finally, pin and baste the lining to the facing and hem of the jacket and sleeves—with the raw edges turned and pressed to the inside, and well back from finished edges. Check to make sure that a little extra length has been allowed, so as to prevent the jacket from being pulled or dragged up. Then with a small felling stitch, sew the lining to hem allowances and facings.

Final pressing should only consist of the removal of creases caused by handling the garment in its later stages of sewing. Touch up the lining by pressing lightly.

10
The Fifth
Design:
The Soft Coat

THE SOFT COAT

This classic-shaped coat incorporates the basic methods of construction suitable for most coats.

It is semi-fitted with the button and buttonhole and single-breasted front fastening, which, when joined at the neck to the collar and set in with facings, forms a small lapel and is worn open at the neck. It has a center back seam, set-in sleeves, and large patch pockets with flaps. The decoration introduced in addition is topstitching on pockets, collar, and edges.

The size and number of buttons may vary according to the pattern chosen. The actual buttonhole described is a piped one made from two folded stripes of the same fabric, this is suitable for most coat-type fabrics and buttons.

New Processes

The new process are:

a. The pockets and Flaps.
b. Topstitching.
c. Piped buttonholes.
d. The collar with facing.

Notions

The following notions are required:

1. Basting sewing thread.
2. Lining.
3. Interfacing—heavyweight for fronts, collar, and pockets.
4. Buttons (including spare ones.)
5. Buttonhole twist for top-stitching (optional).
6. Shoulder pads.

Fig. 122.   Basic soft coat.

INITIAL PROCESSES

The previous processes listed in Chapter Nine are identical to those used for the coat up to and including the making of pockets, which on the coat have in addition flaps and topstitching.

With the marked and separated sections ready, staystitch all curved edges, apply for interfacings to the fronts, back neck, pockets and flaps, and undercollar (once again all cut without seam allowances). Cut the collar interfacing on the same grain as the undercollar in fabric and, if cut in two sections, attach it before joining the center seam. Check to see that the buttonhole and pocket markings show on the right side of the garment fronts.

Staystitch all curved edges, pin and baste darts, and join facings at the shoulder seam.

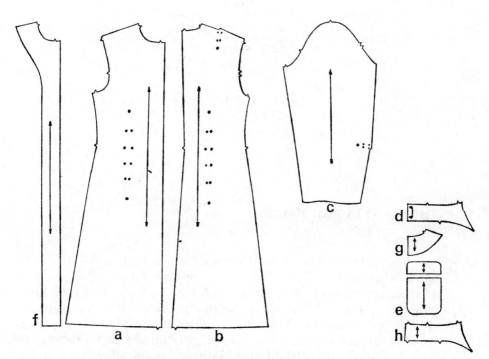

Fig. 123. Basic pattern shapes: front (a), back (b), sleeve (c), collar (d), pocket (e), and facings (f, g, h).

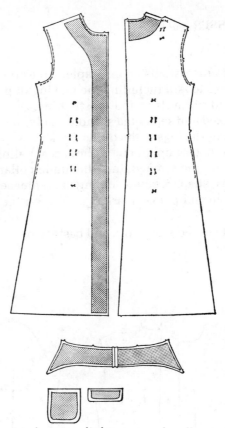

Fig. 124. *Interfacing applied to coat, undercollar, and pocket.*

THE POCKETS AND FLAPS

As in the case of the jacket, the pockets are made before the side and shoulder seams are joined. The pockets are completed in the same way as described on page 147 with the addition of a flap. The flap is lined either in self (same) fabric, if it is thin enough, or with a lining on bulkier woolen materials. The lining piece is sewn to the interfaced top flap, right sides together, with a gap left along the top edge so the flap can be pulled through to the right side. Trim the seam allowances, notch curves, turn right side out, and sew the edges of the gap together by hand. Baste these edges, underpress, remove basting, and press again.

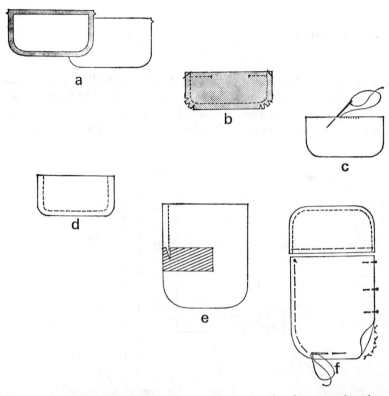

Fig. 125. Flap (a); stitch right side of flap and lining together (b); turn right side out and stitch gap together (c); topstich (d); mark with notched guide (e); baste to marking line (f).

TOPSTITCHING

The flaps are topstitched before being set onto the coat, and the pockets are topstitched to the coat. Again, practice topstitching before working on the flaps themselves (see Fig. 125(a), (b), (c), (d), (e) and (f)).

Use the largest setting on the sewing machine and, if possible, buttonhole twist thread that will show up better. Try to keep the stitching exactly the same distance from the edges. This will call for a little practice. A small marker in cardboard can be a help here, in addition to an accurate basting line, to check the stitching as you go along.

Topstitch the sides and lower edge of the flaps, and pin and baste the pockets and flaps to the marking lines on the coat fronts, so that they are ready for final attaching after the fitting.

PIPED BUTTONHOLES

The next step is to make the buttonholes. As with all new processes, samples worked out before will make it all the easier and lead to better results on the actual garment. This applies especially to the making of buttonholes, and more than one should be practiced to ensure that they

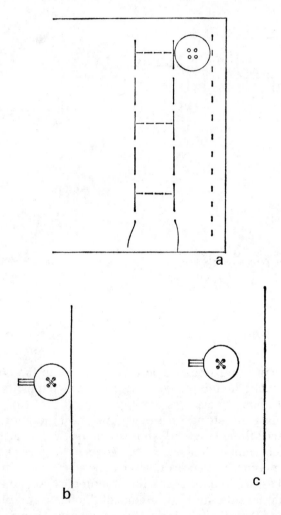

Fig. 126. *Buttonhole placement* (a); *wrong placement* (b) *and correct placement* (c).

are all identical in shape and size and placed in one line equidistant from the edge.

The buttonholes are marked at the center front. A further allowance, approximately the width of the button to the edge of the coat, should be made. This space between the end of the buttonhole and the edge is necessary to allow for the shank of the button and for the garment to close at the center front.

On the sample piece of fabric, mark two or three buttonholes, as shown on Fig. 126(a).

The size of holes must always be slightly larger—3 mm (⅛ in)—than the diameter of the buttons, to allow the buttons to pass through easily and without causing strain to the holes.

Baste vertical lines at each end of the buttonholes as well as horizontal lines. This will enable you to see where to place, start, and finish the piping strips.

Make the piping for the buttonholes by cutting two rectangular pieces of fabric on the straight grain, about 2 cm (¾ in) wide by the diameter of the button plus 2 cm (¾ in) long. Fold the strips in half lengthwise, wrong sides facing, then baste exactly along the center of each strip.

This baste line must be exactly in the middle, otherwise the finished buttonhole sides will be uneven.

Now lay the *raw edges* of both strips to meet right on the basted buttonhole line, on the *right* side of the fabric. The ends of piping strips should extend 1 cm (⅜ in) on each side of the vertical basting lines. Pin, then baste the piping strips in position, on the center basting line (see Fig. 127(a)).

Machine-stitch along this line on each side between vertical basting on either side. Finish off each end securely.

Turn the fabric to the other side, and with small, sharp scissors cut along the buttonhole line to within 6 mm (¼ in) of each end.

Then cut into each corner just to the line of stitching. This must be done carefully and accurately, otherwise a neat finish of the buttonholes will not be possible (see Fib. 127(b)).

Now pull the piping strips through, so that all raw edges are on the wrong side of the garment (see Fig. 127(c)).

The small triangular pieces formed at each end are turned to the back when the piping is in position, and with the garment fabric folded back, sewn to the piping strips.

Underpress and remove all basting marks.

Before marking the buttonholes on the coat front, check to see that the markings are clearly visible and accurately placed on the *right* side of the *right* front.

With the pockets basted in place and buttonholes made, the side and shoulder seams can now be basted together. For ease in handling, prepare sleeves as for the jacket, but do not set in until the collar has been joined to the neckline.

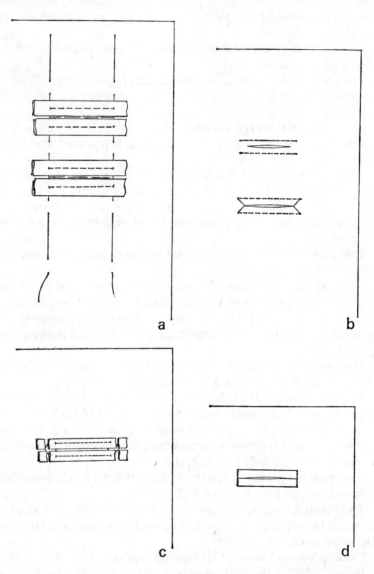

Fig. 127.   Baste and stitch along center of piping strips laid edge to edge on marking lines (a); cut along buttonhole lines (b); pull piping strips through (c); finish ends (d).

THE COLLAR WITH FACING

Baste the top collar (right side facing the right side of the undercollar) on the outside edges, leaving the neck edge open.

Machine-stitch, taking one stitch across the collar points. (This makes for neater corners when the collar is turned to the right side.)

Trim seam allowances, especially at corners. Turn collar to the right side, pull out corners so that both are quite even and of good shape. Baste and underpress, making sure that the outside edge seam does not show on the right side of the top collar. Baste the raw neck edges together with largish stitches.

The collar is then topstitched in the same way as the pocket flap, on the outer edge and sides, at the same stitching distance from the finished edges.

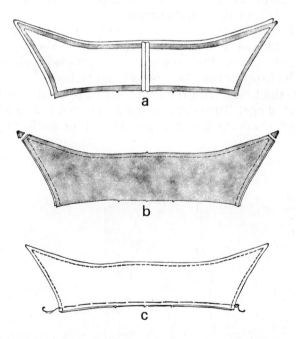

Fig. 128.   Stitch collar (a, b) and topstitch on right side (c).

Pin and baste the collar to the neck edge of the coat, matching notches, undercollar side to right side of coat. Start at the center back and pin/baste to either side at fronts.

Fig. 129.   Baste collar to neck edge.

Lay the facing right side down over the collar and baste, matching front and back of neck edges.

To turn the facing back to its final position for the fitting, it may be necessary to clip neck seam allowances in one or two places.

With curves staystitched and interfaced, an otherwise easily stretched neckline will keep its shape.

Set in the sleeves, pin and baste in the same way as previously. Place and pin shoulder pads, with the center of pads to shoulder seams and extended to the edges of the armhole/sleeve cap seam allowances.

Baste the hems of the coat, sleeves and facings.

Prepare the lining with the hem basted up, because it will not be sewn to hem of coat. Turn the coat inside out, put it on a dress form if possible, and attach the lining in preparation for the fitting.

Fig. 130.   Facing basted over collar.

FITTING AND ALTERATIONS

If your previous fitting for the jacket has been successful, you have by now mastered most of the problems that may arise. Whether you plan to wear your coat over a jacket or not is of great importance from a fitting point of view. If you are, you must of course allow sufficient room for a comfortably fitting coat.

Once again, the shoulder area is of prime importance. The correct positioning of the shoulder seams controlling the "hang" of the garment determine the balance, and attention to this point must be the first step in fitting.

Because the buttons are not yet sewn on, you must lap the buttonhole markings over the buttons and pin one side to the other at buttonholes. Check to make sure you have a true vertical edge from neck to hem, and that both left and right fronts are even in length. Pin, or chalk-mark the edge of the buttonhole side on the left front. When the coat is opened check that the distance from the edge to the mark is even throughout. Place pins into the button positions directly underneath the buttonholes.

Check the collar, see that it is wrinkle-free and even on both sides. Turn the back of the collar up; it should fit just as well as turned down—you may even like it better that way. The pockets are an integral part of the design and must be well-positioned in relation to the proportion of the whole garment. But they are functional, too, so put your hands in them and "feel" that you can use them in comfort.

FINAL ASSEMBLING AND COMPLETION

As before, mark alterations, remove lining, open seams, re-mark (re-cut), and transfer to fabric and pattern. Machine-stitch darts and underpress.

With the pockets firmly basted in final position, topstitch them to the coat, the same distance from the edges as on the flaps. Finish off the ends of stitching securely at the pocket openings. Lay the flaps right side down with the straight edges just above the pocket tops, baste, and

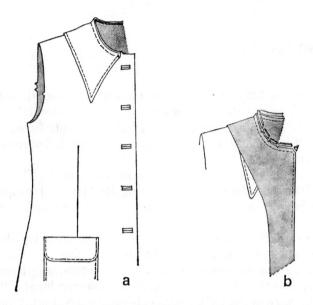

Fig. 131.   *Topstitch pockets (a) and rebaste collar (b).*

machine-stitch close to the edges—no more than 6 mm (¼ in)—and
fasten ends securely. Turn flaps down, press, and make a few firm hand
stitches at the top corners to keep the flaps neat and in a flat position.

Rejoin shoulder and center side back seams (and underarm sleeve
seam if alteration has taken place) and press.

Pin and baste the collar to the neckline as you did in preparation for
the fitting, then lay the facings right side down to the coat and over the
collar. Make sure that all notches meet exactly. Pin and baste in this
position from the center back neck to each side of the front neck edge,
and to center front edges if the facings are not cut in one piece with the
front sections.

Machine-stitch, trim seams and corners. Understitch through the
facing and collar seams at the back neck to keep the collar firmly set in
this position.

Turn back the facings to the inside of the coat, baste and press them.

To finish the buttonholes, mark the wrong side of the holes on the
facing side. Cut along the center length of the buttonholes, then turn in
the raw edges to make an oval-shaped opening. With small felling
stitches, neatly hem the turned-in edges to the back of the buttonhole
piping, without showing stitches on the right side of the garment.

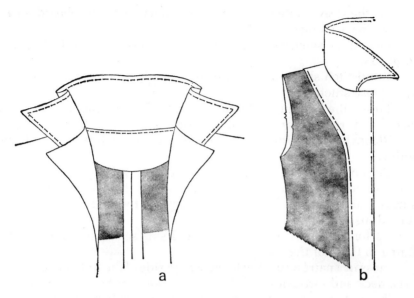

Fig. 132.   Understitch through facing and collar seams (a) and turn facing to inside (b).

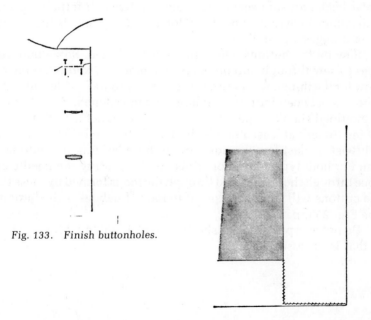

Fig. 133.   Finish buttonholes.

Fig. 134.   Fellstitch facing to hem.

Set the sleeves into the armholes and press on a sleeveboard (seams toward the armholes).

Sew in the shoulder pads as previously described for the jacket on page 153.

Blindstitch sleeve and coat hems and edges of facings to the coat with loose stitches.

Finish the bottom of the facings with felling stitches. Topstitch sleeve and front edges, as for the collar and pockets, if desired.

Remove the basting and press the coat well before sewing in the lining.

Try on the coat again before the last stage of lining it.

The prepared lining, sewn together—with the hem turned up and stitched and all of it well-pressed—is placed to the coat, which has been turned inside out.

As for the jacket, sew shoulder and side-seam allowances of the lining to those of the coat.

Press in a narrow turning to the wrong side of the lining edges at the back neck and through to the hem, as well as on the sleeve hems.

Pin and baste the edges to facings and sleeve hems as shown, and sew back with felling stitches.

The two separate hems (lining and coat) can be held together at the center back and side seams with loose stitches to form a bar or small chain about 4 cm (just over 1½ in) long, which prevents the lining from being dragged up in wear.

Sew on the buttons where previously pinned. Some buttons have holes to sew through and others have a moulded shank on the back to allow for the thickness of the fabric on the buttonhole side and to prevent tightness between buttons and holes when fastened. For a button with no moulded shank, depending on the thickness of the fabric, leave the sewing threads at least 3 mm (⅛ in) long between the fabric and buttons and twist the last few threads around those holding the buttons to the coat. For both types of button, finish off by passing the needle once or twice through the shanks and through the loops formed by these threads. The buttons will then be allowed to move freely over the buttonholes. (See Fig. 255, p. 277.)

Do not overpress the finished garment. Light touching up should be all that is necessary.

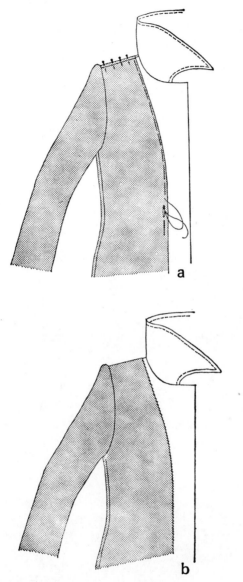

Fig. 135. Baste lining in place (a) and fellstitch lining (b).

II
The Sixth Design: The Shirt

THE SHIRT

This, the last of our six basic garments, is a classic shirt shape, with the collar set onto a band and the sleeves gathered into cuffs. Those of our readers who prefer a sleeveless version can make the shirt with faced armholes as described for the semi-fitted dress in Chapter Eight.

New Processes

The new processes are:

a. Shirt collar on band (stand).
b. Cuffed sleeve with faced opening.
c. Hand-worked buttonholes.

Fig. 136.   The basic shirt.

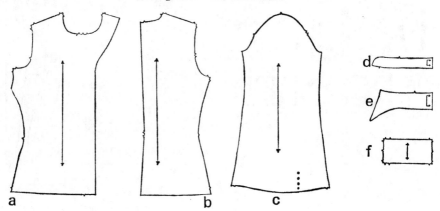

Fig. 137.   Basic pattern shapes: front (a), back (b), sleeve (c), collar (d, e), and cuff (f).

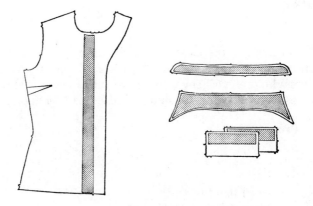

Fig. 138.   Interface button band, collar, and cuffs.

Notions

The following notions are required:

1. Basting and sewing thread.
2. Lightweight interfacing (for a washable fabric use a suitable interfacing).
3. Small shirt buttons (including spare ones).

INITIAL PROCESSES

Once again, the initial processes as previously listed apply to this garment up to and including the staystitching. Then the new processes are incorporated.

After the fitting and alterations, the remaining processes are identical to those for all previous designs, except for making the hand-worked buttonholes.

The sections of the shirt to be interfaced are:

1. The facing allowance on center fronts.
2. The undercollar—for a soft roll of the collar—or both top and undercollar if you prefer a very stiff effect.
3. The collar band on one side.
4. The cuffs on one side.

Staystitch all curves in the usual manner, and then turn the front facing back to the inside and baste it to the neck edge and to the front of the shirt.

SHIRT COLLAR ON BAND

First, lay the top collar to the undercollar, right sides together, then baste and machine-stitch the outer line of the edges, taking one stitch across the points.

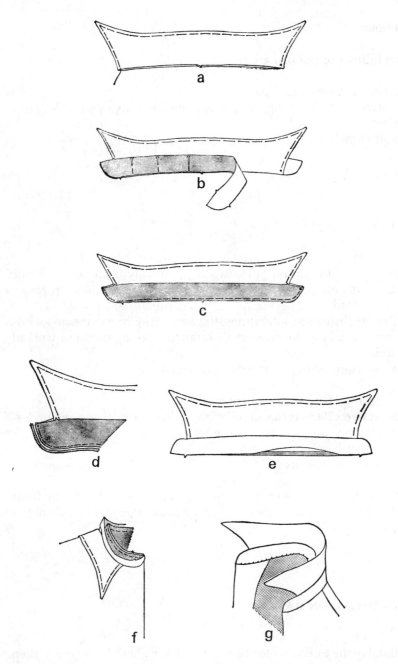

Fig. 139. Turn collar to right side (a); pin band to collar (b); stitch band to right side of collar (c); trim seam (d); turn band to right side (e); baste band to neck edge (f); fellstitch to inside neck (g).

Trim seam allowances, especially at corners. Turn the collar to the right side and pull out the corners evenly. Baste and press.

Lay and pin the interfaced section of the band right side down to the open edge of the interfaced undercollar, right sides together. Place and pin the second band section exactly on top of this on the other side, with the right side down to the top collar.

Pin, baste, and then machine-stitch along this edge and through the collar, making sure that both ends are even and the same in distance on each side from the top collar ends. The neck edge of the band is left open (see Fig. 139(a), (b) and (c)).

Trim the seam allowance and clip the rounded ends to make neat curves and to eliminate excess bulk in this seam.

Turn the band to the right side, baste, press, and also press in the seam allowance on the band/top collar side for easier handsewing to the neck on the inside of the shirt later on.

Pin and baste the other section of the band to the outside neck edge, right sides together, matching the shirt front edges exactly. (To ensure this, baste the collar from the center back to either side of the front rather than in one series of stitches from one side to the other.) Now machine-stitch this seam and trim and clip the seam allowances.

Finally, pin and baste the pressed-in edge of the band to the neck seam on the inside of the shirt and sew it to the neck with felling stitches.

CUFFED SLEEVE WITH FACED OPENING

To prepare the cuffs, fold them over into two equal halves, right sides facing. Machine-stitch both ends, trim seam allowances and top corners, and turn through to the right side. Baste and press. Press in the seam allowance on the interfaced side of the cuff.

Run in a gathering thread around the top of the sleeve caps to ease in the fullness (as described on page 170) and underpress.

Each marked cuff opening is faced with a small piece of the fabric, cut about 6.5 cm (2½ in) wide by the length of the opening plus 2 cm (¾ in). Baste this facing to the opening mark, the center of the facing piece in line with the opening mark, right side to right side of the sleeve.

Turn the sleeve to the wrong side where the marked line is uncovered and still visible, stitch along each side of the mark 3 mm (⅛ in) from it and taper to one stitch across the point at the end. Cut into the line of the opening, turn the facing through to the inside, baste and underpress. Then stitch again, close to the edges of the opening to strengthen it.

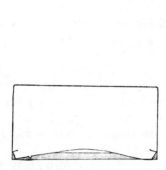

Fig. 140. Turn cuff to right side.

Fig. 141. Gathering thread in sleeve cap.

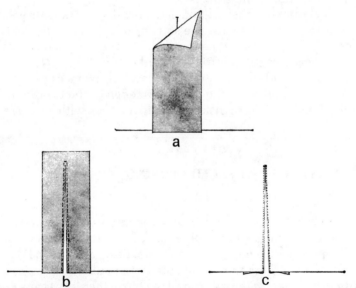

Fig. 142. Place right sides of facing and sleeve together (a); stitch and cut (b); turn to right side (c).

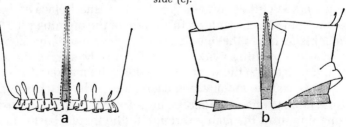

Fig. 143. Gather lower edge of sleeve (a) and baste cuff to sleeve edge (b).

The raw edges of the facings should be overcast and lightly caught to the sleeves.

Now put a gathered thread into the lower edges of the sleeves, draw them up to fit the cuffs, and fasten off. Then stitch the underarm sleeve seams.

Place each of the unpressed edges of the cuffs to the gathered edges of the sleeves, right sides together: the ends of the cuffs should match the sleeve openings. Pin and baste cuffs to the sleeves along these edges, then turn the rest of the cuffs to the inside of the sleeves and baste the pressed-in seam allowance of each cuff to the inside seam line of the sleeves, enclosing the raw edges completely.

Pin and baste sleeves into armholes, and check that the cuff openings lie toward the back of the wrists, in line with your little fingers. Finally, pin and baste the hem allowance before the fitting.

FITTING AND ALTERATIONS

By now you will know what to look for at the fitting stage, and be able to carry out any necessary alterations. But pay special attention to the length of the sleeves and make sure that the gathered, lower parts create the right amount of "pouch effect" over the cuffs, which are an important feature of this design and therefore should not be hidden by the sleeves. If these are too long, pin the excess length out and cut the surplus off at the bottom of the sleeves after the fitting.

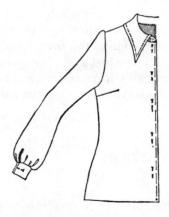

Fig. 144.   Mark position of buttonholes.

Mark the buttonhole positions by pinning these on the front of the shirt vertically, and those on the collar band and cuffs horizontally.

Check that both sides of the front are even in length, and pin the buttonhole markings over the button positions.

FINAL ASSEMBLING AND COMPLETION

When the alterations have been marked and transferred, stitch and underpress darts and seams in the normal manner. Overcast and machine-finish all raw edges. With sleeves taken out of the armholes, remove the basting from the inside of the cuffs. Machine-stitch the cuffs to the sleeves, as basted; replace the inside cuffs, and hem these to the cuff seams with felling stitches. Reset the sleeves and sew them in as described on pages 140–141.

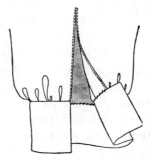

Fig. 145.   Finish cuff.

The hem of the shirt can be blindstitched by hand. Alternatively, you can make two rows of machine-stitching on a narrow turned-in hem. Remember to sew the lower edge of the front facings over the hem.

You will want to try on the shirt again just to make sure all is well and to make minor adjustments if necessary. After that, make sure all basting threads are removed and then press the garment.

HAND-WORKED BUTTONHOLES

The "worked" buttonhole can be made with the appropriate attachment on some sewing machines. Here, we describe the worked type made by hand.

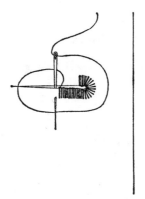

Fig. 146. Hand-worked buttonhole.

First, make sure that the buttonholes are accurately marked on the relevant sections of the garment. Remember to mark them a little longer than the diameter of the buttons.

Cut the marked length carefully—through the facing—and overcast both raw edges to prevent fraying.

At one end of the cut buttonhole, make a small "fan" of stitches, by overcasting and bringing the needle out of the same place, then continue along one edge with a buttonhole stitch (see Fig. 146). To make this, bring the needle from the inside of the buttonhole, through the fabric, about 3 mm (⅛ in) from the edge, with the thread around and under the needle as it comes out; when pulled (not too tightly) this makes a small "purl" on the edge. Repeat these stitches, all along the edge, very very close to each other, and the same length. Make another fan of stitches at the other end, and buttonhole-stitch the other edge. Fasten off securely.

Last, but not least, sew on the buttons and press out the remaining creases on the garment.

FURTHER AND ADVANCED TECHNIQUES

12
Design
and Pattern
Adaptations

Adjustments of commercial patterns to figure and adaptations for
good fit of garments have been described in some depth in Chapter Two.
Together with the guidelines on fitting, much ground has been covered
in this aspect of dressmaking.

When buying patterns, the choice of designs is so large that it would
seem unwise to attempt major adaptations, both from a point of view of
style and fit. Minor however, such as the lengthening or shortening
of sleeves and skirts as part of design and proportion, as well as the
changing of necklines, the adding of lapels, or the adaptation of their
shapes, are more common and desirable.

In this chapter we use our six basic garments once more, to illustrate
by way of examples some adaptations of the design and their respective
patterns.

Fig. 147. Skirt variations.

Fig. 147 shows three varying skirt lengths and the addition of a knife pleat. Shorten or lengthen from the original pattern as shown in Fig. 148(a, b, and c).

V-shaped design lines in Fig. 149 are an addition to the plain slacks in (a), which are shortened in (c). (See Fig. 151 for pattern.)

In Fig. 151 the original semi-fitted dress (a) has a lower neckline, an increase in length (b), and additional adaptations in (c)—a further increase in length, long set in sleeves, a V neckline, and darts joined and followed through to the hemline. (See Fig. 152 for patterns.)

In Fig. 153 the long sleeves on the jacket in (a) become short ones in (b), while (c) shows lapels added to the front of jacket, as shown in Fig. 154.

The coat design used in Chapter Ten is adapted for varying lengths in Fig. 155(a, b, and c); the latter also has an addition of lapels, as shown in Fig. 156.

The long sleeves of the shirt in Fig. 157(a) are adapted to short sleeves with cuffs in (b), and the shirt worn outside the skirt has a tie belt and yoke seamline in (c). (See also Fig. 158.)

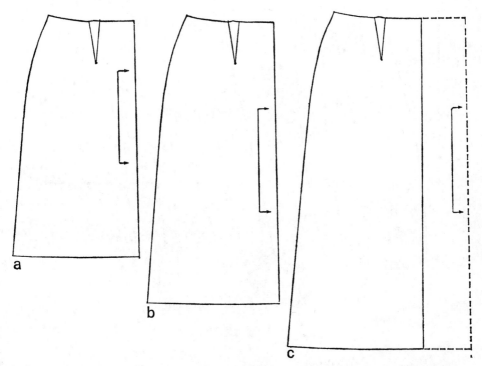

Fig. 148. Lengthen skirt as shown; fold center front to fold of new (broken) line on each side to form an inverted pleat (c).

Fig. 149.   Trouser variations.

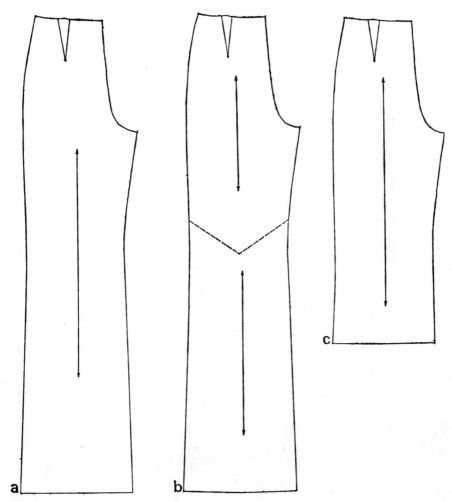

Fig. 150. Cut through design line and add seam allowances on each side (b) or shorten trousers (c).

Fig. 151.   Dress variations.

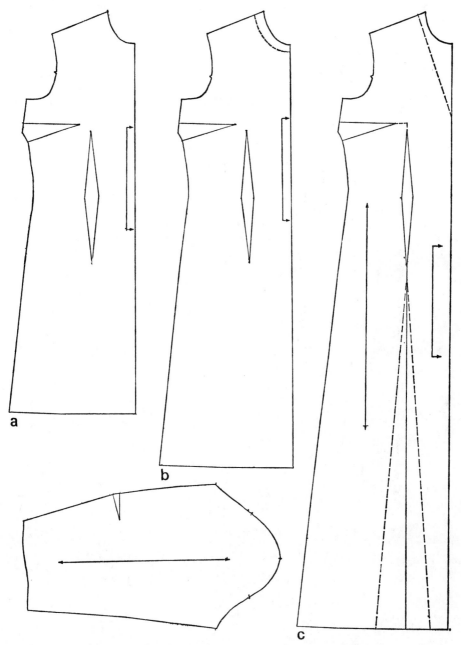

Fig. 152. Lengthen dress as shown; join bust dart to waist dart and continue into seam, as shown by broken lines (c). These are crossed over at either side from the solid center line. The front panel is separated from the side panel, forming a flare when sewn together. After separating them, add seam allowances on each side of the new seam.

191

Fig. 153. Jacket variations.

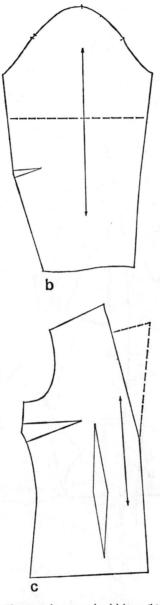

b

c

Fig. 154.   *Shorten sleeve and add hem (b) or add lapel (c).*

Fig. 155.   *Self coat variations.*

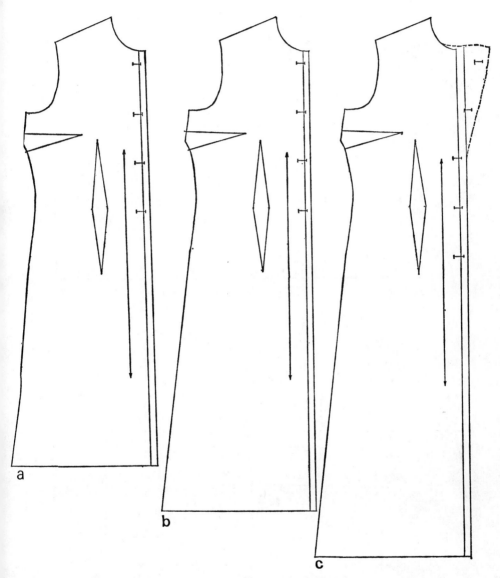

a

b

c

Fig. 156. Lengthen coat as shown; add lapels (c).

Fig. 157.   Shirt variations.

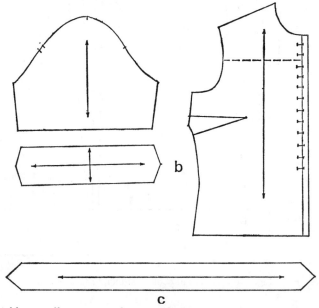

Fig. 158.   Add seam allowances to sleeve and cuff (folded in half and sewn to sleeve) (b);
or cut through for yoke, add seam allowances on each side, and cut belt to fit waist (plus
allowance for belt ends) (c).

13
Figure Types

PROPORTION AND BALANCE

The *Oxford English Dictionary* defines proportion as *due relation of one thing to another or between parts of a thing,* or to put it another way, the balance of one part with another, with all parts related to the whole.

In the context of this book, proportion affects both the human body and the garments with which we clothe and decorate it. The fact that the miraculous structure of the body is such that no two are exactly alike determines our attitude when we are trying to achieve designs of pleasing proportions. Silhouette and shape, their well-balanced division (used as a technical term *balance* also describes the correct joining of parts of a garment) play a vital part and must be related to each other.

Figure types vary from the normal average one—based on a perfect or near-perfect relationship between height, girth, and weight—in many ways. Abnormal or irregular types range from short and slight build to tall, stout, and heavy-boned ones. Figures of average, short, or tall height are additionally divided by an unequal distribution of weight in proportion to height and this weight may also be disproportionately spread on either top or lower parts of the body. Stance—erect, swayback, or stooping, round-shouldered—increases the variety of figure types and proportion of the design must be adapted to suit each individual type.

SILHOUETTE SHAPE

Primarily, fashion decrees silhouettes that prove popular at given times. But, simultaneously, the selection from a range of shapes can be exploited by all figure types to advantage. This, together with a good use of fabric, skillful cutting, fitting, and dressmaking, will achieve satisfaction no matter which figure type we have.

Fig. 159 shows examples of varying shapes ranging from slim, small, and straight to semi-full, full, and long and combinations.

Fig. 159.   Silhouette shapes.

As a general and simple rule, choice of shapes for irregular figures should be based on the aim to draw the eye from those areas which are less in proportion to the rest of the body and emphasizing those parts which are in proportion.

Fig. 160.   *Large skirt and small top for coat.*

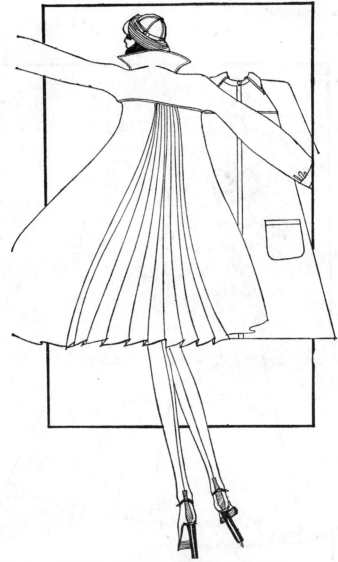

Fig. 161. *Pleats increase full shape of coat.*

Fig. 162.   *Slim shape as dress (a), as jumper and slacks (b).*

The silhouette of the short, full coats (Figs. 161 and 163) are shown in contrast to the slim, close-fitting shapes in Fig. 162, while the full-skirted long coat with a small top (Fig. 160) demonstrates the reverse effect by the fitted skirt and large top.

E

Fig. 163.   *Full shape as raglan-sleeved coat.*

Fig. 164.   *Full-length close-fitting skirt and full jacket.*

DIVISION BY DESIGN LINES

This principle can be extended to both design lines and decorations, acting as dividers. Lines, in both shape and direction—whether straight and hard or curved and soft, short or long, thin or thick, continuous or broken, placed vertically, horizontally, or in oblique position—control

Fig. 165. Design lines.

A   B

Fig. 166. Long seams from shoulder yokes (a); zigzag lines forming insert (b).

Fig. 167. Curved seams forming insets on bodice and skirt.

Fig. 168. Zigzag seams topstitched for decoration (a); yoke and angled seams top-stitched (b).

Fig. 169. *Vertical seams incorporating pleats for fullness in skirt.*

the balance of garments, and their visual effects depend on the prominence with which they are used. Often unequal divisions by design lines and/or decorations, rather than equal halves, produce pleasing proportion.

Within the range of silhouettes, Fig. 165 shows some examples of interesting design lines, introduced to focus additional attention for pleasing eye appeal. Figs. 166–69 also show the combined use of seams as design lines placed in varying directions and positions, attracting the attention of the eye and complementing the silhouette. For example, the yoke and the oblique–vertical seams joined together in Fig. 166(a) emphasize the upper parts of the jacket, while the zigzag and vertical lines on the skirt in Fig. 166(b) stress the lower part of the garment. Acknowledging that the scope and variety of choice of design lines for figure types of good proportion is greater does not imply that less care for and attention to good proportion is demanded. Badly placed seams will reduce the attractiveness of any design, or even ruin it.

DIVISION BY DECORATION

The trimming of garments with lace, fur, leather, braid, flowers, belts, bows, and pockets, as shown in Fig. 170, can considerably enhance the basic shape of clothes. But, as already mentioned, they too act as dividers and draw the attention of the eye onto the decorated sections

Fig. 170.   Decoration.

of the garment—collars, neck, and waistlines, sleeves and hems, and other parts so treated dominate the total look.

This chapter and the illustrations in particular aim to bring about an understanding of the wide range of design details available, and to encourage our readers to make full use of them. Experimenting with all kinds of ideas, with the help of some offered in Chapter Fourteen, will be far more enjoyable than the acceptance of restrictions imposed by dated rules.

Fig. 171. Lace or flower appliqué.

Fig. 172. Fur collar and cuffs.

Fig. 173.   Leather edging (a); braid or leather appliqué (b).

Fig. 174.   *Rickrack braid trimming.*

14
Processes
and Decorations

Following the basic processes carried out in the construction of the six garments, the next step to further and advanced processes will be relatively simple.

Again, make a sample or practice piece of each new method, so any difficulty can be worked out before putting a garment together. This is of course particularly helpful in finding out how suitable the different seams, pockets, etc. are for different weights of fabric.

MARKING

As your confidence and competence in dressmaking gradually increase, you may choose to adopt alternative basic methods to those described in Part Two. These include other ways of marking as follows:

▶ *Tailor's Chalk.* Good on woolens and other surfaces where it brushes off easily. Avoid using colored chalk, because it is harder to remove.

▶ *Tailor Tacking with Loops.* Similar to the basic method given previously.

▶ *Basting.* On single layers of fabric, to mark design detail.

▶ *Tracing Paper.* An easy way to transfer pattern markings on firm but thinner fabrics.

Tailor's Chalk

With the pattern laid on the two layers of fabric, right sides together, pin carefully through fabric and tissue along the design and seamlines to be marked. After all the lines have been pinned, turn the fabric over to the side without the pattern and chalk-mark where the pins show. Use a ruler to draw the straight dart and seamlines. After this side has been marked, turn the fabric back and gently remove the pattern without taking the pins away. Now mark this side in line with the pins, just as for the other side, and remove the pins.

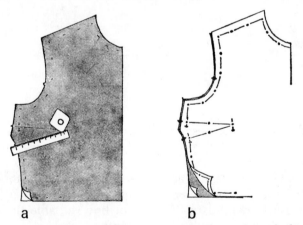

a   b

Fig. 175.   *Tailor's chalk (a); pin and chalk on other side (b).*

Tailor Tacking and Loop

This is almost the same as the method given on page 99, except that there is an additional loop, which makes it less easy for the basting mark to fall out. Using a double strand of basting thread, make a stitch about 1

Fig. 176.   Tailor tacking.

cm (⅜ in) long, leaving a 2 cm (¾ in) loose end. Then, take another stitch, but do not pull it to lie flat—leave it long enough to form a loop of about 4 cm (1⅝ in). Repeat and finish with a 2 cm (¾ in) loose end on completion of marking line.

Cut through the top of the loop and, when marking is finished, lift the pattern off carefully as before. Then, lifting the fabric layers fractionally apart, cut through the thread between them.

When tailor tacking on chalk marks without a pattern, it is not necessary to cut through the loops before lifting the fabric layers apart.

Basting

A single line of plain basting stitches is often used to outline design detail, as we saw earlier for center front and grain positions on single layers of fabric. Basting is also used to hold sections of fabric together before stitching or fitting. In addition, it indicates design lines or notches. A single thread with a knotted end is used and stitches about 2 cm (¾ in) long are adequate.

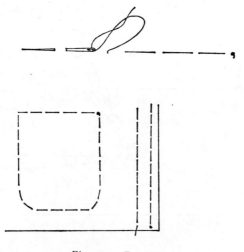

Fig. 177.   Basting.

Tracing Paper

For this you need dressmaker tracing paper and a tracing wheel. Use paper a shade darker or lighter than the fabric to be marked, and test on a scrap of material before to see how visible the line will be and how much pressure to use.

The tracing paper is laid with the coated side down to the wrong side of the fabric, with the pattern laid on top. (A layer of cardboard is

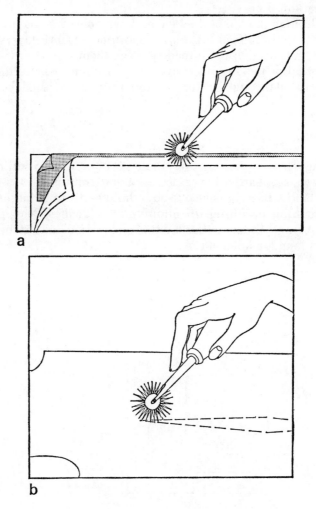

Fig. 178.   Tracing paper (a) and tracing wheel (b).

essential underneath, unless you are using a cutting board, because the wheel will leave marks on a finished surface.)

Mark by following the lines of the pattern, rolling the wheel away from you. For straight lines use a ruler as a guide for the wheel. Two layers of fabric can be marked, which will of course have their right sides together with the pattern laid on top. The fabric must be thin and firm to do this, because more pressure is needed to mark through all the layers.

BASIC HAND STITCHES

All good dressmaking begins and ends with handsewing. Some of the following stitches have already been described, but for easy reference we list them again with their particular uses.

Padding Stitch

This is another basting stitch that holds several layers together firmly, to keep interfacings, facings, and linings in place for fittings. It is a diagonal stitch on the upper side and straight on the other side. (This stitch is not needed when iron-on interfacing is used.

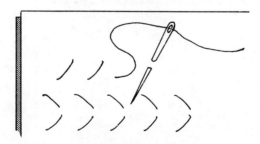

Fig. 179.   Diagonal basting.

Running Stitch

This is a very small, simple hand stitch used for gathering material or easing in fullness. It can be used as a seam where there is no strain on the fabric, particularly on very sheer fabrics when a very tiny stitch is

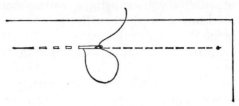

Fig. 180.   Running stitch.

made. In principle, several small stitches are made by passing the needle through the fabric several times at once, then the needle is pulled through. For gathering, a stitch of 3 mm (⅛ in) is average, and use a smaller stitch for a seam.

Hemming Stitch

This slanting stitch shows on the wrong side and is a strong stitch for hems, as the name indicates. One thread of the garment is taken, then the next through the fold of the hem edge, so stitches hardly show on the right side. Stitches should be close together, particularly for heavy cotton fabrics, sheetings, and hems of jeans, for example.

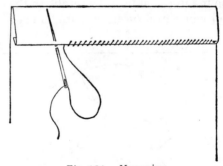

Fig. 181.   Hemming.

Slipstitch

This is similar to the hemming stitch, though not quite as strong. These stitches do not show on the right side, which makes it a good stitch for thin fabrics with a turned-in hem edge. A thread is taken on the garment fabric just below the hem turning, the next is through the fold of the hem along its edge, about 1 cm (⅜ in) long.

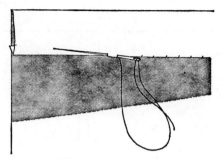

Fig. 182.   Slipstitch.

Felling Stitch

The felling stitch is a tiny version of the hemstitch, used to sew in linings or collar seams, where it is impossible to machine-stitch. These may show, but they are very strong. A minute stitch is taken through the very edge of the hem fold, and one thread is picked up in the garment fabric. These stitches are very close together.

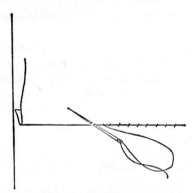

Fig. 183.   Felling stitch.

Blindstitch

The best general stitch to hold down turnings, hems, and facings is the blindstitch, because it holds but does not pull or show the hem ridge on the right side. The turning edge to be hemmed is folded back a little

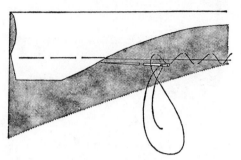

Fig. 184.   Blindstitch.

way and one thread is taken on the garment side and another through the
turning, leaving about 1 cm (⅜ in) between the stitches. The thread is
never pulled tightly, just enough to hold the layers together. It is used
successfully on nearly all fabrics.

Herringbone/Catchstitch

This is another good stitch to hold raw edges of hems, facings, and
interfacings. In this case the edge does not have to have a special finish,
because the stitch itself prevents excessive fraying and is quite secure.
Working from left to right, take a smallish stitch through the fabric from
right to left, then take one or two threads in the underfabric from right to
left; the stitches will cross each other as you go along. An average of
about 1 cm (⅜ in) again, between the stitches. This too is a stitch that can
be used on most fabrics.

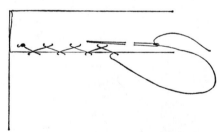

Fig. 185.   Herringbone stitch.

Backstitch

This is a firm holding stitch, used on seams where it is not possible
to machine-stitch, to strengthen neck facings and collars, pockets, etc. It

looks like machine-stitching on the right side, but stitches overlap on the wrong side. A small running stitch is made and taken back the same distance. The needle is brought out further along and then taken back to the end of this first stitch. This is repeated along the seamline.

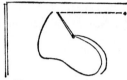

Fig. 186. Backstitch.

Prickstitch

The prickstitch is a variation of the backstitch. The needle is taken back only a fraction, almost in the same place, in fact; then the next stitch is taken only a few threads further along. This stitch is used to sew in zippers by hand, or can be used as a decorative stitch around collar or lapel edges.

Fig. 187. Prickstitch.

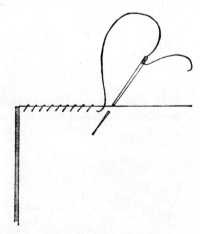

Fig. 188. Overcasting.

Overcasting

This is used to stop raw edges from fraying, as on seam allowances and hem edges. The stitches are taken over the edge with the needle held in a slanting position. Stitches are fairly close together and should be the same size for a neat effect.

Blanket Stitch

This can be used as a finish for raw edges too, as well as being a decorative stitch. Working from left to right, bring the needle out at the edge of the fabric, hold the thread down under the needle, and draw the needle through the loop that has formed. Keep the stitches an even size. The edge will have a chain loop effect to it. This is the same stitch used over several threads to make a *bar tack*.

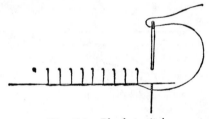

Fig. 189.   Blanket stitch.

Whipstitch

This is a small slanting stitch made on two edges that have to be sewn together, without the stitch showing. It is used frequently when joining lace, or very sheer fabric edges. Again, only one or two threads are taken each side and very small seam or hem allowance is needed.

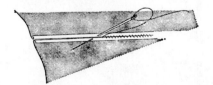

Fig. 190.   Whipstitch.

SEAMS

A seam is the joining of two sections of a garment together, and so is functional, but it can also be decorative and accentuate design lines. Some seams are particularly suited to different types and weights of fabric, and can produce different effects. They can give a more structured or sculptured look, a sharp, crisp appearance, or they can introduce contrast material and color into the finished garment.

Flat Open (Curved) Seam

The flat open seam used previously (see page 103), although basically simple, can also be a curved seam and so needs special attention.

Most curved seams, such as for necklines, princess seamlines, and kimono sleeve seams, need clipping to that the seam can lie flat. On an

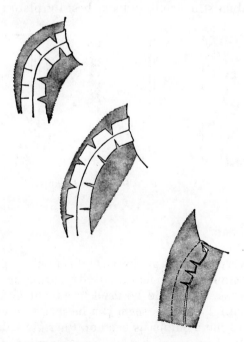

Fig. 191.   Flat open (curved) seam.

inward curve (inward on finished side), clip to the stitching line in spaces of about 1 cm (⅜ in). On an outward curve (outward on finished side) make notches to the line of stitching; these will close up when the seam allowances are pressed open so that extra bulk will be eliminated.

Topstitched Seam

A simple and effective decorative seam is the flat open, topstitched seam. This has been described on page 161, but is elaborated upon here in the following variations:

1. With several rows of stitching each side of the seam.
2. Seam allowances pressed together and stitched through the allowances.
3. A narrow padding strip placed each side of seam under the allowances and stitched through to give a padded effect.
4. The zigzag stitch, too, can look interesting on denim-type fabrics—e.g., double row can be made in a contrasting color.

Topstitching silk with a slightly larger needle on the machine and, of course, a larger stitch setting, looks best for plain topstitching.

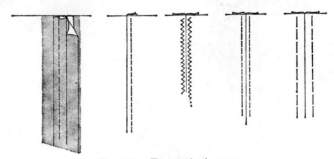

Fig. 192.   Topstitched seams.

Flat Fell Seam

This is a very strong seam, because it is double-stitched. It is ideal for denim and similar cotton fabrics, used on jeans, sportswear, leather, and vinyl clothes, and could be used to advantage on the garments suggested in Part Two. This seam can be made on either side of the fabric, but gives more emphasis used on the right side.

Make a flat open seam, but with *wrong* sides of fabric together. Underpress, then trim one seam allowance to 6 mm (¼ in). Press in a

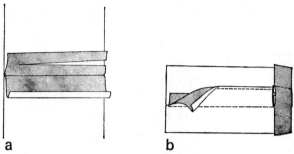

Fig. 193. Flat fell seam.

narrow turning on the other seam allowance and fold over this pressed edge to cover the trimmed seam. Baste down and machine-stitch on the edge of the turning.

French Seam

This seam is for all very fine fabrics, for which a seam allowance should be minimal, and for all lightweight fabrics that need a lot of washing, such as lingerie, children's clothes, and nightwear.

It is a very narrow seam, also stitched twice, so is strong and no raw edges are visible.

Again make a seam with the wrong sides of fabric together, but a very narrow seam 3 mm (⅛ in) is best. If this is found difficult to sew, it can be stitched with a wide allowance and then trimmed down.

Press and turn the fabric so the right sides are together. Press with the seam allowances inside, seamline exactly on the folded edge, and baste and stitch another seamline to enclose the raw edges of the first seam to just under 6 mm (¼ in). It is essential that the seam should be as narrow as possible and that no raw edges show through the second seamline.

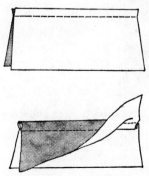

Fig. 194. French seam.

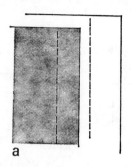

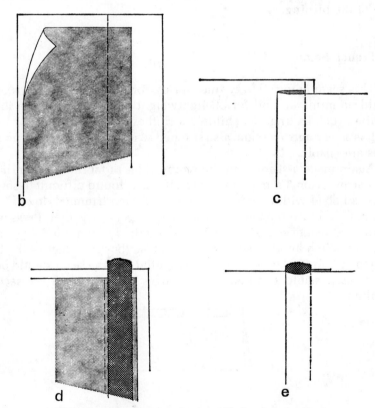

Fig. 195. Welt seam (a, b, c); padded welt seam (d, e).

Welt or Raised Seam

This is an important seam, used widely in tailored clothes. It accentuates design lines, can give a sculptured (structured) look, and is especially effective on plain surface woolens or tweeds with very small designs. Its advantage is that it can be used on quite thick fabrics, so it makes a good coat seam. It looks very like the reverse side of flat fell seam, but because the seam allowance is not turned in there is no additional bulk. The finished width of the welt seam is determined by the width of one of the seam allowances. It is best to cut this first to the desired width, and check to see which side of the stitching line will show on the right side of garment. For example, if a welt seam 1 cm (⅜ in) width is to be made, one of the seam allowances will be cut to 1 cm (⅜ in), the other will be a little wider.

Matching the seamlines, with fabric right sides together, make a plain seam. Underpress, then fold the wider seam allowance over the narrower one and stitch exactly 1 cm (⅜ in) from the first seam, through all the layers. The narrow seam allowance gives the slight raised effect inside the wider one. For a more exaggerated seam, lay a narrow strip of padding next to the first seam and stitch the wider seam allowance over it to enclose the padding.

Lapped Seam

The lapped seam is another good seam, especially for thick fabrics or leather, but workable on most medium-to-heavy fabrics. It is very easy to make and most effective on coat or jacket shapes, because it is a bulkier-looking seam with a tucklike fold which is the lap. When cut-

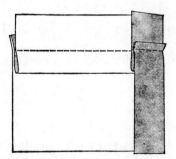

Fig. 196. Lapped seam.

ting, extra fabric is allowed on that side of the seam that laps over the other.

The seam is marked on the overlapping piece of fabric, as well as on a line twice the lap away from it. Fold this section, wrong sides together, so the lines match up, and lay it to the right side of the other fabric section, matching seamlines. Baste in position and topstitch through all three layers of fabric.

Strap Seam

This is a very decorative seam that can incorporate a contrast color or texture for interest. It is a good seam again for leather or leather trimmings and also for reversible fabrics, because no raw edges show on the wrong side.

A flat, open seam is made first on the right side and pressed open. The strap is cut to the width desired, plus sufficient allowance to make narrow turnings. These are pressed in, and a basting mark is made along the center of the strap. Then the strap is laid wrong side down to the seam—the center basting line matching the seamline and the strap covering the seam allowances. Care should be taken not to stretch or distort the strap when it is being topstitched to the seam. With braid or leather trimmings it is usually unnecessary to turn in the edges before stitching.

Fig. 197.   Strap seam.

Slot Seam

This seam, too, can be used with a contrasting color, or different textural trimmings. It can be successfully used on most fabrics that are fairly firm, such as gabardine, flannel, heavy cottons, and tweeds.

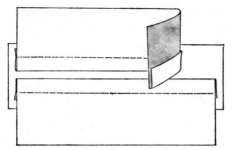

Fig. 198.   Slot seam.

On the two sections to be joined, the seam allowances are pressed to the inside. The fabric for the underlying "slot" strip is cut so that it is slightly wider than the seam allowances together, plus the amount that will show through the gap. This will vary according to the design but it is just as effective if the two sections meet, because the contrast shows through in a more subtle manner. A basting line is made along the center of the slot strip. The two sections to be joined are laid on the strip, with the folded edges of the fabric meeting the center basting line on the strip or, for a wider gap, the same distance each side from the center. Baste in position and topstitch through the fabric and strip, from the fold edge, 6 mm (¼ in) or more depending on the thickness of the fabric.

Piped Seam

This decorative edging for seams, like the previous two seams, can introduce color and contrast very effectively. It can be used on fairly fine fabrics too. Piped with a cord, it gives a firmer, rounder edge; or with plain bias strips, a softer look. For a piped seam without a cord, fold a bias strip along the center, right side out, and baste the piping together, marking off the area that will show. Lay the piping to the seamline on the right side of one section. Match the basted lines, with the raw edges

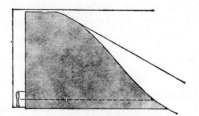

Fig. 199.   Piped seam.

facing the same way as the seam allowances on the main section of fabric. Lay the other sections of fabric right side to right side, seam allowances together and seamlines matching. Stitch together through all layers and press one section of fabric to face the opposite way.

Piped Seam with Cord

First, insert a narrow cord into the piping material. Lay the cord, along the center of the piping on the wrong side of fabric. Fold over the piping to enclose the cord, and baste as close as possible to the cord itself, with a reasonable seam allowance left. Lay the corded piping to the seamline on fabric just as the plain piping was done, and baste the other sections of fabric on top as before. The difference now is that it is sewn together with the zipper foot. This allows the stitching to be right next to the piping, making the corded edge neat and firm.

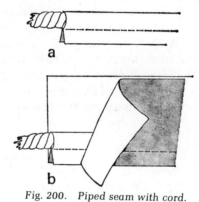

Fig. 200.   Piped seam with cord.

SEAM FINISHES

All well-made seams need a good finish on the inside. Apart from the clean appearance of the finish, this keeps raw edges from fraying and, trimmed to an equal size, no unsightly ridges show after pressing. Various fabrics and garments call for different treatments.

Overcast

An all-purpose finish for most seams, except lingerie and children's wear, which generally have French seams and so need no finishing. Stitches must be even, the size determined by the thickness of the fabric.

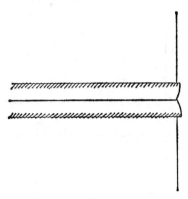

Fig. 201. *Overcast seam.*

Very thick, loosely woven types often need overcasting before seams are stitched together, because they fray very quickly: overcasting before-hand helps to keep the correct seam allowance.

Machine-Finished Seam Edge

This is a narrow turning on the seam allowance, which is edge-stitched. Best for cotton and some rayon fabrics, as it usually gives too thick an edge on other materials and would be bulky and show when the garment is pressed.

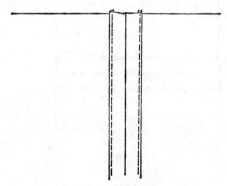

Fig. 202. *Machine-finished seam.*

Zigzag Machine Stitch

This is the nearest domestic equivalent to an industrial stitch, good on most types of fabric (see page 80).

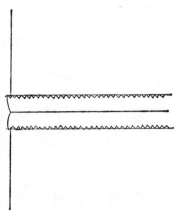

Fig. 203.   Zigzag seam edge.

Bound Seam

These seams have a binding stitched over the edge of turnings. They are mostly used on unlined jackets or coats, because they can be a little too heavy for lighter fabrics and may also hold the seam too tightly.

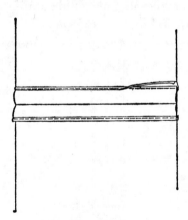

Fig. 204.   Bound seam.

Pinked Seam

Only used on firmly woven cotton and rayon type fabrics, this is made with special pinking shears that have a serrated edge.

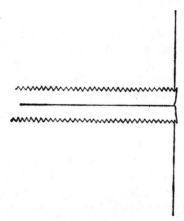

Fig. 205.   Pinked seam.

FACINGS

In most cases a facing is a piece of fabric cut to shape and on the straight grain and is applied to finish the raw edges of necklines, armholes, or openings in a garment.

The basic methods of applying facings have already been described in Part Two. They include the faced slit opening on sleeves (page 178), which is one example of a facing not cut to the exact shape of the main edge to be finished. Facings are also used to finish raw edges on wraparound skirts, shaped necklines, scalloped or pointed edges, false hems—almost any raw edge, in fact, for which a plain turn-back hem cannot be made. They also give added support to shaped edges. Facings can also be interfaced.

The method of attaching a facing does not vary very much, but facing for the different shapes needs some explanation.

The professional-looking facing should be flat along the edge and not roll to show the seam on the right side. All curved or bias edges and loosely woven or stretchy fabrics should be staystitched first, of course, and the interfacing pressed or sewn to the inside of garment before the facing is attached.

Faced Slit Neckline

With the armhole and neck facing described on page 132, the faced slit-opening neckline is as simple, but an often-made mistake is for the opening to be cut before the facing is attached.

The facing is cut to fit the neckline, with an additional placket to cover adequately the length of the proposed slit. Finish the outer edge of the facing with zigzag stitch or overcasting. Mark the slit with a basting line on garment and facing, staystitch and interface the wrong side of neck and slit mark. Lay facing right side to right side of garment, baste and then machine-stitch on seamlines. When the slit mark is reached, stitch a little under 1 cm (⅜ in) at the neck edge, tapering to one stitch across the end of slit mark, and then back on the other side to the neck.

Trim and clip the neckline, cut along the slit marking to the stitching lines, turn facing to the inside and understitch the neck edge as far as possible. Then finish the rest with hand-stitching around the end of the slit. Press and catch loose edge of facing to the garment or topstitch.

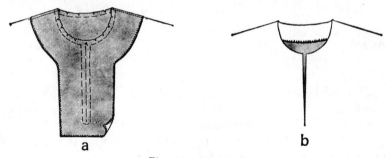

a   b

Fig. 206. Slit neckline.

Scalloped Facing or Pointed Hems and Edges

The scallops are marked on the garment and facing, but *not* cut. The facing is laid right side to right side of hem, matching scallop markings. Again the interfacing, on all but sheer fabrics where it might show to disadvantage, helps to improve the shape—but if a very soft look is aimed for do not interface.

Stitch on the first scallop line, taking one stitch across where the next scallop begins, then cut around the scallop, leaving small seam allowances. Notch the curves and clip to the stitching line between the scallops, right up to the one stitch across. Cutting the shape afterwards

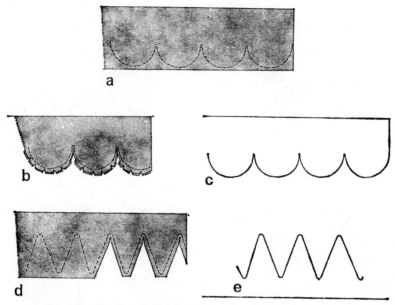

Fig. 207.   Scalloped edge (a, b, c); pointed edge (d, e).

prevents stretching or distortion of shape. Turn the facing through to the inside, and understitch the facing and scallop seam allowances to make a neat, smooth edge.

The same method applies to pointed edges. Points are cut after stitching—and one stitch made across each end of points makes for a neat finish without puckering.

Other hem facings are described in the section dealing with hems on pages 238–43.

One-Piece Armhole and Neck Facing

This type of facing is used for sleeveless dresses or blouses (with or without opening). It is particularly useful for thin or fine fabrics, which need support without any stitching showing. The facing should be fractionally smaller than the top of the blouse or dress.

First stitch the underarm seams of the garment and underpress. Next join the underarm seams of the facing, press, and then finish off the lower edge of facing, but leave shoulder seams open. Then, matching notches, stitch the facing right sides together to the garment around the neck and armholes. Trim and clip the seam.

Pull the facing through to the inside of the garment, through the

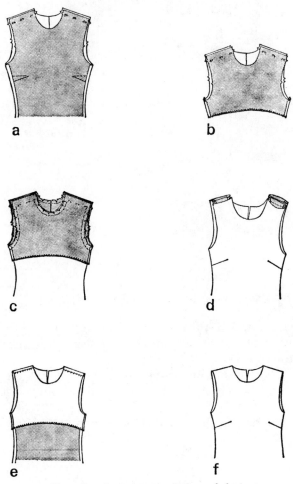

Fig. 208.   One-piece armhole-neck facing.

open shoulder seams. Stitch the garment shoulder seam, press, then fold the shoulder seam of the facing over the garment seam and handsew them together. When completed, no raw edges show.

Self-Facings

Facings can be cut in one with the main part of garment, and then turned back on a foldline.

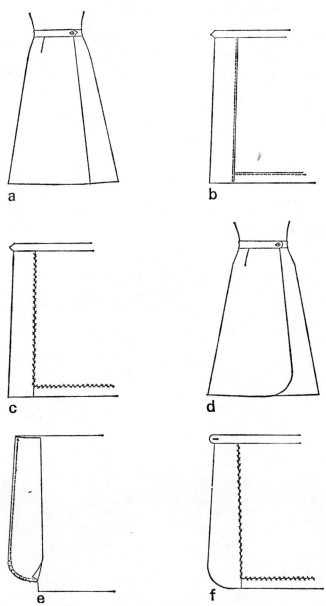

a

b

c

d

e

f

Fig. 209.   Wraparound skirt and facings.

Facing on Shaped Wraparound Skirt

Cut the facing to fit the wraparound, either with a deep facing or a band, cut in one with a fabric hem. If the fabric is thin enough, turn in the loose, raw edge and machine-finish it before attaching it to the skirt; or overcast on frayable or loosely woven fabrics.

Machine-stitch the facing to the seamline; trim and notch seam allowances on curved seams, clip corners on straight ones. Understitch whenever possible, turn facing to inside and press, rolling the seam to the inside if not already understitched.

Hand-stitch the loose facing edges to the inside of the skirt, or bind with bias binding, particularly if the skirt is unlined.

Decorative Facings

Finally, facings can also be used very simply as decoration, by being sewn on the inside and turned to the right side. The edges are turned in and finished neatly and the facings can be topstitched or handsewn to the outside of the garment.

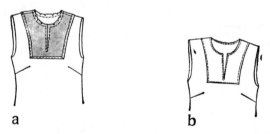

a   b

Fig. 210.   Reversed (decorative) facing.

HEMS

As with most processes, there are several methods of hemming, depending on the kind of fabric and type of garment. On all garments any slight fullness is caught in tiny pleats or tucks and evenly distributed.

Blindstitched Hem

The overcast or zigzagged raw edge and blindstitched hem is good in most cases, because it holds the hem turning flat so there is less possibility of a ridge or excess bulk showing on the right side.

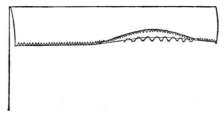

Fig. 211. Blindstitched hem.

Herringbone Hem

This hem is turned up in the same way as the blindstitched hem, except that the raw edge does not have to be finished first. The under-stitch of the herringbone is made through a thread or two of the fabric, the top stitch through the hem turning alone. This is a good hem for most types of fabric.

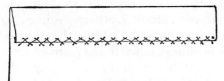

Fig. 212. Herringbone hem.

Plain Hem

This is mostly used now for detail finishing, on small hems of shirtsleeve openings, or household linens or garments that have a lot of wear and washing, such as nightwear, overalls, etc.

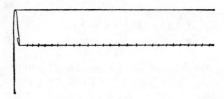

Fig. 213. Plain hem.

Felled Hem

The felled hem is ideal for linings and fine detail, such as on collars and handsewn pockets.

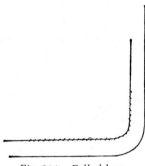

Fig. 214. Felled hem.

Taped or Bound Hem

The raw edge is bound on exceptionally frayable fabrics. Care must be taken not to pull the tape or binding, otherwise dragging will occur on the right side. The tape is sewn to the edge with machine-stitching and the loose edge of tape is blindstitched to the garment fabric. Bias-bound hems have the binding stitched with the folded edge of binding to the hem turning and the other fold sewn to the garment fabric. It can also be stitched to the edge so it will be encased totally—and then it is slip-stitched to the garment. This can cause a slight stretching on some fabrics.

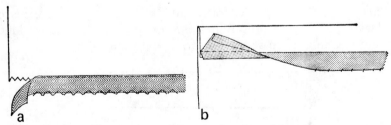

Fig. 215. Taped hem (a); bias-bound hem (b).

Faced Hem

Sometimes called a false hem, this is made either when insufficient fabric has been allowed for a hem or when the hem must be let down. It is also a good way to finish a shaped hem.

Wide bias binding can be used, or a bias strip made from self- or lining fabric, cut on the bias, and joined as shown in Fig. 216. The wide bias is sewn right sides together to the hem edge, pressed open, and then the narrow hem fold on the facing bias is slipstitched down.

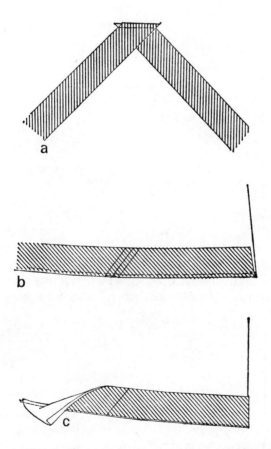

Fig. 216.   Bias strips joined (a), sewn to hem edge (b), and slipstitched to fabric (c).

Circular Hem

This can be blindstitched, herringboned, or bound. In all cases the fullness must be evenly distributed and basted in position, so there will be no uneven lumps in the turning. The turning allowance itself should only be about 2 cm (¾ in). A basting line along the hem edge, as well as near the turning, helps to make a better hem.

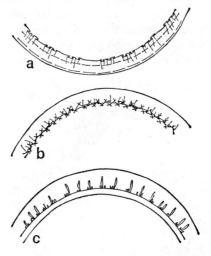

Fig. 217.   Circular hem (a); herringboned (b); bound (c).

Pleated Hem

If the seam is on the inside edge of the pleat, the seam is left open in the hem turning, then turned back and stitched together as shown in Fig. 218. This is essential, otherwise the pleat will not lie properly. The four layers at the hem can be whipstitched together for a neat finish.

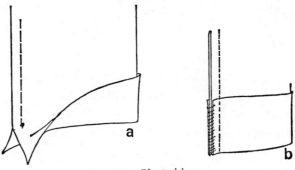

Fig. 218.   Pleated hem.

Hand-rolled Hem

This hem is used for sheer fabrics, scarves, lingerie, etc. Machine-stitch very close to the edge, then roll the fabric between the thumb and forefinger of the left hand, several inches along the edge at a time, then sew with a slipstitch or a whipstitch.

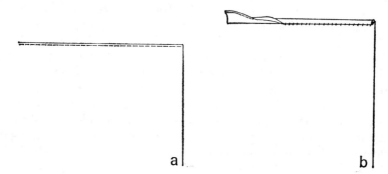

Fig. 219.   Hand-rolled hem.

WAISTBANDS

One simple way of making and sewing on a waistband has been explained on page 116. Here are some other ways of making and attaching waistbands to skirts and slacks.

Topstitched

This method uses machine-stitching instead of handsewing on the inside. The waistband is stitched first to the inside of the seam, right side of band to the inside of the skirt or trouser waist. Then it is turned to the outside and topstitched to the waist seam on the right side (Fig. 220).

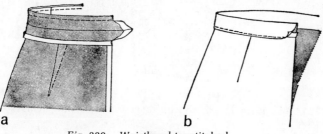

Fig. 220.   Waistband topstitched.

Waistband Interfaced with Canvas

This method is used on thicker fabrics. On the waistband piece, the seam allowances and the center fold line are marked. A piece of canvas or heavyweight interfacing is cut to the finished size of the waistband. This is basted to the band on the wrong side, with one edge to the center fold line. Then it is slightly stitched to the band fabric or machine-stitched 3 mm (⅛ in) from the center line through the canvas or interfacing. The ends of the band should be finished as on page 116 and the seam allowance on the interfaced side of the band should also be finished; it will be left loose and not turned in, to make less bulk at the waist.

Stitch the waistband with the unfaced side, right side to right side of waist, turn band to inside, and baste to the waist seam inside, leaving the finished edge just below the seam.

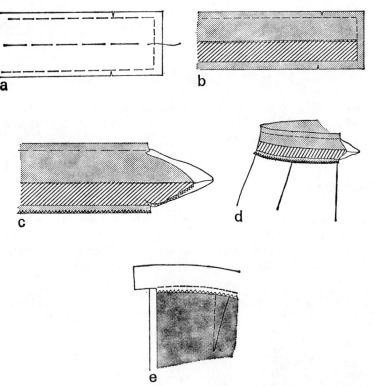

Fig. 221.   Waistband interfaced with canvas or heavy interfacing.

Finally backstitch, or machine-stitch, through the seam crease on the right side, if no stitching is to show, or of course it can be topstitched (Fig. 221).

Grosgrain Waistband

This is a neat and easy-to-apply finish, suitable for a skirt on which no waistband needs to show, or for thin fabrics.

Grosgrain can be bought already curved, or straight grosgrain can be gently stretched along one edge to make a slight curve. This is done by pressing the band under a damp cloth with a warm iron. This curve helps because it sits well in the natural waist curve.

Lay the unstretched or smaller curved edge of the band to the waist seam, the other edge away from the skirt. Turn in the ends and edge-stitch the band to the waist seam. Clip the fabric seam allowance. Turn the band to the inside and press, so the band does not show on the right side. An additional row of machine-stitching can be made at the top through the fabric and band, on the right side.

With the band edges meeting edge to edge, hooks and eyes can be sewn on (Fig. 222).

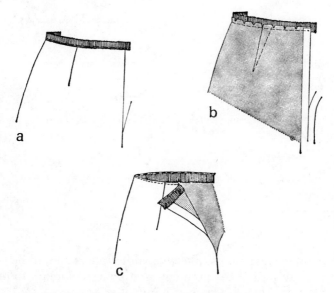

Fig. 222.   Grosgrain waistband.

Waistband Finishes

Here are more ways to finish the ends of a self-fabric band.

With a buttonhole.   If this is a bound type, it must be made before the ends are sewn together.

Curved or tab ends.   The tab point is stitched, right sides together as a plain end. The point and sides are trimmed and then turned through. A curved end is stitched and the curve is carefully notched so the end will be even and smooth (Fig. 223).

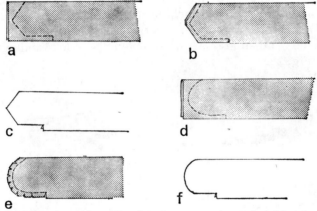

Fig. 223.   *Pointed waistband finish* (a, b, c); *curved waistband finish* (d, e, f.).

OPENINGS

The openings, fastenings, plackets, and zippers should be coordinated with the design of the garment, and be long enough to prevent strain on the ends. They can be nearly invisible, or a prominent feature. Generally they are on sleeves and necks, but are occasionally in the underarm seam on fitted clothes.

Fig. 224. *Variations in openings.*

Faced Slit

The simplest of openings is the *faced slit*. The slit is marked on the garment or sleeve and a facing piece is cut large enough to cover the slit length. Leave at least 3.8 (1½ in) allowance all the way around the opening. Then baste the right side of the facing to the right side of the garment, and stitch around the slit mark, approximately 3 mm (⅛ in) each side, tapering to one stitch across at the point. Cut to the point, turn the facing to the inside, and press. The loose edges of the facing can be sewn to the garment fabric, or finished and topstitched around the opening (Fig. 225).

If this opening is to have loop buttonholes, these can be made and sewn with the looped ends facing away from the slit on the right side. The facing is sewn on top and when it is turned through the loops are in position (Fig. 226).

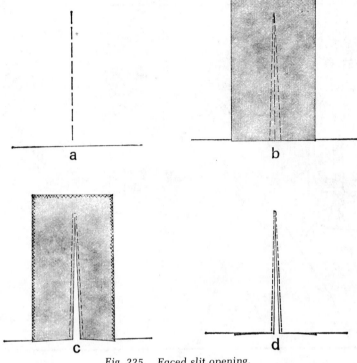

Fig. 225.   Faced slit opening.

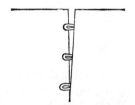

Fig. 226.   Loop buttonholes.

Continuous Opening

This time the slit is cut first. A piece of fabric is cut, preferably on the bias, twice the length of the opening and about 3.5 cm (1⅜ in) wide. The slit is opened out and the strip laid along it, right sides together, and stitched. It should be eased over the point of the slit. Next, the strip is turned to the inside and a narrow hem turned in on it; then it is hemmed to the seamline.

The finished opening is pressed, so that the strip is folded inside, overlapping the underneath (Fig. 227).

This same opening can also be made entirely with machine-stitching. The strip is first stitched to the inside, then turned to the outside and edge-stitched to the seamline.

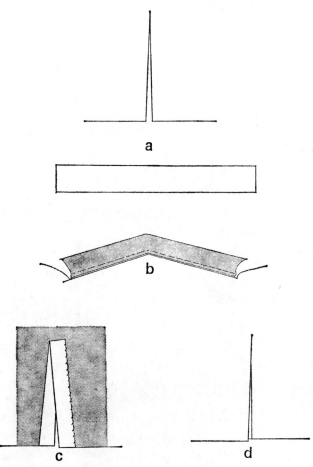

Fig. 227. Continuous opening.

Simple Placket Opening for Sleeves

Cut the opening. Cut a strip for a placket, 4 cm (1⅝ in) wide and at least 2 cm (¾ in) longer than the opening. Press in 1 cm (⅜ in) at one end and along one side of the strip.

On the underside of the slit, make a very narrow hem. Lay the unpressed edge of the placket piece right side down to the inside of the unstitched edge of the slit, the pressed end to the top of slit. Stitch this the length of the opening, then turn it to the right side and baste the

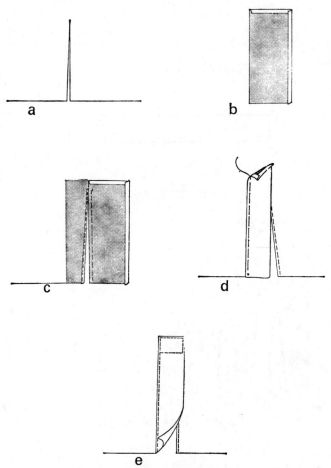

Fig. 228. Placket opening for sleeve.

pressed edge to the slit seam, making the placket end at the top neat and flat, overlapping the end of the opening and concealing it. Stitch along this basted edge and around the placket end, easing in the fullness where the placket is pulled through at the top, or make a tiny pleat (Fig. 228).

Placket for a Neck Opening

Cut two placket pieces, approximately 6 cm (2⅜ in) wide and 4 cm (1⅝ in) longer than the opening to be made. Stitch these each side of the marked opening, right sides to the right side of the garment, with a seam allowance of 1 cm (⅜ in).

Cut the opening, to within 1 cm (⅜ in) of the end, where it is clipped right into the corners of the stitching. Then turn the plackets through to the inside, again turning in a seam allowance of 1 cm along each edge. Sew this to the inside seamline of opening. Leave the overlapping placket end on the right side, turn in neatly, and stitch across the end, or shape to a point, and topstitch (Fig. 229).

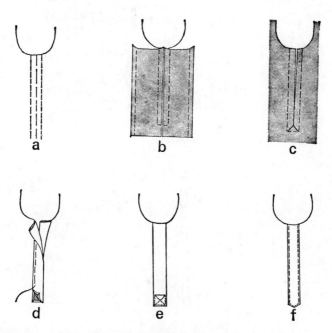

Fig. 229.   Placket opening for neck.

Openings with Zippers

One method for inserting a zipper has been described on pages 109 and 115 for skirt, trouser, and dress openings. The following semiconcealed opening is also generally used and can be machine-stitched or handsewn with the prickstitch.

The opening seam is basted together, and the seam allowances pressed flat inside. Lay the zipper face down to the inside with the zipper teeth exactly on the basted seamline. Baste the zipper tape to the garment through the seam allowances.

Turn the garment to the right side, and stitch with the zipper foot evenly each side of the seam and across the end below the lower stop. Press and remove the basting from the seam.

Alternatively, the zipper can be sewn with a prickstitch, which is

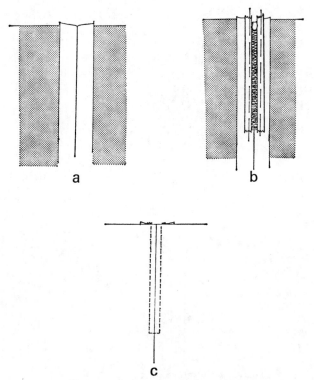

Fig. 230.   Semi-concealed opening.

better on very fine, soft fabrics, or where machine-stitching should not be visible (Fig. 230).

Inserting a zipper in a fly-front opening is a little more complicated because there are facing pieces sewn as well. First stitch the facing to the right side of the opening, then clip and press the seam. Make the fly shield for the other side; this is made from two facing pieces shaped like the one already stitched to the opening.

Lay the zipper right side down on the faced side of the opening with one edge to the seamline and the other toward the raw edge of facing.

Stitch this side of the tape, using the zipper foot, close to the zipper teeth, and stitch the same side again but on the edge of the tape.

Turn the facing to the inside, baste, and stitch it down, leaving the unstitched side of the zipper tape free.

Press in the other side of the opening, then baste it over the free edge of the zipper next to the teeth. Baste the fly shield behind this, matching all the seam edges inside. Stitch through all the layers. Clip the lower end of the seam, and make a few stitches in the same place at the end of the opening to strengthen (Fig. 231).

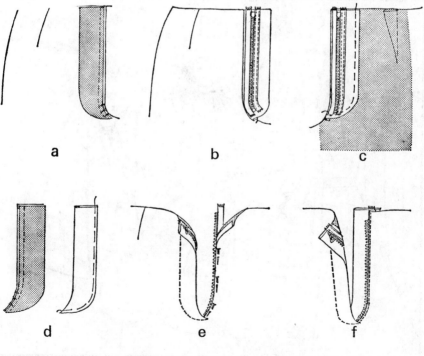

Fig. 231. Fly front.

POCKETS

These fall into three main groups.

1. The patch pocket, with or without flap, which is set on the garment.
2. The set-in pocket, which has a special opening of one kind or another made in the garment.
3. The pocket incorporated into a seam. Because pockets are important decorations, great care should be taken in placing and making them so that they will be well integrated in the design.

Pocket shapes and sizes can vary enormously but, as a general guide for size, top pockets are usually smaller than lower pockets.

Sizes generally vary for pockets on dresses, jackets, etc. from 9–15 cm (3½–6 in) and large patch pockets on coats and skirts from 20.5–25.5 cm (8–10 in).

Fig. 232.   Pocket variations.

Patch Pocket with Flap, Cut in One Piece

This is a simple variation of the basic patch pocket described on page 146.

Interface the pocket on the wrong side, and cut a facing to the shape of the flap plus 3.8 cm (1½ in) below the foldline. Machine-stitch the flap facing to pocket, right sides together. Turn to the inside, underpress, and baste back the turnings of the pocket. Use a herringbone stitch for the raw edge of the flap on the inside. Hand-stitch or topstitch to garment.

To introduce further detail, the edges could be bound with contrast fabric or braid, or topstitched in a contrasting colored thread (Fig. 233).

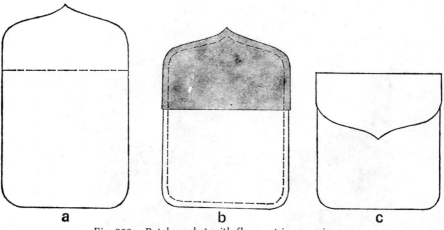

Fig. 233. Patch pocket with flap, cut in one piece.

Pocket Set in Seam (Concealed)

One of the easiest pockets to make, this is used on many types of garments.

Mark the pocket opening on both sides of the seam (use the widest part of your hand as a guide for width).

Cut a pocket bag with seam allowances in lining, or self-fabric if it is a thinnish type, slightly longer than the opening (use your hand again to find the right depth).

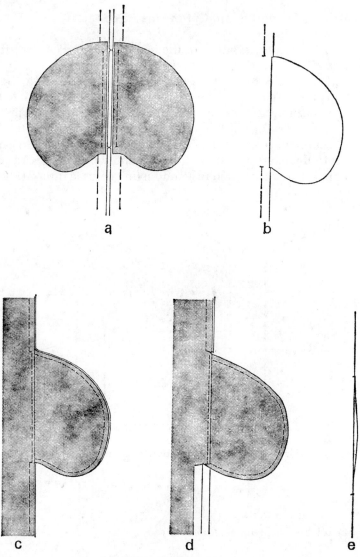

Fig. 234.   Pocket set in seam.

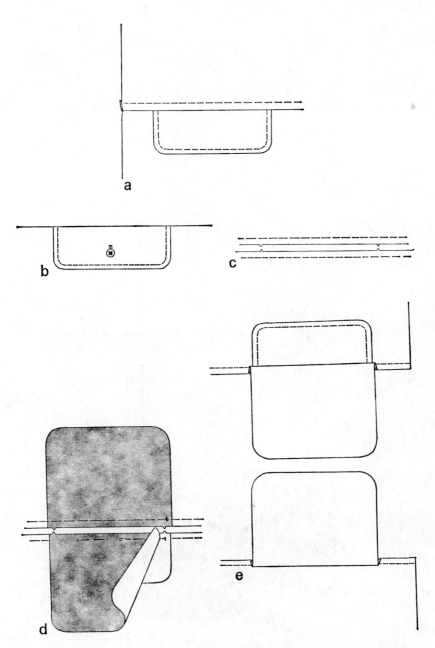

Fig. 235.   Pocket with flap set in seam.

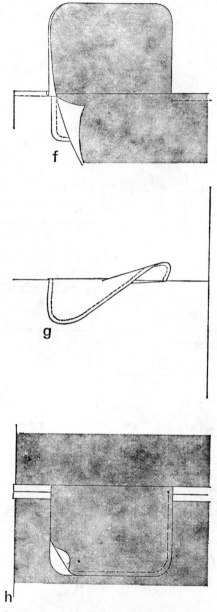

Fig. 235 (cont.).   Pocket with flap set in seam.

Lay the two halves of the bag—raw edges level with edges of seam allowances—right sides together, and machine-stitch to seam allowances (between seamline and seam allowance edges of garments).

Press both halves of the pocket bag toward the seam edges and away from the garment sections, then place the garment seams right sides together and join up to, and from, the pocket-end markings, thus leaving a gap to form the opening.

Clip one side of seam allowances, above and below the pocket opening. Press the garment seam allowances open and stitch the sections of the pocket bag together. Strengthen each end of the opening with small hand stitches (Fig. 234).

Pocket Set in Seam, with Flap

This procedure is show in Fig. 235. It is similar to the method described above and is used for a seam pocket with a flap, which can be varied with topstitching, buttonhole, or other decorations, though all are made on the flap beforehand, and it is sewn into the seam of the garment.

Cut a pocket bag, one-half deeper (by the width of the seam allowance) and slightly longer than the opening.

Cut flap pieces with seam allowances, interface on wrong side, and machine-stitch these together. (This is identical to the pocket flap on the coat design on page 161.) Turn through, press, and, if it is to be decorated, do so now.

Mark the pocket opening on both seams of garment.

Lay the unstitched edge of the flap between opening marks, right sides together; level with the seam allowance edge of garment. Baste in position on the garment and flap seamline.

With right sides facing, lay the deeper half of the bag over the flap and baste them together. Then baste the second half of the bag to the opposite seam, edge of bag to edge of garment seam allowance.

Machine-stitch on both sections, leaving the turnings on the pocket bag free. Press both halves of the bag (not the flap) toward the seam edges (and away from the garment sections) and join the garment seam to and from the opening ends.

For a plain seam, clip into one seam allowance each side of the pocket and press the seam open.

For a topstitched seam, press seam allowances together.

Finally, machine-stitch sections of pocket bag together (Fig. 235).

Welt Pocket

The welt pocket, illustrated in Fig. 236, is frequently used on tailored garments. It can be placed vertically, horizontally, or diagonally. Any decoration should be made before the welt is sewn onto the garment—the same as for the flap.

The placing and marking of this type of pocket is most important, because it is not set into an existing seam but has an opening cut through the garment so that mistakes are hard to rectify.

Mark the welt shape on the garment. Then mark a second line, just under 1 cm (⅜ in) above the welt line—call this the pocket line.

Cut the welt piece (twice the depth of the finished welt size, plus 1 cm (⅜ in) seam allowances all around, and equal to the length of the pocket opening. Interface on the wrong side. Fold this piece in half lengthwise, right sides together. Machine-stitch each end, clip and trim seam allowances, turn through to the right side, and press. Baste loose edges together.

Cut the pocket bag, with seam allowances, again slightly longer than the opening, one-half deeper than the other.

Lay the welt piece, right side down, with raw edges to the pocket line (the folded edge facing lower edge of garment). Baste in position, then lay the deeper section of the bag above the welt, with opening edge meeting the welt edge. Lay the other half of the bag on top of the welt, the opening edge level with the welt edge, again to meet the pocket line.

Machine-stitch along the welt seam through all layers, but stitch the top line (bag section only) slightly shorter at both ends. This keeps the ends of the opening from showing when the welt is turned up and in final position.

Cut into the pocket line and diagonally into corners (as for piped buttonhole on page 164).

Pull bags through to the wrong side and machine-stitch or hand-finish the ends of pocket opening. Press the seams, turn the welt up, and prickstitch or machine-stitch welt ends to the garment. Finally, sew the pocket sections of the bag together (Fig. 236).

Flap Pocket

Almost the same method used for the welt makes this pocket. The basic differences are that the flap is sewn above the pocket line as it faces downward—instead of below the pocket line for the welt, which faces upward.

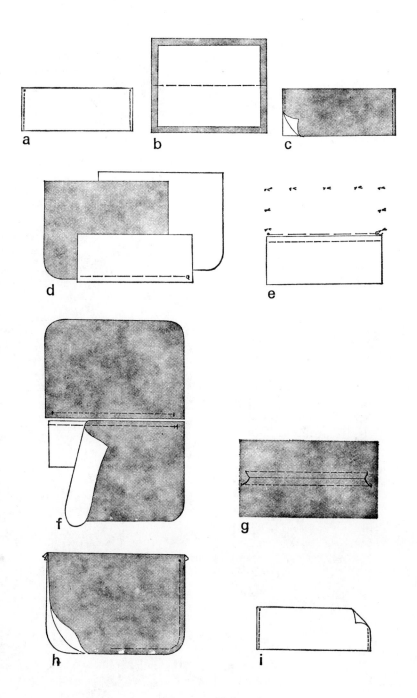

Fig. 236. Welt pocket.

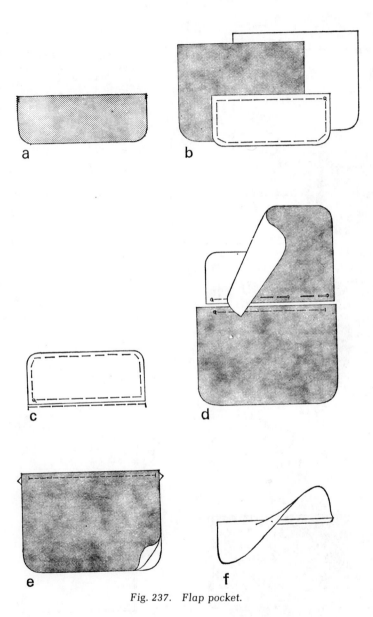

a

b

c

d

e

f

Fig. 237. Flap pocket.

As before, first make up the flap, then pin the right side to the right side of the garment, with the basted edge to the pocket line and the finished edge facing away from the pocket marking. Sew the deeper bag section on top, exactly over the flap, the seam allowance extending beyond the flap at each end. Machine-stitch the length of the finished flap.

Sew the lower pocket bag on, with opening edge to pocket line below the flap, all these edges meeting.

Stitch the lower section slightly shorter, again to ensure that the ends of the opening do not show when the flap is turned down. Cut

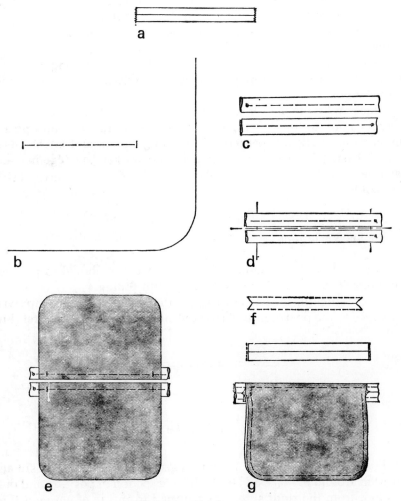

Fig. 238.   Piped pocket.

between the stitching and, diagonally to the corners, pull the pocket bags through to the wrong side. Machine-stitch or hand-finish the ends of the opening and stitch the pocket bag together. Then press flap down in position on the right side (Fig. 237).

Piped Pocket

This pocket is very much like a piped buttonhole opening, with the addition of a pocket bag.

Mark the opening on the garment. Cut piping strips at least 3.2 cm (1¼ in) wide, and slightly longer than the pocket opening.

Cut two sections to form the pocket bag, one of them 1 cm (⅜ in) deeper than the other.

Fold piping strips in half, right sides out, and baste along the center of each strip. Lay each piping strip, with raw edges to pocket marking, on the right side.

Place and baste pocket bag with opening edge to pocket line—the deeper section to top. Machine-stitch on basted line. Cut into pocket line, and diagonally into corners. Turn through, press, and stitch ends of piping. Last, join seam allowances of the pocket bag together and machine- or hand-stitch the ends of the pocket opening on the right side (Fig. 238).

Pocket Variations

The pockets so far described can be easily combined to produce variations. The first example is the flap with piping.

Before stitching the flap and bag, lay the prepared piping strips with raw edges to the pocket line. Then continue as for the flap pocket (Fig. 239).

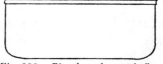

Fig. 239.   Piped pocket with flap.

For a piped pocket with a single bag section, make a piped slit and topstitch around it. Place and baste the bag section in position and then topstitch from the right side, when turned to inside of garment (Fig. 240).

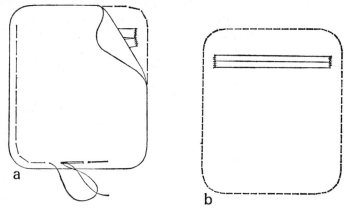

Fig. 240.   Piped pocket with single bag section.

Similarly, for a pocket with flap and a halfbag section, sew the bag over the flap and, when turned to the inside, topstitch to the garment. Machine-finish the lower opening edge (Fig. 241).

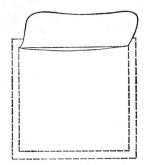

Fig. 241.   Piped pocket with flap and single bag section.

Front Hip Pocket

This pocket is made before the side seams are joined. The pocket edge should be staystitched first, then interfaced on the wrong side to stop stretching and to keep the shape.

One pocket bag section is stitched right side to the right side of the skirt front. If the edge is curved it must be clipped. Turn the bag section to the inside and understitch the seam. Place the front skirt over the hip and the other pocket section, at the waist and side. Stitch the skirt to the hip pocket section where it overlaps at the waist and side. The pocket edge opening should stand slightly away from the underneath section to allow room for a hand. Stitch the pocket bag sections together and join the front to the back skirt (Fig. 242).

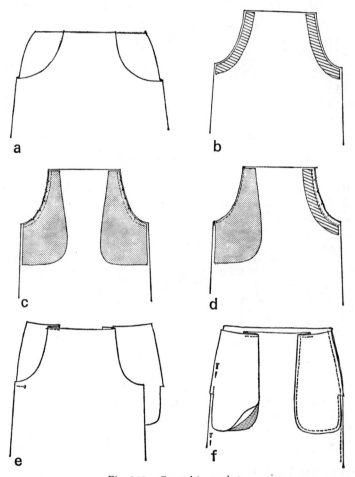

Fig. 242. Front hip pocket.

Porthole Pocket

Finally, there is a very decorative, but easy-to-make pocket called a porthole pocket. This can have piping cord inserted around the edge and a contrast fabric or embroidered backing, which makes it popular for children's clothes. A circular one is described, but of course the method would be as valid for other shapes—an oval or rectangle shape, perhaps.

Mark the circle for the pocket opening on the right side of the garment. A compass or plate can be used to make an accurate shape. A facing piece and pocket bag are cut large enough to contain the circle plus an allowance of at least 5 cm (2 in) on three sides, with a much deeper allowance on the lower edge to make the pocket bag. The pocket opening is marked on the facing piece and laid right side down to the right side of the garment, with the pocket opening matched. Baste in position and stitch.

Cut away the center of the circle, leaving a seam allowance of 1 cm (⅜ in), and clip this in turn to the stitching line. On the circle shape this will have to be clipped at every centimeter, so the seam allowance can be turned back neatly.

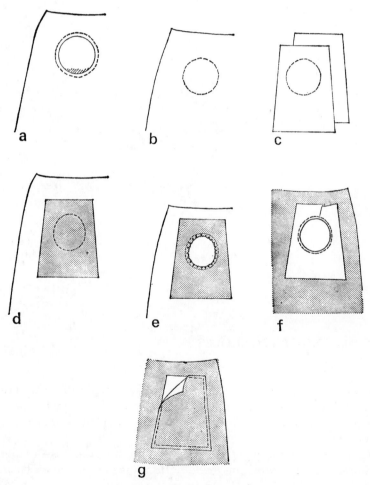

Fig. 243.   Porthole pocket.

The facing is turned to the inside, pressed back, and the edge is topstitched. The back pocket bag section is then sewn to the facing edge inside (Fig. 243).

Porthole Pocket with a Raised Edge. For a piped edge, which gives a raised effect, the cord is sewn in when the facing has just been turned through to the inside. The cord is laid between the facing and the garment fabric, right next to the stitching line on the inside. Push it well up to the seam and baste it in position, keeping the facing well to the inside. This will give a good raised edge. Stitch on the basting line with the zipper foot, which can lie close to the cord, keeping it firm.

Then the pocket is finished exactly the same way as the previous one (Fig. 244).

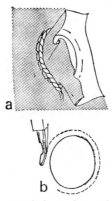

Fig. 244.   Porthole pocket with raised edge.

BUTTONS AND BUTTONHOLES

These, like many other processes of dressmaking, fulfill a functional purpose while at the same time being decorative. The choice of size and type is most important, because badly placed or sized buttons can spoil an otherwise good-looking garment.

There are two main types of hand-made buttonholes—bound (or piped) and worked. Machine-made buttonholes are made on basically the same principle. Bound ones have the edges finished with fabric;

worked ones are made with thread. Bound, like the piped version on the coat design on page 161, are made on the garment with an interfacing only and faced afterward. Worked buttonholes are cut and sewn through the garment, interfacing, and facing, when the garment is finished.

The buttonholes described are bound, as loops, tailor-worked, as thread loops, and set-in-seam buttonholes.

Fig. 245. Buttons and buttonholes.

Button Line

Button sizes are known by "line" sizes. "Line" is a small measurement first used probably in the eighteenth century, and refers to the standard measurement for all buttons. The average sizes shown in Fig. 246, and all others, correspond to the metric and traditional measures of the button diameter.

Further button varieties, among other forms of fastenings are described on pages 321–22.

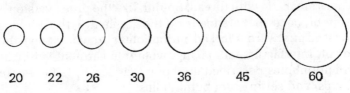

| 20 | 22 | 26 | 30 | 36 | 45 | 60 |

Fig. 246. Button "lines."

Button Placement

Before making buttonholes, it is essential to have the button and buttonhole allowances properly placed, to keep the balance of the design. The making of a piped buttonhole and a simple worked one has been demonstrated on the coat and shirt in previous chapters, but there are basic rules about placing them which apply to all. It is worthwhile to mention them again. Sometimes button markings are left off patterns, and occasionally you may wish to add buttons when you are adapting a pattern.

There must be a sufficient allowance between buttons and holes for fastening to avoid gaping at openings. They must be placed evenly. They must be large enough, without being clumsy—and remember that the buttonhole must be 3 mm (⅛ in) longer than the button, to allow it to slip through without strain and allow room for the button shank.

The allowance for material between the buttonhole and the edge of the garment should always be at least half the size of the button plus 1 cm (⅜ in), which often corresponds to the actual size of the button. This

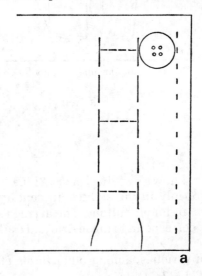

Fig. 247. Button placement.

allowance is essential to ensure that the button does not fasten off-center, or overlap the edge of the opening. Buttonholes can be placed vertically or horizontally across center lines. Placed horizontally, they are more practical, because garments so fastened are not so apt to gape when used with average-size buttons. The vertical position is used mainly on tab and shirt fastenings. An added help is to make a cardboard template of the button size, as a check for accurate placement.

From the center front/back line, the allowance is measured to the edge, with a seam allowance or self-facing added to this (see Fig. 247).

Parallel to the center front/back line, and on its opposite side, an edge line is marked, according to the width of the button. The distance from the top neck edge to the first buttonhole is also equal to the button width (if applicable according to the design). Horizontal buttonhole lines are marked between the center front line and the line parallel to it, but should extend 3 mm (⅛ in) beyond the center line into the allowance for the button shank.

For a double-breasted fastening, decide on the width of the allowance and follow the general principles of a single fastening. Mark the center front line and measure and mark the allowance, to the edge of the opening, providing for a button width to the *beginning* of the first row of buttonholes. On the opposite side of the center front line, mark the beginning of holes exactly the same distance away from it (Fig. 248).

Tabs with vertical buttonholes, should have the top button position equidistant from the side and top edges.

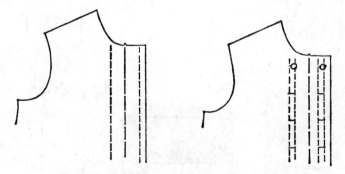

Fig. 248. *Double-breasted button placement.*

Bound Buttonhole

This is similar to the piped buttonhole described on page 164, the difference being that a much narrower binding edge is possible, because it is made with only one piece of fabric. It is suitable for use on thinner fabrics, or almost any that are not very loosely woven and fray easily.

Cut a rectangular piece of fabric, on the bias or on the straight grain, 5 cm (2 in) wide by a length equal to the diameter of the button plus 2 cm (¼ in). Mark a line at the center on the wrong side. Place this piece right side down to the right side of the garment, matching the center line to the buttonhole line and overlapping 1 cm (⅜ in) at each end. Baste marking lines 3 mm (⅛ in) each side of the center line (this distance can vary depending on fabric and size of button, so first try it out on a sample). Machine-stitch along the basted lines and across each end to make a rectangle. Cut very carefully through the center, stopping 3 mm (⅛ in) before each end, then cutting diagonally into the corners. Accuracy in stitching and cutting will produce neat binding edges, now turned through to the wrong side.

Press the seams toward the opening, press the binding piece, and pull each end so that tiny pleats are formed. Then sew these down firmly to the binding. A small backstitch can be made for extra strength on the

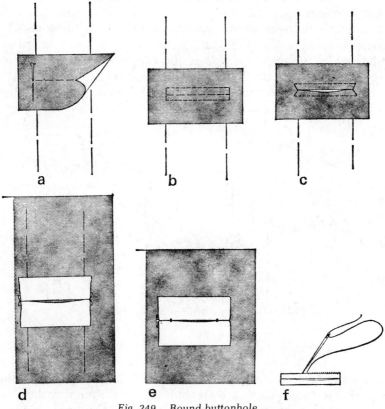

Fig. 249.   Bound buttonhole.

right side, through the binding seam. Finish the back of the buttonhole, when covered by the facing, in the same way as the piped version, by cutting a slit, then turning in the raw edges and hemming the turned-in edges to the binding (Fig. 249).

Loop Buttonhole

This is a very easy method, especially suitable for silk and lighter-weight fabrics often used for evening wear. Loop buttonholes can be made from ribbon, but are generally cut on the bias in self-fabric, because pulling through the ribbon on the straight grain is a little more difficult. A longish strip of fabric cut on the bias, about 2 cm (¾ in) wide, and long enough to make the loop, is required.

This is folded along the center of the length, right sides together, and stitched 6 mm (¼ in) from the fold. Leave threads at one end, thread

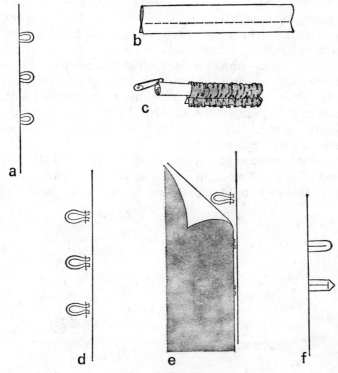

Fig. 250.   Loop buttonhole.

them through a bodkin, and pull the material through to the right side, working it with your fingers. If you do not have a bodkin, a small safety pin can sometimes be used.

The loops can be cut (Fig. 250d) or left in one continuous piece. Either way, the loop must face away from the edge. Sew them in position, on the right side, and sew the facing right side down on top. When this is turned to the inside of the garment the loops will be placed in the right direction. Naturally, without a separate facing the loops can be sewn to the inside of the garment, facing the right way. If the tubing is pressed when it is turned through, a flat tablike loop can be made if the end also is pressed where it folds naturally into a point (Fig. 250).

Tailor-Worked Buttonhole

This has an eyelet hole at one end, since it is intended to accommodate a *tailored button*, sewn on with a longish shank, as is usual on coats and suits. Make the eyelet hole at the beginning of the buttonhole with a stiletto, cut the line, then overcast the slit opening and hole over a narrow, strong cord, called *gimp*. This, when held in place next to the cut edge, is worked with a buttonhole stitch, using heavier twist or silk. Working from left to right, insert the needle into the slot, bringing it out below the overcasting. Bring the thread from the needle eye around and under the needle point from right to left. Draw the thread up to form a *purl* on the edge. Do not pull too tightly, and continue in the same manner around the buttonhole, keeping the stitches close together so that the purls cover the edges completely. Work a bar tack at the end and buttonhole stitch over it (Fig. 251).

With more practice, this gimp can be left free and the buttonhole stitch worked over it. Before the final end bar is worked, the ends of the gimp are pulled up to tighten the opening, then sewn in with the bar.

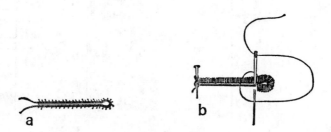

Fig. 251. Tailor-worked buttonhole.

Thread-Loop Buttonhole

The thread-loop buttonhole is used at neck edges on lingerie, baby clothes, and under a collar where the buttonhole should not be seen.

On the opening edge sew a few threads, rather like a loose bar tack, and just big enough for the button to slip through. Next work a blanket stitch over the threads, as shown in Fig. 252.

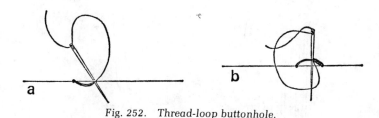

Fig. 252.   Thread-loop buttonhole.

Slot or Seam Buttonhole

This is a buttonhole set in a seam. It is very easy to make and is good for jersey fabrics. It can be made in braid, ribbon, and self-fabric, and is versatile; it can be used to add a self-facing when none has been allowed and can also be used horizontally, with or without a facing.

Basically, a band is cut twice the width of the button, plus seam allowances, or with enough turn-back to form a facing. Similarly, the garment section can have a facing cut in with it, or just have a seam allowance. Buttonholes are marked on the wrong side of band, which is then laid right side down to right side of garment, seam allowances matching. This seam is stitched between buttonholes, and the ends are stitched securely. The seam is pressed open, band turned to inside, seam allowance turned in—the hem to seamline, but not over it (Fig. 253c–e).

Figure 253(f)–(g) shows a facing cut in one piece with the garment. The band is stitched to the center line, then the seam is pressed open and the facing pressed back at the same time. The turned-in edge of the band

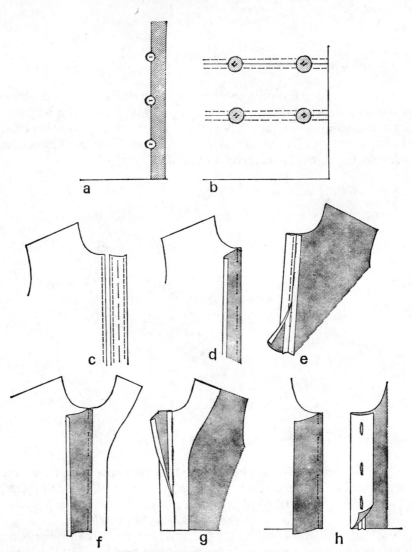

Fig. 253.   *Slot or seam buttonhole.*

is sewn back to the seamline. In Fig. 253(h) the facing has been cut in one piece with the band, so after the seam has been stitched and pressed, the facing side is turned in to the wrong side and blindstitched to the garment. The buttonholes are cut in the facing and hemmed, as in the bound and piped buttonhole methods.

The horizontal slot/seam buttonholes are marked in the seam, stitched, and pressed as on the band, the back finished through facing as above.

Sewing on Buttons

As already mentioned on page 167, mark the button placing with a pin through the buttonhole. For buttons with two or four holes, start with a few stitches on the button-mark position, then sew through the holes and back through the fabric, fairly loosely. On four-hole buttons these stitches can cross several times or be sewn to make two parallel sets of threads. In both cases, the thread is wound several times around those holding the button to the garment, to form a shank. Buttons that have their own shanks attached do not require loose stitches.

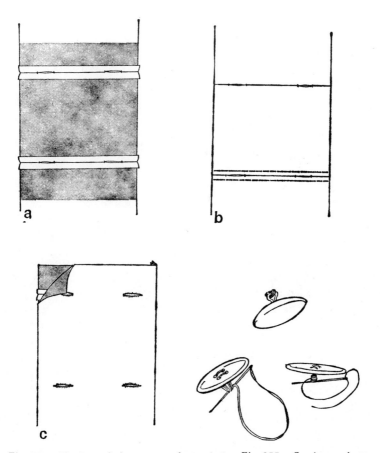

Fig. 254.   Horizontal slot or seam buttonhole.   Fig. 255.   Sewing on buttons.

Fig. 256. *Collar variations.*

COLLARS

There are three main categories of collars: (1) the flat, (2) the stand-up, and (3) the rolled collar.

Peter Pan, Eton, and sailor collars fall into the first group; and in the second are shirt, turtleneck, and mandarin collars. The rolled type includes the shawl and lapel collars with their variations.

On collars with rounded edges, what is necessary is careful notching and stitching to retain the shapes, a stitch across sharp points to allow for a good turnthrough, and on most, except very soft shapes, a good interfacing on the undercollar.

Collars that stand up must have both ends equal, because even a slight difference in the measurement is very obvious at the neck.

Two ways of attaching two different collars have already been described on pages 165 and 176—attaching a collar with a front and back facing, and attaching the shirt collar set on with a band. With all the varying shapes and ways of attaching collars, there are common essential points in constructing all collars:

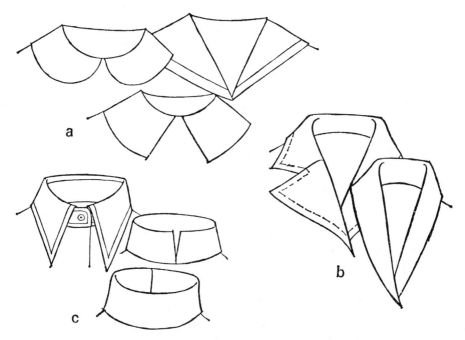

Fig. 257   Collars: flat (a); rolled (b); stand-up (c).

1. Staystitch the neckline of the garment.
2. Clip the neckline to the staystitching before attaching the collar, and match it to the neckline seam without allowing puckering.
3. Where possible, understitch the collar for a good turned edge.
4. Check to see that both ends of the collar are the same length and shape.
5. Match the collar markings exactly to the corresponding marks on the garment back.

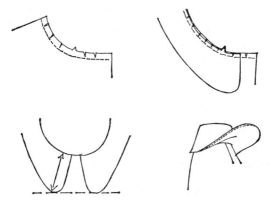

Fig. 258.   Attaching collars.

Three other ways of attaching the collar to the neckline are to apply it (1) with a front facing only, (2) without any facing, and (3) with a bias binding or bias strip.

Attaching a Collar with a Front Facing Only

Pin and baste both edges of the collar to the neck edge from the front to the shoulder seam. Clip the top collar where it meets the shoulder seam. Then pin and baste the undercollar only to the back neck edge of the garment. Fold back the facing over the collar at the front. Pin and baste, then stitch all the way,around. Clip the neck edge, turn the facing to the inside, and press and then underpress the back neck seam toward the collar.

Turn under the seam allowance of the top collar at the back, and with a felling stitch sew it to the back seam line. Slipstitch the shoulder edge of facing to the shoulder seam of the garment (Fig. 259).

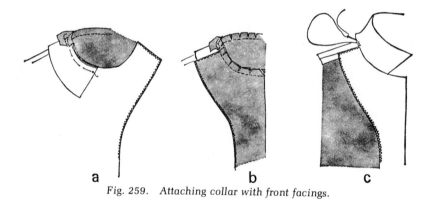

a   b   c

Fig. 259.   *Attaching collar with front facings.*

Attaching a Collar without Facings

This is a similar method, except that the undercollar edge is stitched all the way around the neck, and then the top collar seam is turned in and hemmed to the inside back neck seam. One major point to note here is that the top collar must have fractionally more allowed than the normal top collar allowance so that it will roll over well and lie correctly.

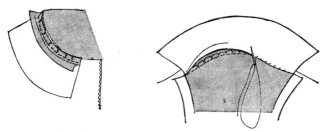

Fig. 260.   Attaching collar without facings.

Attaching a Collar with a Bias Binding or Bias Strip

Pin and baste both edges of the collar neck to the garment neckline. Baste the bias binding or strip, right side to the right side of the collar. Stitch, clip, turn to the inside. Press the seam allowances and bias toward the garment. Slipstitch the hem to the inside neck.

If there is a narrow turn-back on the open neck, the bias should overlap it slightly before it is stitched, so that it will look neat when it is turned to the inside.

All these methods apply equally to necklines with or without openings, of course. The figures will help show the variety of shapes and necklines where they apply.

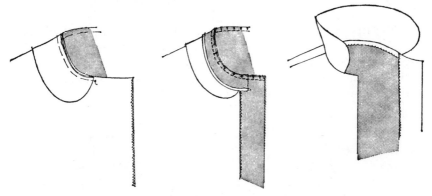

Fig. 261.   Attaching collar with binding or bias strips.

Turtleneck Collar

This soft, rolled-type collar is very easy to make. Cut on the bias, the fabric is folded in half lengthwise, right sides together. The ends are stitched, corners trimmed, and then it is turned to the right side. One edge has the turning pressed in. The other edge is laid to the neckline, right sides together, and stitched. The seam allowance is clipped and pressed upwards. Then the pressed-in edge is slipstitched to the inside neck seam. This collar can also be cut deep enough to make a turned-over polo-neck collar and sewn in the same way. Hooks and eyes are sewn to the edges, which meet edge to edge; buttons and loop buttonholes work very well too.

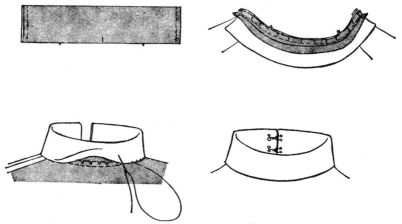

Fib. 262.   Turtleneck collar.

Shawl Collar

For this shape, the edges of the collar should be staystitched as well as the edge of the neckline (or sew a narrow tape to the seamline), because all the edges are on slanting cut lines, and these stretch very easily. The nearest way is to set the collar on with a front and back facing and to understitch the neckline.

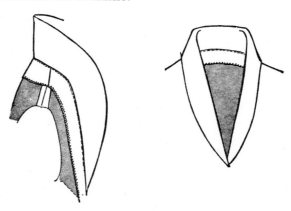

Fig. 263.   Shawl collar.

A Facing and Lapel Collar

Sewing the collar on with a front and back facing is one way of making the lapel collar. Another is to stitch the top collar to the front and back facing, stitching the undercollar to the garment. Special care must be taken with this basically simple method when stitching the collar and lapel seam where it joins. It must be absolutely accurately marked, otherwise it does not fit or turn through properly (Fig. 264).

First the undercollar is sewn right sides together to the neck edge and the seam clipped and pressed open. Next the top collar is stitched, right sides together, to the front and back facing, with the seam clipped and pressed open like the first one. The top collar/facing is laid with the undercollar and garment section, right sides together.

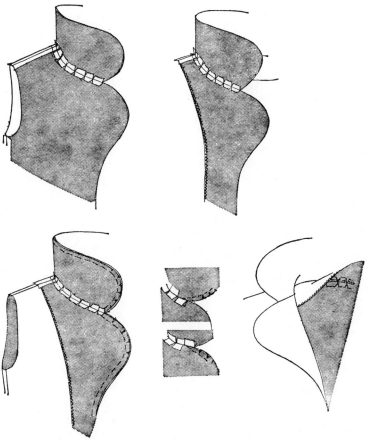

Fig. 264. Lapel collar with facing.

Pin and baste all around the edge of the collar and the facing edges. When stitching, turn down the neck seam where it meets the lapel and facing so that it does not get caught in the stitching. Leave the machine needle in the fabric, lift the presser foot, and turn up the turning again before stitching around the rest of the seam. Trim away any excess seam at the same point before turning the collar and facing to the right side.

The seam allowances of the undercollar and top collar are back-stitched together as far as possible. The facing is hand-stitched to the shoulder seam and the front facing edge is lightly caught to the garment inside.

SLEEVES

There are many different designs for sleeves and ways of cutting armholes and constructing them. Several basic variations are (1) the *set-in sleeve*, already described for the coat, jacket, and dress shapes; (2) the *raglan sleeve*, with the sleeve and top shoulder cut in one piece, or with a center seam from the neck to wrist; (3) the *dropped armhole*, which, as the name implies, has the armhole seam set low on the top arm; (4) the *kimono and dolman sleeve*, sometimes cut very low and cut in one piece with the bodice (these last two have their own variations —such as the *batwing*—but the basic shape has a sleeve with the armhole starting at or just above the waist); (5) a narrower fitted version of the dolman, in which a sleeve is cut in one piece with the bodice with a gusset under the arm (sometimes called the *Dior sleeve*); and (6) a classic *shirtsleeve* and armhole.

Set-In Sleeve

This should be smooth and fitted to the armhole, with no puckering or twist from off-grain cutting or fitting. All design detail, such as cuffs, buttonholes, and openings, should be made before the sleeve is set in. Puffed, pleated, and gathered tops to sleeves should be gathered or pleated to fit the armhole, then basted and stitched to hold the fullness in the right position before it goes into the garment. The stitching-in and pressing is the same as for a plain sleeve.

Fig. 265.   Sleeve variations.

Raglan Sleeve

This sleeve is made with a top shoulder dart or seam. The dart or seam is stitched first, and pressed open. For a close-fitting raglan sleeve, the underarm seam is stitched on the sleeve and on the garment, then the raglan seams are matched and stitched. The seam is clipped and can be pressed open, both seam allowances pressed together, up or down, and may also be topstitched. If the raglan is looser-fitting under the arm, the sleeve sections can be sewn to the front and back bodice parts first, then the underarm and sleeve seam can be stitched together. The dart or top sleeve seam is sewn last.

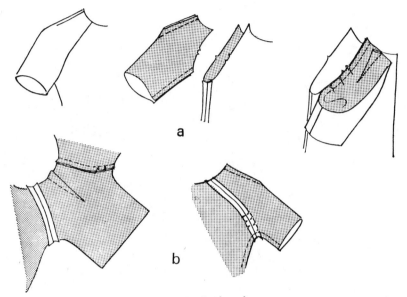

Fig. 266.   Raglan sleeve.

Dropped Armhole

Sleeves can be set in two ways with this type of armhole: the sleeve underarm seam and garment side seams can be stitched first, with the sleeve then pinned in the same way as a set-in sleeve; the difference is that there is usually no cap to the top of the sleeve and it needs to be carefully matched to the notches.

If this armhole is slightly deeper, as when there is a very full gathered sleeve, or when the garment side of the armhole is to be topstitched, the sleeve is better and more easily sewn to the armhole before the side and underarm seams are joined.

Stitch and press the shoulder seam of garment first. Lay the sleeve right side to the right side of the armhole; pin, baste and stitch. For a topstitched edge, press both seams toward the garment and stitch on the right side. On a flat open seam, the underarm seam may need clipping if there is a curve. A gathered sleeve can have the seams pressed toward the gathering or both seams pressed up.

Finally, the side seams of the garment and underarm seams of the sleeves are sewn as one seam.

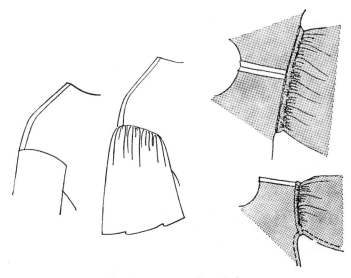

Fig. 267. Dropped armhole.

Dolman and Kimono Sleeve

In these easy sleeves there is no armhole seam; sleeves are cut in one with the bodice (the kimono seam is set very low). The shoulder seams are sewn first, then the underarm and garment seam. No difficulties here, but if the shaping makes the sleeve less deep, a strengthening tape or staystitch should be made at the underarm itself, and the seam should then be clipped to the staystitching.

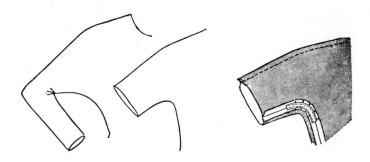

Fig. 268. Dolman/kimono sleeve.

Dior Sleeve

This is a fitted version of the dolman sleeve, which must have a gusset under the arm to allow for movement. A diagonal slash line is made at the underarm, about 9 cm (3½ in) into the bodice part where a sleeve seam would normally be. The end of this cut is staystitched with a small piece of fabric sewn on the wrong side at this point to strengthen it.

A gusset piece to fit the slash line is cut on the bias, about 10 cm (4 in) square. The shoulder underarm and side seams are stitched on the garment. The gusset is basted into the opening left by the slash lines. This is the neatest method if it is stitched from the inside, but it is quite hard to turn back the corners and stitch on the machine, so a hand stitch at these points may be necessary. The gusset can be edge-stitched from the right side, which is easier, but the stitching will show.

On thin fabrics, the slash line may be faced and a two-piece gusset made, each gusset piece being sewn in before the underarm seam is sewn.

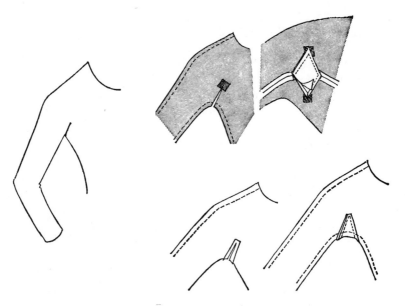

Fig. 269.   "Dior" sleeve.

Shirtsleeve

Sleeve construction is different for the classic shirt type. The cap of the sleeve is much shallower and it is set in with a flat fell seam on the right side, before the underarm seam is sewn. This is then stitched as one seam with the garment side seam.

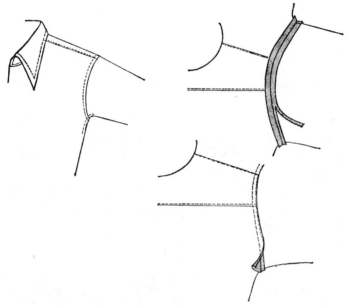

Fig. 270.   Shirtsleeve.

These are the basic ways of setting in the main sleeve types. The sleeve shapes themselves vary, but this is mostly a question of cutting. As already pointed out, any decoration is made before the sleeve is set in. The main functional and decorative process associated with sleeves are *cuffs* and *openings*.

Openings

Openings have already been described (see pages 248–51). The faced slit, continuous opening, and placket opening are all made at the edge of the sleeve in line with the little finger of the hand. An approximate measure is halfway on the back between the underarm seam and the center of the sleeve edge. A fitted sleeve can also have an opening in the underarm seam, with a zipper closing, or hooks and eyes.

Basic Cuffs

One general point should be made here: all bound or piped buttonholes, topstitching, or decoration should be made before the cuff is sewn to the sleeve.

Again, there are various shapes of cuff, but they are sewn to the sleeve the same way.

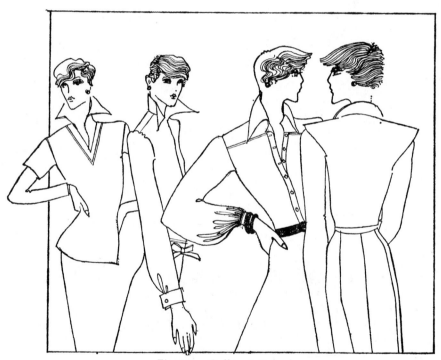

Fig. 271.   Cuff variations.

Band Cuff. The fabric is cut and interfaced on the wrong side. For a crisp look, the interfacing can be cut to the seam allowances, or cut to the finished size of the cuff. The fabric is folded lengthwise, right sides together, and stitched across the ends. Then it is turned to the right side and pressed, with the seam allowance pressed in on the outside cuff.

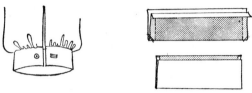

Fig. 272. Band cuff.

Shirt Cuff. This is cut in two pieces, interfaced as before; if there is a curved edge it is notched before being turned through and pressed.

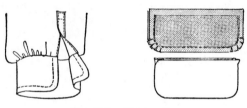

Fig. 273. Shirt cuff.

French Cuff. This is cut double the length of the shirt cuff so it can turn back. The turn-back can be extended slightly in width for a link fastening or slight flare.

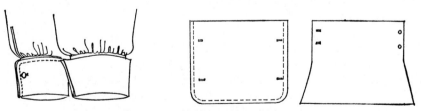

Fig. 274. French (turn-back) cuff.

Attaching Cuffs to Sleeves. The sleeve has the opening already finished before the cuff is attached. The edge of the sleeve is gathered or pleated to fit the cuff, and the cuff edges should have markings match exactly.

For a machine-stitched finish, press under the seam allowance of the outer side of the cuff. Lay the underside of the cuff seam to the inside of the sleeve (the right side of the fabric to the inside); pin, baste, and stitch the seam and press it toward the cuff. On the outside, baste the pressed-in edge of the cuff to the seamline on the outside and stitch it.

For a hand-finished cuff, machine-stitch the outside of the cuff, with the right side to the right side of the sleeve, and press the seam toward the cuff. On the inside, hem the inside cuff edge to the seamline.

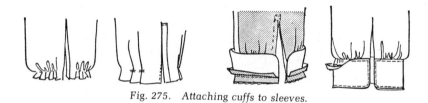

Fig. 275.   Attaching cuffs to sleeves.

PLEATS

To be perfect, pleats must be made of the right fabric. Soft drapable fabrics can have unpressed pleats, otherwise you should use a crisp fabric that presses well—not bulky or with a rough, textured surface. The best are garbardines, polyester blends, worsteds such as flannel, and other close-woven, firm but light fabrics. Velvets, spongy crêpes, thick wools, and stiff fabrics are out.

Various types of pleating include knife pleats, which are flat, even pleats all the way around or in groups; box pleats; inverted pleats; kick pleats (small ones to allow movement in straight skirts); unpressed pleats; and commercially made pleats such as accordion and fine knife pleats.

Fig. 276.   Pleats.

Whenever possible, the hem should be made first and on all but the last four types, the pleating section should be laid on a flat surface. Pin the pleats in position, checking to make sure they are on the grain line and are lying smoothly. Baste each pleat, a basting line across hip level and at waist, then press the whole section. (Fig. 277).

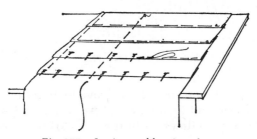

Fig. 277.   Laying and basting pleats.

Pleats can be stitched to hip level on the inside or each pleat can be edge-stitched on top. On some of these, such as box pleats, the excess layers can be cut away inside; but care must be taken that enough support is left for the pleat (Fig. 278).

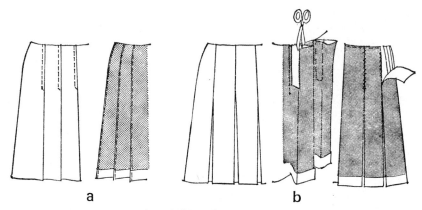

Fig. 278.   Edge-stitching pleats (a); cutting away bulk (b).

Accordion or fine knife pleating made commercially also has the hem made before pleating. To ensure a good fit, a tape should be cut to the waist size; then the pleating is eased in and basted to the tape before the waistband is attached (Fig. 279).

Fig. 279.   Taping waist.

For all-over pleating on bodice or sleeve sections, the pattern is laid on the pleated fabric and then cut. Basting around the edge keeps the pleats in place, and sometimes the lining is cut to the shape of the section and stitched to the pleating before the garment is assembled (Fig. 280).

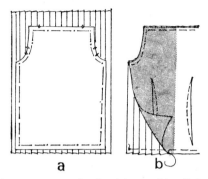

Fig. 280. *Laying pattern on pleating* (a); *attaching lining to pleating* (b).

The small kick pleat is usually cut as an extension of the seam from the waist, or at the lower edge of the skirt. The pleat from the waist has more support; but on thicker fabrics the other way is best, with a tape or lining sewn from the top of the pleat to the waist, or a row of stitching made across the top of the pleat to the garment (Fig. 281).

Fig. 281. *Kick pleat.*

Some inverted pleats are sewn with a separately cutback piece called an *underlay*. The seam is stitched to the pleat mark, the pleat allowance is pressed back, and the underlay is stitched to the seams. All pleated hems in which the seam is on the inside fold of the pleat must be turned up as described earlier, so that they have a sharp edge without bulk (Fig. 282).

Figures 277–82 show some basic points we have been discussing.

Fig. 282. Inverted pleat.

DECORATION

Well-applied decoration integrated with the design can add individuality to a garment. The decoration can be simple binding or fine
beadwork, but if it does not enhance the design do not use it. Fashion

Fig. 283. Decoration.

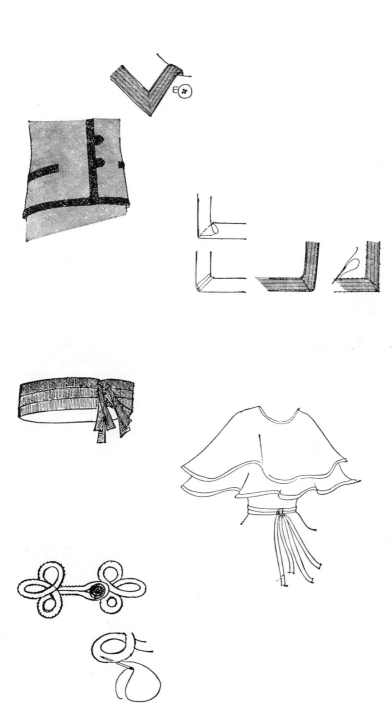

Fig. 284.   Braid, ribbon, frogging.

ideas found in magazines and newspapers can be inexpensively worked out this way.

Braid, wool textured in finish, mixes well with tweed. Chanel produced a classic of the century with soft tweed suits bound and trimmed with braid. Use of braid is functional, too, because it can enclose raw edges at the same time, be made into button loops, or form seam buttonholes. **Ribbon** can be used in this way too, as well as being inserted into seams as a piping. Belts made from ribbon, sewn together in different tones, are very effective for evening clothes. **Narrow braid and buttonhole loops** make froggings, or edge necklines. **Satin binding** can edge wool crêpe and, as a narrow binding on sheer fabrics, solve the hemming problem and can give shape to soft lines.

The wider braids and ribbons can be sewn on by machine-stitching on the edge, or handsewn with a felling stitch or slipstitch. This applies to the flat, narrower ones too, but if they are of the cord, or round loop shape, they will have to be handsewn (Fig. 284).

Tucking—from narrow pin tucks to wider flat tucks—is made on the fabric before it is cut to shape. This is usually most successful for sections that are completely tucked; smaller groupings can be marked on the pattern. The all-over tucking is made on the fabric, cut much larger than the pattern shape. A notched guide is a help to check the distance between the tucks, which must be marked on the straight grain. Narrow pin tucks can be made by folding the fabric on the tuck line and pressing the fold. The tuck is machine-stitched very close to the edge. Basting along the tuck line is another method; and flat tucks are marked, then

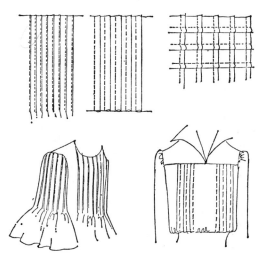

Fig. 285.   Tucking.

basted the depth of the tuck—all on the right side. (They can also be made across as well for an interesting detail.)

Perhaps this type of pleating is most effective on bodices and on sleeves, where fullness can fall from the end of the tucking (Fig. 285).

Ruffles and gathering on thinner fabrics can be made in various ways. Ruffles have the hem made first; this can be done with a small zigzag stitch or with the rolled hem attachments on the machine. Other fancy edging stitches on the machine can be made on the ruffle too. The ruffle is gathered up by machine-stitching, using the largest stitch and pulling up the thread to fit the edge it is to be sewn to. If there is a ruffler attachment this can of course be used.

For a collar or cuff, the ruffle is laid right side down to the right side of the fabric, with the gathered edge to the edge of the fabric, and basted in position. The other side of the collar or cuff is then basted right side down over the ruffle, edges meeting. After being stitched on the basted line the collar or cuff is turned to the right side.

A ruffle in a seam is stitched the same way, with the gathered edge to the seam edge and right sides together, the other section right side down over it. Press the seam allowances away from the ruffle. For a circular ruffle cut the length of the edge, sections must be seamed together for wider hems. A small inside circle will make a fuller ruffle. This inside edge is staystitched first, and the outer edge hemmed by hand or on the machine. The seam above the staystitching must be clipped, then sewn the same way as a gathered ruffle (Fig. 286).

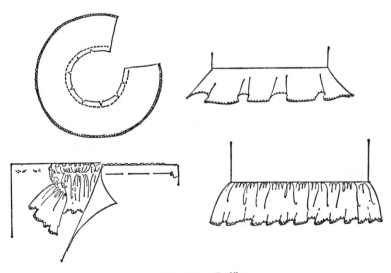

Fig. 286.   Ruffles.

Godets are flared inserts, often bias cut, and are sewn into slash lines in a skirt. A slash line should be staystitched at the point, and the adventurous sewer can set a narrow satin piping in the seam! Pleating and lace can be set the same way as godets (Fig. 287).

Fig. 287. Godets.

A tape or ribbon sewn to the inside of a full garment can have a cord or elastic drawn through for a **gathered waistline.** (Fig. 288).

Fig. 288. Gathered waistline.

Lace can be handsewn to an edge with a whipstitch or inserted between bands of fabric. It can also be sewn with a zigzag stitch if it is

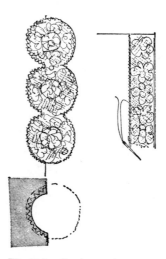

Fig. 289. Sewing on lace.

sewn to the right side; otherwise it is stitched with the right side of lace to each right side of sections to be joined, with narrow plain seams (Fig. 289).

Smocking can be simulated on the machine by drawing up even rows of gathering, and using some of the embroidery stitches on the machine. Hand-smocking has a variety of stitches, the most popular being a honeycomb stitch. This can be made for yoke pieces or cuffs on dresses of soft fabric (Fig. 290).

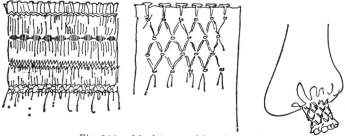

Fig. 290. Machine- and hand-smocking.

Embroidery stitches on the machine, including the basic zigzag stitch, can be used to good effect on denim-type fabrics, or other plain surfaces used as edging stitches, or to introduce a contrast color. Yokes, collars, pockets, and belts can be finished this way (Fig. 291).

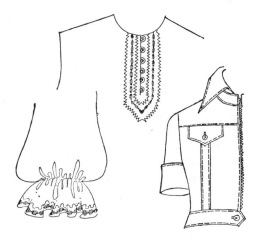

Fig. 291. Decorative stitching.

Beads can be sewn on singly with a backstitch and securely fastened off or sewn threaded on a cord, then whipstitched over the cord.

Sequins can be sewn in with a backstitch through the center hole of each one (Fig. 292).

Fig. 292.   Beads and sequins.

Belts in self- or contrasting fabric can be made from either a long or two narrower lengths of fabric, interfaced on the wrong side and top-stitched on the right side. For tie belts, the fabric can be cut in two sections for one with shaped ends, or folded in half lengthwise, both with right sides together. These are stitched all around in the first type, just leaving a gap to pull the belt through; the other has just one long seam, stitched across one end as well, then the belt is pulled through like a large tube. The gap and end are whipstitched. Belt backing can be bought, to make stiffer belts, and buckles made or bought (Fig. 293).

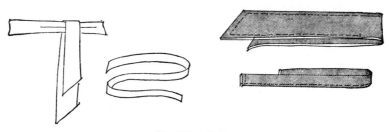

Fig. 293.   Belts.

All decoration, must be worked out at the original planning stage. It must never look as if it was a last-minute thought (Fig. 294).

Fig. 294. Smocking, ruffles, and gathers.

15
More about
Fabrics

METRIC AND YARDAGE CALCULATIONS

When buying fabrics, the distinction made between length expressed in yards and width in inches changes to meters and decimal parts of a meter for length (e.g., 2.25 m) and centimeters for width (even when greater than 1 meter—e.g., 140 cm).

Using the metric system, fabrics can be bought in multiples of 10 cm (0.10). Because this is rather less than ⅛ yd, it provides greater accuracy in fabric calculations for any chosen design.

The following charts on page 308 list the nearest conversions.

SEWING WITH SPECIAL FABRICS

Some popular fabrics need special handling, and although they appeal to the beginner their difficult textures, weaves, or designs need special attention in cutting and construction.

In this section we will deal as simply as possible with these fabrics, which are: checks, plaids and stripes, velvet, chiffon and other sheers, lace and crêpe, knitted fabrics, mohair, and (although they are technically not fabric) leather and its imitations.

Checks, Plaids, and Stripes

The main problem here is in laying out and cutting. Because it is the matching of these at the seams that is important, it follows that patterns should be chosen that have as few seams as possible, with good, unbroken lines. Some checks and plaids are smaller and even, which makes matching a little easier. Even so, more fabric must be allowed; for these allow an extra 0.25 m–0.50 m (¼–½ yd) and on the larger and more uneven plaids as much as 0.5 m–0.90 m (½–1 yd). Matching stripes needs slightly less extra allowance than checks and plaids.

Planning the position of the plaid is important, for a larger or more dominant check will affect the design, and should be placed accordingly. Pockets, sleeves, and pleats too will be affected. When laying the pattern on the fabric, mark on the pattern the position of these checks and, particularly, mark where the stripes or checks meet the seamline. Mark these in accurately with a pencil, in one or two places (near notches). With an uneven plaid or stripe, the pattern will also have to be laid the same way, and not up and down; this is why more fabric must be allowed.

With the checks, plaids, and stripes marked in this way, the other sections can be laid on, matching the marked pieces to the fabric checks, etc. (Fig. 295).

Unless cutting is on the true bias, straight, or equal slant, the plaids will not match all along the seam. Similarly, matching at seams can be

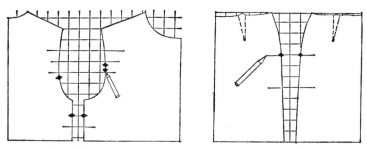

Fig. 295.   Mark where stripes/checks meet on seamline.

achieved horizontally, but not always with the vertical bars matching.

It is safer to cut all these uneven and large checks and plaids on a single layer of fabric not forgetting to reverse the pattern pieces for the other section. Because sleeves cannot always be matched on both front and back bodices, it is better to match the front; again the notches will help in matching the same check lines. Figs. 295–96 will show some of the possibilities. It goes without saying that you should always look for a pattern that has been designed for plaids and checks as well as for plain fabric!

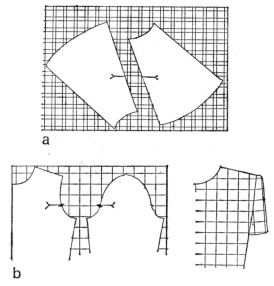

Fig. 296.   Reverse pattern on single layers (a); match sleeve and bodice (b).

AVAILABLE FABRIC WIDTHS

cm	in	cm	in	cm	in
65	25	115	44/45	150	58/60
70	27	122	48	175	69/70
90	35/36	127	50	180	72
100	39	140	54/56		

FABRIC WEIGHT
Gram per square oz. per yard meter

METERS TO YARDS—ROUNDED TO THE NEAREST EQUIVALENT

meter	yard	meter	yard	meter	yard
0.15	⅛	3.20	3½	6.30	6⅞
0.25	¼	3.35	3⅝	6.40	7
0.35	⅜	3.45	3¾	6.55	7⅛
0.50	½	3.55	3⅞	6.65	7¼
0.60	⅝	3.70	4	6.75	7⅜
0.70	¾	3.80	4⅛	6.90	7½
0.80	⅞	3.90	4¼	7.00	7⅝
0.95	1	4.00	4⅜	7.10	7¾
1.05	1⅛	4.15	4½	7.20	7⅞
1.15	1¼	4.25	4⅝	7.35	8
1.30	1⅜	4.35	4¾	7.45	8⅛
1.40	1½	4.50	4⅞	7.55	8¼
1.50	1⅝	4.60	5	7.70	8⅜
1.60	1¾	4.70	5⅛	7.80	8½
1.75	1⅞	4.80	5¼	7.90	8⅝
1.85	2	4.95	5⅜	8.00	8¾
1.95	2⅛	5.05	5½	8.15	8⅞
2.10	2¼	5.15	5⅝	8.25	9
2.20	2⅜	5.30	5¾	8.35	9⅛
2.30	2½	5.40	5⅞	8.50	9¼
2.40	2⅝	5.50	6	8.60	9⅜
2.55	2¾	5.60	6⅛	8.70	9½
2.65	2⅞	5.75	6¼	8.80	9⅝
2.75	3	5.85	6⅜	8.95	9¾
2.90	3⅛	5.95	6½	9.05	9⅞
3.00	3¼	6.10	6⅝	9.15	10
3.10	3⅜	6.20	6¾		

Sewing the parts together accurately means pinning them in the first place, with all stripes and checks matching where marked. Pin on the bars of checks and stripes and lift the seam allowance from time to time, to see if at the seam itself the stripes and bars are matching. Baste the seam carefully, and machine-stitch at a medium pace. Sewing threads and trimmings should match in the dominant color of the fabric (Fig. 297).

Fig. 297.   Lift seam allowance to check that stripes match (a); unbalanced stripes (b); balanced stripes (c).

A chevron effect is made by cutting the fabric on the bias. Try a fold on the bias first to see just how the plaids or stripes will look. The fabric with an uneven plaid must be reversible and cut separately. Balanced plaids also have the pattern pieces cut individually, on a single layer, with the pattern turned over to have right and left sections. As with all plain bias fabrics, care must be taken not to stretch the seam when it is stitched. The sections should be laid flat on a table, without distorting the seams, and the pieces should be pinned and basted together firmly to avoid slipping (Fig. 298).

Fig. 298.   Chevron.

Velvet

Velvet is a queen among fabrics, with its lustrous pile and sheen. It is not too difficult to sew correctly if a few directions are remembered. First, there are several types of velvet and cotton velveteen; these include corduroy, velour, and plain velveteen. There are rayon velvets, which are softer and silkier in feel, and pure silk velvet, which can range from a "Lyons" type, very rich and fairly substantial in handling, to a panne velvet, which is thin and very shiny. "Street" velvet, developed for outer wear but with the rich look of a Lyons type, is sometimes without a one-way pile, making it simpler to lay out and cut.

Because most velvets have this definite pile surface, the sheen on the pile as it lies one way will be very different from a section cut the other way; the shading will be quite different, often going from very pale to dark. The pattern pieces must be laid out and cut one way to avoid this. If the pile smooths in an upward direction, this will give a deeper tone; when it is smoothed downward the shading is lighter. For this reason velvets are generally cut with the upward direction of the pile. As with the plaids, more fabric must be allowed. If no meterage/yardage for velvet is shown on the pattern instructions, make sure that the design is suitable for velvets. The cutting is done with the napped (pile) surface inside, and the direction of pile marked on this wrong side with chalk. When you are preparing to make up velvet, you should do the pinning in the seam allowances with the pile, and not across it, because that could cause marks. When possible you should use the very finest pins, or better still, fine needles. Basting is best done with a fine thread and needle, as for all hand-finishing, and all sewing is done in the direction of the pile or nap. There should be a light tension on the machine; about 10 stitches for 2.5 cm (1 in); needle size 14; cotton thread for the cotton velvet types and pure silk for the luxury velvets. The seams cannot have a turned-in finish, because this is too bulky and would leave marks after pressing; a zigzag stitch, hand overcasting, or bias seam binding are best. For facings use lightweight lining on velveteens, or organza on the finer velvets.

Pressing is the most problematical point. Velvet cannot be pressed in the ordinary way, because this would shine or flatten the pile surface. A needle board is best but expensive: the velvet is laid face-down on the needle surface and pressed in the direction of the pile under a damp cloth. If you don't have a needle board you can stand the iron on end, place a damp cloth over it, and draw the wrong side of the fabric across the covered iron to steam-press it.

Most of these directions apply to other napped fabrics in woolen cloth, and in general these are cut one way, but with the nap running down—corduroy cut this way shows less wear but, on the other hand, not so deep a color.

The same cutting and layout principles apply to one-way printed fabrics. Check that the print is the right side up—large flowers upside down on one section are very obvious! Satin fabrics can also have a shading problem, so if in doubt, cut these one way as well (Fig. 299).

Chiffon and Other Sheers

This group includes chiffon, which is very soft; voile and lawn, which are semi-soft; and crisp sheers such as organdie. Many will have to be lined, and the lining should be of a type to give depth to the fabric.

Again, choose a pattern with as few seams as possible and one specially designed for the fabric, for the best results.

Chiffon has a tightly woven selvage that should be clipped at intervals to keep the fabric from lying unevenly. Mark with tailor tacking —any other method will show through to the right side and be difficult to remove. The very soft fabrics will have to be pinned and sewn through tissue paper so they won't slip; cutting must be done with very sharp shears or scissors.

Full skirts can also be cut across the width instead of lengthwise —this eliminates some seams. A double hem lends weight and looks neater, with no raw edges visible through to the right side. The alternative is a very narrow, rolled hem. If a lining has been sewn together with the sheer fabric, the facing is made in the lining fabric, but if not, a fine bound edge in the same fabric can be neater than a facing.

To sew through tissue paper and fabric, cut strips of it and lay them underneath the basted seam; then stitch through both, tearing the paper gently away from the seam afterward. Use average to loose tension, and the same pressure. The stitch length should be short—about 16 stitches to 2.5 cm (1 in), and a very fine needle, size 9 or 11, should be used, with fine pure silk thread.

Seams can be made and finished so little is seen through to the right side. The French seam is ideal, but another way is to stitch a plain seam, press both seam turnings together, and stitch again close to the other seamline through the turnings. Trim away surplus turnings.

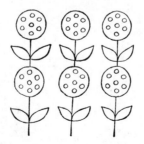

Fig. 299. One-way print.

One method for hems is a very narrow machine turning, then turned again and slipstitched. Another is a hand-rolled hem. On the machine this can be a very narrow machine turning, then another just as narrow and stitched again. A double hem is one that turns the depth of the hem, and is turned again so that the raw edge is right on the inside of hem fold; then it is slipstitched in place. Buttonholes can be made on the machine; otherwise loop buttonholes are more successful.

Lace

Lace comes in various weights and patterns. It can be backed onto net, which accentuates its design, or sewn to a lining, which takes away its transparency. The pattern lace may require some matching up; if so, pay attention to the seams and front openings and, of course, choose a pattern without too many seams and design lines. As on sheers, facings for the heavier laces can be in lining fabric. On the lighter ones you can make a narrow bound edge in chiffon or silk, or face it with net. Chiffon can also be used as a backing to give light support (or semi-transparency) to a soft type of lace. Mark with tailor tacks. The tension on the machine should be slightly loose; the pressure adjusted to the fabric. A medium to long stitch should be used with a fine needle, size 11, and mercerized cotton thread, or pure silk for the very fine laces. Finishing on seams and hems can be as for the sheers; you can make a faced hem, in the same lining, or use net for the whole garment. If the lining is sewn in with the lace, seams are pressed open and finished with zigzag or overcasting through both seam allowances. On unlined laces, zigzag close to the steamline and trim. On some large-motif laces, for an unseamed look, the motif or pattern is cut around and matched to the other section, then it can be handsewn with a hemming stitch on the right side, or stitched with a small zigzag stitch on the machine.

Press lace under a cloth, because the openwork of the lace can catch on the iron tip (Fig. 300).

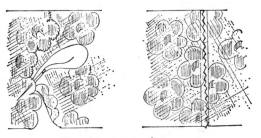

Fig. 300.   Joining lace.

Crêpe

This material is a spongy texture fabric that is rather stretchy. Before it is cut out it needs to be pinned to the pattern very carefully so it won't slip. Slanted seams and necklines should be basted singly while still flat on the table and staystitched immediately to prevent excessive stretching. Bias seams are tricky, because the hem will drop very unevenly, so the garment needs to hang for at least a few days before the hem can be measured and cut. As before, a pattern designed with this fabric in mind is best, and the cutting is all-important. On the machine use a medium to light tension, a stitch length of about 12–14 stitches to 2.5 cm (1 in), fine mercerized thread, and a fine needle. Some slanting seams—those in a halter top, for instance—can have a very narrow tape sewn in with the seam to stop stretching. The same method can be used on shoulder and waist seams, too. Press with care, and never damp because this can shrink the fabric alarmingly, or flatten and shine it, so press under a dry cloth on the wrong side.

Knitted Fabrics

Knitted fabrics, developed from the basic wool jerseys, now have the look of hand-knits as well as crochet and rib patterns. Doubleknit jersey is easy to make up because it is firmer (see page 55). The finer and softer knits need more attention, and circular and bias seaming should be avoided, when possible—the circular shape in particular would just go on dropping, and look very saggy. Check to see where the rib is and which is the "grain" of the knitted fabrics. Avoid stretching the fabric when cutting out, remembering that knitted material stretches more in the width than in the length. The tension on the machine should be medium to light with 12–15 stitches to 2.5 cm (1 in), or use a small zigzag stitch. Size 11 needle is required for the fine single knits, and a size 14 needle for heavier knits with a mercerized thread. Very thin nylon and silk jerseys need smaller stitches, a fine needle size 11 (changed as soon as it becomes slightly dull), or a small zigzag stitch. Sew slowly and evenly, otherwise stitches may get skipped.

With all these knits, seams at the shoulder and waist should be taped. Zigzagging the hem or overcasting it and then blindstitching it is best, because it stretches easily with the fabric.

Mohair

Mohair is delicious to look at and difficult to sew! Usually it is best if this is completely underlined first and, on the very lightweight, loose-woven types this underlining could be in organza or a very light polyester blend. Mounting a fabric like this is done by basting in the underlining as soon as the sections have been cut. Baste the underlining around all the outside edges, the underlining to the wrong side of the fabric. Sew in a few big diagonal basting lines across to keep the material flat. Then do the darts and seams as if the two layers were one piece of fabric. A lining is sewn in afterward in the normal way. On the machine use an average to light tension, about 12–15 stitches to 2.5 cm (1 in), size 14 needle, and mercerized thread. It is a help to have paper on both sides of the fabric between the presser foot and plate; this keeps the foot or teeth on plate from catching in the loops of the mohair. Press the fabric under a dry cloth, because it will flatten or shrink otherwise. Bound or piped buttonholes can be made with a matching ribbon or firm fabric.

Fur Fabrics

These look very difficult but in fact are not. Some of the points to watch are the same as for velvets and other pile fabrics. The pile and backing is usually manufactured, and either knitted or woven. Obviously, with the bulkiness of the fabric, you must pay attention to the type of collars and sleeves if you are not using a pattern specifically designed for this fabric. The bigger lapel type of collar is possible, though not with sharp corners, which would be hard to make up. Facings are better cut in one piece with the garment, made in lining fabric, or you can bind the edges in braid. The fabric should be cut one way with the pile running down, and the very thick pile types should be cut singly. Stitch with a loose tension, light pressure, larger stitches—about 10 stitches to 2.5 cm (1 in)—a needle size 16 or heavier, and heavier-weight mercerized thread.

All sections will have to be firmly basted first, so they won't slip or "creep"; stitching is always in the direction of the pile. To pick out pile caught in the seam on the right side, use a pin; on the wrong side, darts and seams can have the pile shaved so that they will be flatter. Not much pressing is needed for these fabrics, but if a hem or seam must be pressed, use a velvet board, or terry towelling, and lightly steam-press without touching the fabric.

Leather

This has obvious differences from fabrics. In the first place, leather is made up of sections of animal skins, so are individual and have to be chosen to match one another in weight and color. The skins are not very large, so the pattern must be bought or worked out first so you can see how many skins you'll need. Leather also needs interfacing to hold and support the shape. Pieces must be cut singly, with 1 cm (⅜ in) seams; and the pattern must be laid to the lengthwise or crosswise right side of the leather. Suede leather has a napped surface, and the tops of all pattern sections should point to the neck of the skin.

Only pin in the seam allowance, or use transparent tape to hold the pattern to the leather. Mark with chalk on the wrong side all design lines, darts, etc., and make sure of fitting and accurate marking before sewing, because stitches show if they are removed, or the leather could split! Stitch with a slightly loose tension—about 8–10 stitches to 2.5 cm (1 in). Use a 14 or 16 needle—always new if no leather needle is available—and use a heavier-weight mercercized thread. Seams can be sewn with a special adhesive leather tape, to strengthen and prevent ripping. They should be held, before stitching, with paper clips or sticky tape, instead of pins. Seams and darts are trimmed, pressed, and glued down so they will stay flat.

All seams and darts and the hem, which is also glued and not sewn, are hammered lightly so they will be flat and stay in place. Bound and piped buttonholes can be made—seam buttonholes are ideal, because they eliminate extra stitching. Press with a warm, dry iron over paper or a medium-weight cloth.

Leather Imitations and Vinyl

These materials have some points in common with leather. Pinning should be done only in the seam allowance, with tape or paper clips to hold the layers together; work in general as for leather. Use very sharp scissors, mark on the wrong side with chalk. The tension on the machine should be medium with a stitch length of 8–12 to 2.5 cm (1 in). Any topstitching should be larger; use size 14–16 needles, depending on the weight of the material, and heavier-weight mercerized thread. When the leather or vinyl surface is down on the throat plate, or to the presser foot, use tissue paper between them to prevent sticking. As for leather, stick down all seam allowances that are not topstitched. Hems can be done with a blindstitch that catches the garment side with its backing material. Bound or seam buttonholes work best.

For all leather and leather imitations, welt, flat fell, and topstitching on seams are good; as well as being decorative, they hold down the seams and support the shape.

FABRIC AND DESIGN SUITABILITY

With all this information it is apparent that certain fabrics are more suitable than others for the various types of garments. As a brief guide starting from the inside, so to speak, *lingerie fabrics* should be the very lightest and smooth so as not to interfere with the lines of the dress or skirt shapes. *Housecoats, dressing gowns,* and *nightwear* all make up well in the washable manufactured fibers, especially the ones mixed with cotton to give softness.

Shirts and blouses can be made in fine jersey, cotton, silk, and similar-weight manufactured fibers. *Skirts and suits,* which have a more tailored look, make up well in all the worsted type woolens, heavy denim and cotton gabardine, lighter-weight tweeds. Corduroy is good, but its slightly bulkier look, like that of thicker tweeds, must be taken into account (for instance, pleating is not possible). The same fabrics, apart from the thicker tweeds, are suitable for *trousers. Dresses* too follow the same fabric suggestions, with fluid, softer lines made up in jersey, cool crêpe, and similar-weight mixtures. Shirt dresses make up well in most fabrics; gathered skirts and pleated dresses need thinner, flat-surface fabrics; some fine wool crêpes look ideal, but in fact are rather too springy. Cottons and single jerseys are best for gathering and some of the new blends are fine for pleats. These softer fabrics, through to the sheers, are best for evening and special-occasion wear, looking very good on the full-skirted and sleeved designs.

Jackets look well in flannel, denim, velour, tweed corduroy, or velveteen—these weights are good for all the tailored and soft tailored shapes. *Coats* can be made in all the woolen fabrics—from the worsted to the heaviest-weight fabrics—with body in them; they will wear and hang well.

This general outline does not exclude experimenting with fabrics, but always work out if a fabric will pleat; hold a collar shape; is not too loosely woven; or if there are fine points or shapes to sew. Hold the fabric and see how it falls and if it is heavy or springy to handle. Denim, silk and corduroy all make coats as they are firmly woven, the difference is to see the purpose and the design worked out to its best advantage.

Linings, Underlinings (Backings), Interfacings, and Interlinings

Linings.   These are essential for a good professional finish on most types of garments. A lining helps to keep the shape and prevents excessive wrinkling. It also reduces the need to finish some seams, except on the most frayable types of fabric, because it covers the inside of the garment.

Lining is constructed separately and is joined only at major seams. It should be suitable to the garment fabric in qualities like weight, washability, and color. Today there are polyester lining materials that are extremely versatile and easy to work with. Color for a lining is usually chosen as near as possible to the background color of the fabric. Sometimes for thinner or transparent fabrics a darker or lighter shade can be used to enhance a design and give depth to the fabric. For coats and jackets, a contrast color or printed lining can be used to match a dress or shirt; however, plain or printed, the color should blend.

Underlinings (Backings).   This is a confusing term because it can be taken to mean lining, which it is not. Underlining is cut exactly as the garment and sewn with the garment fabric *as one layer.* This gives support to a design shape, may be used to back a very loosely woven fabric, or simply to add body to a rather limp fabric that needs a more structured look or is difficult to handle.

Thin cotton lawn, organza, or lightweight polyester blends are the most usual types of backings used.

Interfacing.   These can be of the iron-on type, and can be woven or nonwoven. They are applied to support necklines, collars, pockets. They add crispness and body, strengthen buttonhole areas, and give prominence to shaping in design. Interfacing is always used between the facing and outer fabric. The iron-on interfacings are the easiest to use, but are not suitable for very fine or semi-transparent fabrics because they add a certain stiffness. This must be taken into account when support is needed but a soft look is desired. On most of the heavier-weight cottons iron-on interfacings work very well, because they suit the weight of the fabric. For woolen fabrics there are heavier interfacings, and iron-on types are available for the heavier tweeds and coatings. Of the other non-iron kinds, canvas, hair canvas, and wool canvas are all traditional interfacing fabrics for wools and tweeds. These are preferred by some dressmakers because they are more flexible and "move" with the fabric. For silk and similar fabrics, fine organza can be used if collars or cuffs need interfacing, for a softer look lawn is good as well as being suitable to interface other fine cotton fabrics. Some people now use manufactured blends almost exclusively for all their interfacing.

Interlinings. These are heavier types of material primarily used for warmth. The lining pattern is used to cut the interlining. Sometimes it also helps shape a garment as well as adding warmth. In any case, it is constructed separately and sewn to the garment before the lining is attached. Today there are fabrics available that can be used as *both* lining and interlining; these for example, may have a warm, furry inside, with a shiny, satiny side meant to serve as the lining that will be the finished inside of the garment.

16 Notions

Bindings, belts, buttons, zippers, and all functional and decorative additions to a garment are called *notions*. The basic ones listed here are in general use; some others are listed in the glossary. One point common to all notions—do not use nonwashable ones on washable garments.

THREADS

Among notions in the most functional sense are the **threads** that hold the dressmaking together. There are specific threads for various weights and types of fabrics; **polyester-cotton** blend is proving to be extremely good for manufactured materials because of its "give." Color

Fig. 301.   The total look.

matching should be as near perfect as possible, but always choose a
spool of thread that looks slightly darker than the fabric, because when it
works in with a single strand it is lighter.

The size number indicates the suitability to fabric weight. For example, size 8 to 36 is for heavy fabric such as sailcloth; 36 to 40 cotton
thread is for medium-heavy materials like corduray or denim; 60 to 70 is
for lighter-weight fabrics like gingham; and very sheer fabrics like lace
or chiffon call for 70 to 150 thread or silk thread.

Basting cotton is a soft, breakable thread, used because it is less
likely to mark the fabric when it has been pulled out. For velvet, as has
been mentioned before, however, the fine silk thread must be used to
avoid marking the material.

Buttonhole twist is a much thicker, silky finish thread for hand-
made buttonholes and hand topstitching. A similar **silk twist** is available
for machine topstitching. **Glimp thread** is a fine linen cord covered in
silk or cotton and used to strengthen the edge of the buttonhole.

FASTENINGS

The basic **hooks, eyes, and bars** are usually in black or white metal, graded from a very small size for invisible neck fastenings to larger sizes for skirt waists, belts, and coats. The hook is used with the eye for edge-to-edge closings, and with the bar for overlapping closings. **Trouser hooks and bars** are much larger and designed to be set in the waistband. Special hooks and eyes are available for fur and fur fabrics.

Snaps are made of metal, and also range from very small to larger sizes. They are used where buttons cannot be placed and the edge needs to fasten and lie flat. Like hooks, they can be used in conjunction with buttons to relieve excess strain on the buttonhole and button itself.

Velcro, a brand name for a special fastening strip, is made of two tapelike strips with gripping pads which stick to each other when they are pressed together. This is ideal for sports clothes and outer wear, which need unfastening quickly and simply.

Zippers are perhaps the most popular of fastenings, with different weights and lengths for different garment types and fabric weights. The lengths are from 10 cm (4 in) to 61 cm (24 in) for dress openings, the shortest usually for neck openings; 20.5–23 cm (8–9 in) for skirts; side seam openings in dresses need about a 30.5–35.5 cm (12–14 in); and back neck openings to below the waist need from about 46–61 (18–24 in), depending on the style and size. Skirt and dress weight zippers for woolen and firmer fabrics need medium-weight zippers, and lighter-weights exist in a large range, made with metal or nylon teeth, making them suitable for natural or synthetic fabrics.

The question of the right weight of zipper is most important, because too heavy a type will drag on lighter fabric, and lightweight zippers will not take the strain of heavier garments and fabrics.

Separating zippers for jackets and coats are available in a standard range of sizes and basic range of colors. Color choice is again very important; a large choice is available, and the zipper should match as nearly as possible the background or dominant color of the fabric.

BUTTONS

The wrong choice of buttons can ruin the look of a garment. They should be matched carefully to the color and design of the garment, and the choice depends on the importance of the closing.

Some buttons have either two or four center holes, and are sewn through these with a hand-made "shank" between the back of the button and the fabric. The others are of the dome or covered type, with a shank moulded on the back. The first group include most of the tailor-type buttons in bone or plastic substitute. These plain bone buttons have always been much favored in French couture, because they can be dyed professionally to exactly match the fabric and do not detract from the design of the garment.

A button-covering service is available in most good notion departments in stores and specialized shops, and "do-it-yourself" sets are sold on cards. With all covered buttons, washability should be taken into account, and rustless moulds used.

Fancy buttons are sold in different color ranges and a large selection of designs—military-style buttons in metal, diamante buttons for evening—a fascinating choice to be made wisely.

BELTS

As with buttons, many stores have a belt-making and covering service. For those making their own, belt backing and buckle covering sets are available in notions departments. Whenever possible bought belts should be chosen at the same time as the buttons with a fabric sample and design or pattern illustration.

BINDINGS AND BRAIDS

These are used decoratively on the outside, or to finish insides of garments. Bias, straight seam, and satin bindings, wool, silk, and cotton braids can be used imaginatively and functionally.

Bias binding is sold by the yard from rolls, or ready-cut on cards, in regular or iron-on fabrics. The bindings can be in plain cotton, in a softer silkier finish, or in nylon. A soft satin one is sometimes obtainable in black, navy, white and pastel shades for special edgings.

Straight seam binding is about 1 cm (⅜ in) wide with a silky but firm texture, and does not stretch. It is therefore used as a stay tape in seams, and to finish raw edges, make loops, etc.

Wool braids come in many patterns, usually about 1 cm (⅜ in) to 3–4 cm (1¼–½ in) wide. They can be used to good effect on tweed and wools with a surface, for finishing raw edges on unlined jackets and coats as well as lined ones, and of course on reversible garments. These and silkier ones can be made into froggings as well.

Cotton braids and similar weights in synthetic fibers include rick-rack, a zigzag narrow braid widely used for trimming children's clothes, and other types of decoration. A narrow rayon **round braid** (soutache), almost like a cord, can be used to make buttonhole loops, and is sometimes sewn in with the lining seam to strengthen it, particularly on fur coats.

GROSGRAIN RIBBON

Grosgrain is a corded ribbon used as a trimming, or to back openings, as on knitted garments.

A stiff grosgrain is available to finish the waist of skirts, or inside the fabric waistband as a stiffener. A ready-curved type is sold that fits a natural waist curve.

PIPING CORD

Piping cord is made from white cotton and comes in various widths, from very fine up to 1 cm (⅜ in). It is usually covered with a bias strip, to be inserted into piped seams or used decoratively as a finish to neck and hemlines.

TAPE

Narrow plain cotton tape is used as a stay for waistlines, seams, and any stretchable edges. Being narrow, it can be successfully sewn in with the garment without creating too much bulk on the seam.

PADDINGS

Wadding is obtainable in synthetic or natural fiber. Apart from being warm, it can be used very effectively as a quilted edge or to pad seams, apart from the wider all-over quilting. It can also be used to make shoulder pads.

Shoulder pads can of course be bought ready-made. They come in different shapes and sizes for coats, dresses, or jackets. An additional shaping can be given to fiber pads if they are pressed gently over a sleeve board or pad under a dampish cloth.

All these trimmings are used to enhance the design and to give the construction of the garment a professional look. Looking around notions departments and keeping an eye on current fashion ideas will give you the opportunity to experiment with them and use your own ideas.

Glossary

DRESSMAKING AND FASHION TERMS

Accordion pleats. Graduated pleats, from narrow to wider.

Allowance. Extra fabric padded (1) to a seamline, (2) to accommodate pleats, gathers, tucks, or (3) for movement and comfort in wear of garment.

Appliqué. Pieces of fabric sewn on to another with decorative stitches.

Armhole. The opening in a garment for the arm. Armholes can be faced or sleeves set into them. (Also called a *Scye.*).

Asymmetrical. A design of two unequal sides of a garment.

Backstitch. Continuous handstitch, as in machine-stitch.

Backstitching. Reversing the sewing direction at the beginning and end of seams to secure the stitches and thread ends.

Balance. (1) The correct hang of a garment from the shoulder, dividing the front from the back section or the correct hang of a sleeve set into an armhole. (2) The correct joining of two or more parts of a garment making them equal on two sides. (See *Notches.*)

Basting. Joining parts of a garment with temporary hand stitches in preparation for fittings and before machine stitching.

Belt loop. Made in fabric or thread to hold belt in position.

Bias. Diagonal to straight grain of lengthwise and crosswise threads of fabrics. Fabrics cut on the bias achieve greater elasticity and "give." Material cut at 45° to selvage gives the true bias.

Bias Binding. Strips of fabric or tape cut on the bias grain for seam binding and encasing of raw edges, and for decoration.

Bishop sleeve. A full-length sleeve, wide at the bottom and gathered in to a cuff or band.

Block pattern. Master pattern without design lines.

Bodice. The upper part of a dress, above the waist.

Body Measurements. The actual measurements of the body without allowances for movement and comfort in wear of garment.

Bolero. A short jacket originating in Spain.

Boutique. French for small shop, now associated with selling fashion garments and accessories of a particular type.

Box pleat. A pleat with two sides of folded edges facing outward.

Braid. A woven trimming for decoration, finished on both edges, made in a variety of widths and weights.

Breakline. A line on which a lapel folds back against the front part of a garment.

Buttonhole loop. Narrow strips of fabric stitched and turned through.

Button Line. A standard measurement for all buttons.

Button placket or allowance. Material added to the edge of a garment beyond the position of buttons and buttonholes on each side of an opening.

Cap sleeve. A very short sleeve, usually cut as an extension to the shoulder seams and sometimes in one with the bodice.

Circular skirt. A skirt cut with the waist and hem circumference based on a true circle.

Clip. To cut into corners or curved seam allowances, enabling seams to lie flat when pressed open.

Collar band. That part sewn to the base of the neck up to the crease line.

Control of fullness. Removal of excess material at a given point at one end, creating fullness at the other for shape, by means of darts, seams, tucks, folds.

Cording. A cord inserted into a piece of fabric for decoration.

Cording Foot. A special attachment used on the machine allowing the corded fabric to be stitched close to the seam into which it is inserted.

Cross-grain. See *Bias*.

Crotch. That part of pants or slacks where the legs are joined together.

Dart. A stitched fold, tapering to a point at one or both ends, used to give shape to garments to fit the contours of the body. (Called an open dart if left unstitched at one end.)

Décolleté. A very low-cut neckline.

Directional. Cutting, stitching, and pressing *with* the grain of the fabric.

Double-breasted. A front fastening with two rows of buttons set equally apart from the center front line.

Drape. Soft folds, forming pleats or gathers on garments.

Dress form. A form made in varying materials, corresponding to the shape of the human torso from neck to thighs.

Ease. (1) Allowances on certain parts of patterns, over and above body measurements, ensuring tolerance for movement and comfort in wear of garments; (2) extra length added to one side of a seam joining two parts of a garment, to create shape, in place of darts; (3) allowing an extra amount of fabric for decorative fullness by gathering.

Edge-stitching. Topstitching close to edges.

Eyelet. A small hole made in garment or accessory and finished by hand stitches, or a metal ring (as in a belt to hold the prong of a buckle).

Facing. Material sewn to raw edges, in self or other fabric.

Fastenings. Buttons, hooks, eyes, and bars, snaps, Velcro, etc. used to keep garments closed.

Fitting. Adjusting prepared garments to fit individual figures.

Fitting lines. Final seamlines.

Flare. Additional width of fabric at lower ends of a garment for extra fullness.

Fly.   The buttoned or zippered front opening of trousers.

Fly fastening.   A concealed opening, the type of fastening not being visible on the right side of a garment.

French chalk.   Powdered chalk.

Fraying.   Small, loose threads that unravel on cut edges of fabrics.

French dart.   A bust dart placed diagonally at lower end of bodice side seam.

Frog fastening.   Looped braid or cord used for decorative fastening of garments.

Fusing.   The melting of iron-on interfacings and canvases to fabrics by application of heat and pressure.

Gatherings.   The shortening of a fabric length by drawing it up on a line of stitching.

Gimp.   A thick thread used to strengthen and raise buttonhole stitching. It can also be used for embroidery.

Godet.   A triangular-shaped piece of fabric sewn into lower parts of garment for extra width.

Gore.   A panel of fabric that is narrower at the top than at the bottom. Mostly used for skirt designs.

Grain (straight).   A term denoting the lengthwise (warp) and crosswise (weft) threads of fabric crossing each other at right angels. Fabrics are *off-grain* if warp and weft threads do not cross each other at right angles, or are *off-grain* if not placed and cut on the straight grain.

Grosgrain.   A webbing or heavy ribbon used to finish waistlines on skirts and trousers.

Gusset.   A triangular-shaped piece of fabric inserted to allow extra movement, usually at underarm seams on sleeves cut in one piece with the bodice, or at crotch seams.

Hanger appeal.   A trade term to describe the look of a garment when seen on a clothes hanger.

Haute Couture.   French for "high sewing." A term now mainly used to describe the work of well-known French designers, though couture-made garments embrace all those made for private clients. Couture garments may have many fittings and are finished with a considerable amount of handwork.

Hem.   The edge of that which had been folded under.

Hemline.   The line on which an edge of fabric is folded.

Hemming.   The hem sewn back to the main part of the garment.

Interfacing.   Material used for shaping, reinforcing, and stiffening parts of a garment to give strength and body, placed between the outer fabric and facing and/or linings.

Interlining. Material used primarily for warmth; sometimes also for shaping.

Inset. A piece of fabric, braid, or other trimming set into a seam, mainly for additional decoration.

Inverted pleat. Two sides of pleats with folded edges facing inward. The reverse side of a box pleat.

Jet pocket. A pocket opening made with folded piping strips, in self- or contrast fabric.

Joining. Stitching together of fabric pieces on sewing lines.

Kick pleat. A short pleat at the lower end of skirts, mainly for extra stride room. Usually cut on as an extension to center and side seams and forming a knife pleat.

Knife pleat. Folded edge of one side of a pleat facing either to the left or right side.

Lap. To place and then secure one piece of fabric *over* another (*over-lap*) or *under* another (*underlap*).

Lapel. The upper part of a front edge of a jacket or coat folded back from the neck.

Layering. Trimming of seam allowances to narrowing widths to reduce bulk.

Layout. Pattern pieces placed on the fabric for cutting according to the width and type of fabric.

Lining. Material, constructed separately, which fully or partially covers the inside of a garment.

Link buttons. Two buttons held together by strands of treads forming a long shank, used as cufflinks or front fastenings on coats and jackets.

Marking. To transfer symbols on patterns—sewing lines, darts, notches, pocket positions, etc.—to the fabric.

Match. (1) To join and bring together construction markings; (2) checks, plaids, and stripes; (3) colors of fabric and trimmings.

Miter. (1) Forming of diagonal seam at a corner; (2) the addition in length to one side of a dart to equal the length of the other, if placed on a diagonal seam.

Modeling. (1) Designing three-dimensionally by pinning and marking muslin on a dressmaker form; or (2) displaying garments on the body.

Needleboard. A board with a surface of fine steel wires for pressing velvet and other pile fabrics preventing the nap or pile from being flattened. (Also called *Velvet board*).

Notches.   Placed as guide marks on seams of patterns and cut-out fabric to ensure correct balance.

Notions.   All things such as zippers, threads, bindings, etc. necessary to finish garments.

Off-grain.   See *Grain.*

Overcasting.   Handstitching of raw edges preventing fraying of the material.

Overlock.   A special machine-stitch used in the trade for overcasting raw edges.

Pad Out.   To build up parts of a garment with soft material.

Padding stitch.   Diagonal stitch used in tailoring, holding canvas to the fabric, especially on collars and lapels for lasting shape.

Peplum.   A loose piece of fabric, from waist seam to hips, mostly on jackets. A peplum has a fluted effect; a *basque* has a flat shape.

Picot.   A special edge finish on hems, made by cutting through machine stitches.

Pinking.   Cutting seam edges with serrated (or "pinking") shears to prevent fraying.

Pin-tuck.   A very narrow edge-stitched tuck.

Piping.   A folded piece of fabric inserted into a seam for buttonholes, pockets, and other decorations.

Pivot.   (1) Turning at square corners when machining; (2) swiveling of darts from bust point.

Placket.   A piece of fabric sewn on to openings of garments for a neat finish.

Plaids.   Patterns of checks and lines woven into, or printed onto, cloth.

Pleat.   A fold on fabric, stitched down, left loose, or pressed into a crease. All pleats are based on three main types: the box, inverted, and knife pleat.

Pleating.   The forming of patterns of pleats.

Pressing.   The removing of creases or creating of creases on fabrics by heat and pressure, as in dry pressing, or by the use of moisture, as in damp and steam pressing.

Presser foot.   An attachment to the sewing machine which puts pressure on the fabric and ensures an even flow of stitching.

Princess line.   A garment shape, cut to fit close to the body and flared toward the hem, using only vertical seam lines.

Pucker.   Too tightly stitched and held seams, giving a "wavy" effect.

Purl.   A twist in the thread to form a knotlike edge.

Quilt.   Several thicknesses of fabric sewn together, or soft material inserted between two outer layers of fabric and stitched through all, forming a pattern with a raised effect.

Ready-to-wear.   A term embracing all types of garments made without fittings for sale in shops and stores.

Reinforcing.   Strengthening of corners or slashed openings with extra stitching, tape, or interfacings.

Ribbon.   A strip of fabric in varying widths, finished on both edges.

Rick-rack.   Type of braid with zigzag edges and serrated effect used for decorative purposes.

Ruffle.   A piece of fabric with one edge gathered, the other left flat, giving a fluted effect.

Saddle stitch.   Decorative stitching often made with special threads, large on the right side, small on the wrong side of the fabric.

Scallop.   Edgings forming decorative semi-circles.

Seam (line).   A sewing line holding parts of a garment together. (For types of seams see Chapter Sixteen.)

Seam allowance.   A given amount of material on garments, between (stitching) sewing lines and cutting edges, added to sewing line to allow for seaming.

Seaming.   Joining two or more parts to form one.

Self-fabric.   This refers to using the same fabric as the garment.

Self-facing.   Hems or facings cut in one with the main sections of a garment, rather than separately.

Selvage.   Finished lengthwise edges of fabrics.

Shank.   Space between button and fabric, taken up by strands of thread or lower part of button.

Shape.   (1) Created by the use of darts, seams, and fullness to accommodate structure of body and limbs; (2) the silhouette and line of a design.

Shirring.   Gathering material with elastic thread.

Slash.   To cut into fabric.

Sleeve cap.   The upper part of the sleeve.

Slot.   Two rows of parrallel stitching, set apart for insertion of ribbon or elastic.

Smocking.   Gathering of fabric with decorative stitches.

String.   A piece of string, thread or similar mark on selvages, used to denote faulty or damaged section of fabric. Shops and stores allow extra length in compensation.

Stitches.   For most types of stitches see Chapter Sixteen.

Swatch.   A composite collection of small pieces of fabrics.

Symmetrical.   A design of two equal halves.

Tailored.   Garments made in part by shaping and moulding with an iron and the use of interfacings to maintain shape.

Tailor tack.   Marking sewing lines, darts, notches with double threads through both halves of parts of cut garment, leaving loop between each stitch, pulled apart and cut.

Tension.   The relative tightness or looseness between top and bottom thread in machine-stitching.

Toile.   A copy of a garment, made in unbleached calico or muslin. Finished toiles are often bought by manufacturers for copying of designs.

Top-pressing.   Final pressing of finished garment.

Topstitching.   Machine-stitching on right side of garments for decoration and/or extra strength.

Tracing.   Marks transferred from one part of pattern to another, from pattern to fabric or one part of fabric to another, using a tracing wheel (see Chapter Four).

Trimming.   (1) Cutting back widths of seams or excess fabrics; (2) decorating garments with buttons, belts, braid, and other materials.

Tuck.   A straight and even fold stitched either outside for decoration or inside for body shape.

Turning.   Same as *Seam allowance.*

Turn-up.   Material folded and turned up at bottom of trousers.

Underlining (backing).   Material treated as one piece with fabric piece; generally used to strengthen very lightweight fabrics.

Underpressing.   Pre-pressing of sections and opening of seams with an iron—progressively—when making garments, before final top pressing.

Understitching.   Topstitching of facings through seams holding facing to main parts of garment. Keeps facings inside garments and prevents them from rolling back and showing. Also called machine backstitching of facings.

Unit construction.   A method of making up two sections of a garment, first machine-stitched separately, or two layers of fabric sewn together on all sides except for an opening, and turned through from wrong to right side.

Velvet board. See *Needleboard.*

Vent. A lapped hem opening on lower parts of a garment.

Welt. A strip of fabric sewn to a pocket opening, stitched down on three sides and left open at the top.

Wing seam. A curved design line beginning at the front or back armhole and extended to the waist.

Working drawing. An accurate drawing of a design, clearly showing all seamlines and details.

Yoke. A shoulder piece on front and/or back of garments, or a waist piece at the top of skirts and trousers.

FABRIC DESCRIPTIONS

This comprehensive list will help in identifying fabrics, and in the most suitable selection for any chosen design or purpose. The Glossary of textile, dressmaking, and fashion terms (see pages 325–33) will assist in clarifying the finer points of cloth constructions and finishes and in the construction of fabrics.

Alpaca. The fiber from the fleece of the alpaca or llama of South America. A soft, very fine quality fabric with a smooth, lustrous surface. Mixtures with wool and cotton are used for lightweight garments.

Angora wool. Long, soft wool spun from the hair of the Angora goat or rabbit. Very good for knitting yarns. Angora wool is used to make mohair fabric.

Art silk. An old name for rayon (artificial silk).

Astrakhan. Wool or lamb's fur of a curly nature coming from Astrakhan, in the USSR. Also a pile fabric made to imitate Astrakhan or Persian lamb cloth. The foundation cloth is either knitted or woven and contains mohair, sometimes cotton or rayon.

Banlon. Registered trade name of a bulked nylon yarn-knitted fabric.

Barathea. A fabric made from woolen and worsted or silk and manufactured fibers, with a twilled rib weave. Usually in black.

Batiste.   A smooth, soft, lightweight plain-weave cotton fabric, also sometimes made in linen or rayon. Suitable for shirts and soft dresses. Available in white, colors, and prints.

Bedford cord.   A strong, smooth, generally woolen fabric with lengthwise cords. Best for suit and coat weights.

Bengaline.   A plain-weave, ribbed fabric resembling poplin. Wool, cotton, silk, or rayon, in dress and coat weights.

Bird's-eye.   A weave pattern (see Textile Glossary, page 347).

Blazer cloth.   A cloth similar to flannel and melton.

Botany.   A fine wool from the merino sheep. Also cloth woven from Botany wool.

Bouclé.   A woven or knitted, usually woolen fabric with a roughly curled loop effect on the surface, produced by means of fancy yarns.

Broadcloth.   A fine, close, plain-weave woollen cloth. Smooth and lustrous, and highly napped one way, this produces different light reflections so that all pattern pieces must be cut in one direction only.

Brocade.   A heavy, rich fabric and elaborate, slightly raised, jacquard-weave patterns. Often made in silk or rayon, satin-backed, sometimes incorporating gold and silver threads.

Broderie Anglaise.   Open embroidery work is the characteristic of this cotton fabric.

Calico.   A plain-weave cloth without finished surface available in light, medium and heavy weights. Coarse in handle, creases easily. Mainly used for making toiles. (See Glossary, page 332).

Cambric.   A fine, muslin type fabric of firm, plain weave and glazed surface finish.

Camel hair.   A very fine wool fabric woven with camel's hair, and wool fibers. Slightly napped, soft, and combines qualities of warmth with light weight.

Canvas.   An unbleached, strong, firm plain-woven cloth. It is made in cotton and flax, also in wool, hair, and rayon in a variety of weights and for many uses, particularly for interfacings in tailored garments.

Cashmere.   Fabric woven from a soft, very fine wool of goats in the Himalayan region. Expensive, but used for many types of outer-wear garments.

Cavalry twill.   A strong, double twill-weave fabric with pronounced diagonal cords, in wool, rayon, and cotton.

Chambray.   A plain fabric, woven with colored warp, and white weft threads. Usually in cotton, but can be made with fiber blends. Washes and handles well.

Cheese cloth.   A coarse muslin fabric.

Cheviot.   A rough, heavyweight, twill-weave woolen fabric, not unlike tweed.

Chiffon.   A plain-woven sheer fabric, soft, lightweight, and delicate, with a "floating" quality. Not easy to handle.

Chintz.   Glazed surface sheen fabric normally used as a furnishing fabric, but occasionally also for clothes. Closely woven, good-quality cotton, brightly patterned. Finished for stiffness, though this is not permanent.

Ciré.   This fabric has a bright, shiny, wet-look surface appearance, produced on satin by application of wax, heat, and pressure.

Cloqué.   Raised pattern effect on the surface of fabric resembling embossing.

Corduroy.   *"Cor du Roi"* gave the name to this fabric. Worn by the servants of French kings. A ribbed cotton velvet, very strong and durable with a short, one-way pile. Ribs vary from thin, pin needle cord to thick-wale cord and elephant cord.

Crêpe.   The name denotes the structure of this type of fabric. It is woven with highly twisted yarns to form a crinkled surface effect. Wool, cotton, and manufactured fibers are used for crêpe fabrics, including: *Alpaca crêpe*—a soft full rayon type with the appearance of a woollen fabric; *Bark crêpe*—with the appearance of tree bark, woollen or rayon; *Canton crêpe*—rough-looking, with much crosswise stretch; *Chiffon crêpe*—soft, smooth, plain weave; *Crêpe de Chine*—a sheer washable silk crêpe; *Crêpe Georgette*—lightweight, semi-sheer, made in wool, silk or manufactured fibers. (see also *Marocain*.)

Crepon.   Woven or knitted with puckered, blistered surface effect, achieved by chemical or heat setting processes. Light to medium in weight.

Delaine.   Lightweight, plain-weave wool fabric, often printed.

Denim.   A very strong and hard-wearing twill fabric, woven with colored warp and white weft yarns with a slightly stiff, but firm handle. Obtainable in medium to heavy weights. Makes up and washes well. Suitable for many types of garments.

Dimity.   A crisp, sheer, corded cotton fabric.

Doeskin.   A one-way napped fabric, reflecting light in different directions. Close twill or satin weave, made in wool, cotton, and rayon with a very fine, suedelike surface.

Donegal (tweed).   Originally hand-spun in County Donegal, now used as the term for this type of tweed of herringbone or twill weave construction, incorporating colored spots or "slubs."

Dotted Swiss. Sheer cotton fabric with woven dots.

Drill. A double-weave strong cotton fabric of medium weight.

Duchess satin. See *Satin*.

Duck. Closely woven, heavy canvaslike cotton fabric with a slight rib effect. Also made in linen.

Dupion (douppion). A slub fabric made from silk, or simulated in manufactured fibers. The use of two threads woven as one produces the irregular slub effect.

Duvetyn (duveteen). Soft, velvetlike napped fabric, similar to suede, from silk or wool fibers, with good draping qualities. (See *Pile fabrics*.)

Etamine. Woolen fabric that is soft, lightweight, in plain, open weave.

Face-cloth. A woolen or worsted fabric, finished with a soft, smooth, regular nap.

Faconne. Silk or rayon fabric with a small jacquard design.

Faille. Flat, ribbed fabric, with flatter ribs than found in *grosgrain*. Made in silk or rayon.

Felt. A nonwoven fabric, mainly made from wool fibers, by pressure, moisture, and heat.

Flannel. An all-wool or part-wool fabric of plain or twill weave, with a soft handle. It has a slightly raised surface, but not one-way. A firm cloth that makes up well.

Flannelette. Made from cotton, with raised surface as flannel. It is soft, warm, and cozy and launders well. Also made in manufactured fibers.

Fleece. Long-napped fabric from the fleece of sheep. Often used as the inside of sheepskin coats. Rather bulky and not easy to handle.

Foulard. Soft, lightweight silk fabric with a twill weave. It is also made from wool, cotton, or rayon fibers. Often used for ties and scarves.

Fur fabrics. Pile fabrics, woven or knitted from manufactured fibers to imitate natural fur.

Gabardine. Describes the structure of the twill weave, with a diagonal rib. The fabric is firm, made mainly in wool, worsted, and cotton. The rib effect is less pronounced in cotton gabardine. Extensively used for suits, coats, trousers, casual and sportswear.

Gauze. A sheer, lightweight fabric, with an open lace like effect produced by the weave. Made in cotton, linen and rayon.

Georgette. See *Crêpe*.

Gingham.   Cotton, with woven colored check or plaid designs. Sometimes blended with silk or rayon. Crisp, but soft to handle. Washes extremely well.

Gossamer.   A gauze weave, very lightweight silk or cotton fabric.

Grosgrain.   Firm, stiff, closely woven fabric with a pronounced horizontal rib, heavier than in poplin or faille. Silk or manufactured.

Guipure.   See *Lace.*

Harris tweed.   This fabric is spun, dyed, and finished in the Outer Hebrides. Made from pure Scottish wool.

Homespun.   A coarse, plain-weave wool or cotton fabric with a handwoven look. The thick yarns used produce a heavyweight fabric suitable for coats and suits.

Hopsack.   A coarse, plain-weave cloth of wool or cotton, not very closely woven. Some hopsack may be of a basket weave. Primarily suitable for coats and suits.

Houndstooth.   Woven tweed-type fabric with a toothlike design.

Interlock.   A lightweight, circular-knitted cotton cloth.

Irish tweed.   A fancy tweed fabric, woven with homespun yarns.

Jersey.   A knitted fabric of wool, cotton, rayon, silk, or synthetic blends, so weights range from sheer for lingerie to heavy for coats. Stretchability of lighter weights (single-knit) make jersey most suitable for draping, but it is firm enough for tailored garments in heavier weights (doubleknit).

Knits.   Any knitted fabric made by the interlocking of loops of one or more yarns (see Glossary, page 347).

Lace.   Open-work fabric, made with bobbins, needles, and hooks, either by hand or machine. Made from nearly every fiber, the threads are formed into designs, such as: *Alençon Chantilly*—light, delicate, usually with floral pattern, backed to a fine net; *Cluny Venice*—coarser, stronger, with geometric designs, mainly in cotton without backing; *Guipure*—rich, stiff, heavy-textured lace.

Lamé.   A brocade woven with natural and manufactured fibers and containing metallic yarns for decorative purposes, hence suitable for evening wear.

Lawn.   Lightweight, sheer, thin and fine cotton or linen of plain weave. Crisper than voile, less crisp than organdy. Ideal for many lightweight garments, or as backing for extra body. In white, colors or prints.

Linen.   Woven from the strong flax fiber, in three main weights: handkerchief, which is sheer; medium dress weights; and heavier suiting weights.

Madras.   Cotton with plain weave, in multicolored checks and stripes; not colorfast and bleeds in washing and sunlight. Used for shirts, blouses, and dresses.

Marocain.   Heavy dress weight in silk or manufactured fibers: *moss crêpe*—mosslike finish; *satin crêpe* or *satin bark crêpe*—heavyweight type; *wool crêpe*—soft, from wool fibers only. (see also *Crêpe.*)

Marquisette.   An open-weave mesh fabric, very lightweight. It is made in cotton, silk, or nylon, often suitable for evening wear.

Matelassé.   This, made in cotton, wool, silk or rayon, is woven on dobby or jacquard looms to produce patterns with a quilted effect.

Melton.   Heavily felted, nonlustrous woolen fabric with slight one-way nap. The finishing processes ensure that this is a solid cloth, so garments wear well.

Merino.   Very fine wool from the merino sheep used for worsted cloth.

Milanese.   A warp-knitted fabric, the product of the "Milanese" machine.

Mohair.   Luxurious fabric from the fine, soft, silky hair of the Angora goat. Made in plain and twill weaves, its characteristics are strength, lightness, and lustre.

Moiré.   Any fabric, often silk taffeta, finished with a watered/wavy surface effect.

Moss crêpe.   See *Crêpe.*

Moleskin.   A strong twill fabric, resembling the skin of the mole in touch and appearance.

Mousseline de soie.   Silk or rayon muslin with firm and crisp finish. Most suitable for evening wear.

Mull.   Soft, thin cotton muslin, semi-sheer. Coarse and loose weave, finished without stiffening agents.

Muslin.   Usually cotton with twill or gauze weave, muslin is a coarser version of mull. Sometimes dressed with starch, which is not permanent.

Needle cord.   See *Corduroy.*

Net.   An open-weave, meshlike fabric. Can be made in cotton, rayon, silk, or nylon in weights from light to heavy.

Nonwoven fabrics.   Any fabric in which fibers have been bonded or fused together rather than spun, woven, or knitted.

Nun's veiling.   A soft, lightweight plain-weave cloth, not unlike flannelette in feel.

Organdy.   Thin, stiff, transparent fabric in plain-weave cotton.

Organza. As *organdy*, in silk or rayon. Both suitable for evening wear.

Ottoman. Heavy, crosswise corded fabric with larger and more rounded ribs than *grosgrain*. Can be made of wool, cotton, or rayon, with silky appearance.

Paisley. Any wool, cotton, or rayon fabric that is printed with the traditional scroll design originating from Paisley in Scotland.

Panne velvet. See *Velvet*.

Peau de soie. The "skin of silk." A good-quality heavy, dull satin dress material made from silk, but also from manufactured fibers or blends.

Pile fabrics. Any material woven with looped yarns, raised on the surface and cut or uncut, to stand up to form a rich texture. Fur fabrics, velvet, velour, corduroy, etc., are all pile fabrics.

Piqué. Crisp, mainly cotton fabric with raised lengthwise or diagonal ribs, as in *Wale piqué*, *Waffle piqué*, or honeycomb (diamond shape) weave or birds-eye effects.

Plissé. Plain or printed cotton, with a blistered surface effect achieved by a special finish. Made in a variety of weights.

Poplin. Smooth, firm, ribbed, plain-weave cloth originally made in silk, but can also be in wool or rayon, though it is mostly a medium- to heavyweight cotton fabric.

Poult. A stiff, ribbed silk or rayon material heavier than taffeta.

Prints. Can be any fabric with printed patterns applied by various methods after the cloth is made.

Rattinet (ratieen or **ratiné).** A pile wool fabric, with a surface effect of small round knobs. Mostly suit and coat weights.

Raw silk. See *silk*.

Repp (rep). A ribbed fabric produced by weaving with a thick weft into a thin warp.

Sailcloth. Strong and slightly stiff, mostly heavyweight fabric, made of cotton, linen, or nylon. Used largely for play clothes and casual wear.

Sateen. A cotton cloth woven with the normal satin weave used for silk and rayon satin. Glazed for high lustre.

Satin. Satin weaves make a large range of lustrous fabrics in silk or manufactured fibers, extensively used for dresses, linings, and lingerie. These include: *crêpe satin*—soft, drapy; *duchess satin*—stiff and solid; *lining satin*—light in weight; *panne satin*—very high lustre; *slipper satin*—fairly stiff; and *washable satin*.

Seersucker. Lightweight, plain-weave cotton fabric with crinkled surface effect. Can be laundered without ironing. It has no right or wrong side.

Serge. Twill, or plain-weave cloth of wool, worsted but also other fibers, with a roughish texture. Suit weights, hard wearing.

Shantung. Plain-weave, rough silk caused by use of uneven yarns, giving this fabric a slubbed effect. Made in cotton rayon and blends to simulate this slub.

Sharkskin. Wool, worsted, silk, rayon, and synthetic fibers are used for this cloth, which is medium to heavy in weight and most suitable for tailored garments and sportswear.

Shot silk. Silk characterized by changing color effects.

Silk. A selection of silk fabrics includes: *Jap silk*—very lightweight, soft plain silk, mostly used for linings; *Pongee*—a rough, strong, natural silk fabric; *raw silk*—the continuous filament from the silkworm before processing to remove the gum. The uneven weave produces a rough surface effect.

Spun silk. Made from silk waste.

Stretch fabrics. All fabrics constructed to achieve elasticity and stretch when pulled, returning to the original shape when released. Stretch qualities include comfort, shape retention, and crease-resistance. Stretchability varies from: *warp*, or parallel to selvage, good for trousers; *weft*, or across the width of fabric, good for skirts and tops; *two-way* stretch, in both directions, used mostly for swimwear and foundation garments.

Suedette. Velveteen, napped one way and finished to simulate suede (leather).

Surah. Soft twill-weave, lightweight silk, but also made in rayon or synthetic fibers.

Taffeta. A plain, closely woven, smooth and crisp fabric. Originally in silk, now mainly made with rayon or synthetic fibers: *faille taffeta* has a crosswise rib; *moiré taffeta* has a wafered, wavy surface effect; and *paper taffeta* is lightweight and stiff.

Tarlatan. Cotton cheesecloth, with plain weave and starched finish.

Tartan. Colorful checks denoting Scottish clans.

Terrycloth towelling. Cotton fabric with uncut or looped pile (not one-way) mostly on both sides. Very absorbent and therefore popular for beachwear.

Thai silk. Woven in Thailand, with traditional patterns.

Tricot. A plain warp-knitted fabric made with a single thread. Mostly made in cotton, rayon, or nylon. It is light in weight and very suitable for underwear and T-shirts.

Tulle. A stiff, fine, netlike sheer fabric in silk, nylon, or rayon. Popular for bridal wear.

Tussore (Tussah). Wild silk, rough and coarse, quite loosely woven.

Tweed. Genuine tweed is made with pure virgin wool. It has a rough surface, is usually woven with two or more colors, often forming patterns of checks and plaids. There are now not only woolen tweeds; cotton, silk, and synthetic tweeds are also available. The term "tweed" sometimes now covers almost any fabric that has a roughened look.

Twill. A basic weave fabric with a diagonal rib in natural, manufactured fibers and blended yarns.

Velour. Has a velvety texture, and is a soft, thick fabric closely napped one way. Wool velour is similar to broadcloth, most suitable for suits and coats. Nylon is also used to make this cloth. (*See also* Pile fabrics.)

Velvet. A one-way pile fabric in silk, rayon, cotton, or nylon, sometimes in natural fibers backed to synthetic ones. Velvet is double-woven face to face, and cut apart on the loom by a knife placed in position resembling a shuttle. Types of velvet include: *chiffon velvet*—lightweight with silk or rayon backing; *Lyons velvet*—a stiff velvet; *mirror velvet*—a calendered, highly polished velvet; *panne velvet*—has a flattened pile, is very lustrous in appearance. (*See also* Pile fabrics.)

Velveteen. A cotton one-way weft pile velvet; the fibers are cut after weaving and form the dull surface. (*See also* Pile fabrics.)

Vicuña. A soft woolen cloth from the hair of the South American goat, of high quality, made in dress and heavy weights.

Virgin wool. Wool that has never previously been processed.

Viyella. Registered trade name: part wool, part cotton fabric, with slight nap. The cotton content makes it more washable.

Voile. A soft, light semi-transparent fabric, usually a plain weave, or variations of a plain weave. Similar to organdy and lawn, though less stiff, with good draping quality.

Vynel "fabric." A type of plastic and not strictly a fabric. Vynel films are used either on their own or with bonded woven or knitted backing. They can be embossed to simulate natural leather.

Waffle cloth. See *Piqué*.

Whipcord. A closely woven worsted, with a diagonal rib, similar to gabardine, but the ribs are more pronounced. A strong fabric with a lot of body.

Wool crêpes. See *Crêpe*.

Worsted. Made from best-quality wool fibers, the highly twisted yarns make a strong, firm and smooth cloth.

TEXTILE PROCESSES

Before fabrics became available to the consumer, both natural and manufactured made fibers undergo a great many processes to make up the finished cloth. It would be inappropriate to give detailed descriptions of these processes in this book. Some basic facts, however, will help in understanding the variety and differences found, and offer our readers some knowledge about fabrics which we all too often take for granted.

Raw, greasy wool fibers from the fleece of sheep, and impure cotton and flax from harvested plants, are taken through processes which include sorting, selection, and blending, cleaning or "scouring" (the removal of grease), drying and "carding," to name but a few.

Carding is a combing process, which, for example, distinguishes woolen from a worsted cloth. The even and smooth yarn that makes worsted cloth firm and strong is the result of combing long wool fibers of high quality—from the merino sheep—to make them all parallel to each other. This produces the characteristic lustre of worsted. In woolen cloth, on the other hand, the relatively short fibers are not so arranged and the yarn spun from these fibers is of a "fluffy" nature. The length of fibers—from as short as just over 1 cm (½ in) in the case of natural fibers, to as long as hundreds of meters/yards in silk and manufactured fibers —is a most important and determining factor in the structure of yarns.

Manufactured fibers are made by forcing a liquid chemical substance through fine holes in a nozzle called a spinneret and solidifying the filaments formed in this way by various means. The name "spinneret" is taken from that of the gland in the head of the silkworm through which the liquid silk is extruded; this liquid is what solidifies and forms the cocoon. The basic method of making synthetic fibers is thus borrowed directly from nature.

There are two main types of yarns:

1. Continuous-filament—more or less ready for weaving or knitting.
2. Staple-fiber (spun yarns)—thousands of filaments from a number of spinnerets brought together to form a thick ropelike structure. This is then cut into exact lengths, and the mass of cut fibers is baled and sent to mills for final spinning. These spun yarns have advantages compared with continuous-filament yarns: they are suitable for a

greater variety of fabrics, and they enable fibers of different sorts to be blended together. Furthermore, the necessary production processes are fewer and staple fibers can therefore be made at much higher speeds, and so more economically than continuous filament of the same fiber.

From Fibers to Fabric

Basically, processes for most prepared fibers fall into three main groups.

1. The twisting of fibers, which are then spun into yarns.
2. The intertwining of yarns with varying constructions, by weaving or knitting, to form fabrics.
3. The treatment given to fabrics by bleaching, dyeing and printing, and finishing processes to affect appearance, handle, and performance (see Textile Glossary).

A comprehensive list of fabrics from natural fibers and their descriptions has already been given. The following are the main groups of manufactured fibers, separated by chemical and spinning processes.

MANUFACTURED FIBERS

1. Viscose Fibers for Rayons

Viscose is a regenerated cellulose, usually made from chemical wood pulp from spruce pine trees. It is the original manufactured fiber, developed in continuous-filament form since around 1900, leading to the popularity of silk stockings and later to be replaced by nylon as well as being widely used in dress fabrics.

Rayon staple fibers were first developed in the 1930s and are now used for all kinds of dress fabrics, linings, pile fabrics and braids and ribbons. The raw material in staple form is spun on the cotton and worsted system. It is frequently blended with nylon, polyester, and natural fibers, and remains one of the most important synthetic fibers.

2a. Acetate

This is often described as the "nearest to silk." Made from chemical wood pulp, as the basic raw material, acetate has quick-drying qualities and was extensively used for women's underwear until the advent of nylon. It is now often used for knitted and woven dress fabrics and linings. Acetate fibers are often blended with other fibers, including wool, especially for knitting yarns, and are claimed to improve washability.

2b. Triacetate

This is a chemical product very much like acetate, with quick-drying qualities. Because it is thermoplastic (having fibers that soften on heating), fabrics can be "heat-set," so are good for permanent pleating, with washing stability and wrinkle-free drying. This is used for woven and knitted dress fabrics and linings, particularly for washable garments.

3. Polyamides

Polyamides comprise the nylon group, and were first produced by Dupont and the American Chemical Company.

Nylon, originally made from coal tar, is now made almost entirely from petroleum chemicals. Nylon is immensely strong and hard-wearing, and as a thermoplastic fiber can also be heat-set for size and shape retention in wear and wash. Early nylon fabrics did not absorb moisture very well, and had a lot of static elasticity, which, though harmless, was unpleasant. These problems have been remedied to a large degree. Knitted fabrics that are more porous, such as now used for shirts, improve the feel and handle of nylon. With the advantages in laundering, quick drying—without wrinkles—it is a much-used fabric for lingerie, overalls, stockings and tights, in both woven and knitted forms; it is also used for household and industrial purposes.

4. Polyester

Noted for its easy-care qualities, polyester is often blended with wool and worsted, for shape-retention qualities, and with cotton for things like rainwear and shirts. It is used extensively for knitted jersey fabrics, for men's trousers, jackets, and women's wear, as well as for woven dress goods. Polyester staple fibers are blended with wool for suitings, giving high performance in wear—including shape retention. There is also a wide range of uses for polyester fibers for domestic and industrial purposes.

5a. Acrylics

These are textured yarns, made from staple fibers only. Acrylics are made from petroleum chemical products, but also sometimes from natural gas. They produce a soft feel and warmth, nearer to that of wool, than any other synthetic fibers. The process of "bulking," the making of air gaps to absorb moisture, makes this the chief characteristic.

Acrylic fibers, like other synthetics such as nylon and polyester, are thermoplastic, so that they can be pleated and have good shape retention. The main outlets are for knitted jumpers, cardigans, and knitting yarns, as well as woven dress goods.

5b. Modacrylics

Modacrylics have flameproof qualities, but are as yet only developed to a limited scale, and are mainly useful for garments that are likely to come into contact with fire.

6. Elastomerics

Also called elasto-fibers, these replace rubber for stretch fabrics. Mainly used for foundation garments and swimwear, elastomerics are based on polyurethane, derived from petroleum chemicals. They are always blended with other fibers, such as nylon or polyester. These produce strong, hard-wearing fabrics, light in weight and perspiration-resistant.

NONWOVEN FABRICS

All fabrics that have not been woven or knitted come under this heading. Both natural and synthetic raw material sources are used for their production. The oldest of these is *felt*, made from wool fibers, also from fur or mohair, or sometimes mixed with cotton or rayon. A web of short fibers, subjected to heat, moisture, friction, and pressure is held together by the interlocking of the scales of the fibers. The term "felting" is applied to the shrinkage of wool, which allows the making of felt from fibers without spinning or weaving. Simultaneously, of course, the characteristic shrinkage of wool offers the advantage of disposing extra fullness for shape when constructing garments, particularly in the case of tailored ones. The disadvantage of shrinkage of wool garments in washing is well known, but finishing processes alleviate this problem.

Other nonwoven fabrics include the *bonded* type from synthetic fibers, which have become particularly popular for interfacings. These are produced by bonding a prepared web of fibers with chemical agents, such as starch, glue, resin, and others, and compressing them into a flat sheet.

Thermoplastic fibers are also bonded by heat-setting—the fusing of fibers by application of heat. Two layers of fabric can also be bonded back to back, to form a single one for the following main reasons:

1. The inner layer of the fabric acts as a built-in lining for warmth and shape retention.
2. Two faced fabrics are bonded for reversibility.
3. Open-weave type fabrics are strengthened for ease in construction.

Foam Laminates are produced by bonding processes, building up a layer of fabric to a synthetic foam for thickness, extra strength, and insulation without increase in weight; they are especially used as coat interfacings, but are also found in dress goods.

The variety of thicknesses in all nonwoven fabrics is considerable and they can also be made in differing degrees of stiffness.

Strictly speaking, plastic materials, which include *vinyl*, are not fabrics, though they are generally accepted as such. They are made from plastic films, and not fibers. These films may remain unsupported or have a woven, knitted, or bonded backing added to them.

There has been an increased use of plastic in recent years. It has the advantages of being resistant to soiling and can be cared for and cleaned easily. Its recovery from creasing, high durability, waterproof qualities, and low cost have made this material popular for clothing too.

TEXTILE TERMS

The great majority of fabrics in common use are woven, which means that yarn strands are interlaced at right angles to one another. The many different ways in which this interlacing takes place, and the quality, structure, and color of the yarns used, determine the feel and performance as well as appearance of fabrics. Many more are knitted, a construction of the interlocking of loops of one or more yarns, and are either "circular" or "warp-knit." The use of one yarn makes a single-knit; two or more makes a doubleknit. Novelty knits can have tweed effects, looped and bouclé surfaces, lacy, crocheted, and open, fishnet appearances. Other fabrics still are bonded by chemical processes as previously described. The great variety available is further extended by numerous finishing processes.

In dressmaking, you will want to know something about the fabric you choose so that you can link its characteristic performance with the selected design to obtain the best from both. Even though the finer technical details of fabric constructions are not important to you, and can be quite confusing, a basic understanding of the main differences of materials can only be an advantage and help to achieve garments that are a great pleasure to wear.

Weaves

Dobby. Geometric designs woven by special looms; for example **Birds eye,** a twill weave forming a diamond pattern with small dots in the center resembling the bird's eye.

Gauze Leno. An open-effect weave, produced by the Leno loom for lightweight fabrics like **Gauze, Net.**

Jacquard. A loom with perforated patterns, which enables every individual thread to weave differently from all others in a given design. Thus intricate shapes of patterns can be produced as in **damask,** in which patterns stand out from the ground with a contrasting lustre.

Pile. A combination plain and twill weave, with an additional warp thread forming a loop on the surface. This is cut as in **velvet,** flattened as in **panne velvet,** or left uncut as the **terrycloth.**

Plain. This and the following two weaves are the basic methods used. The difference between them are the way the warp (lengthwise) threads cross the weft (crosswise) threads. In the plain weave, the weft yarn is passed over the warp yarn and under the next alternately. Closely woven, this is the strongest of all weaves. All others are variations of these three. The **basket weave** is one of them, using double yarns instead of single ones. This makes a loosely woven fabric that stretches easily. Plain-weave fabrics include **bastiste, broadcloth, cambric, lawn.**

Satin. Similar to the twill weave, but with longer gaps in the interlacing between warp and weft threads. The weft thread is passed under four or more warp threads and then over one. This helps to produce lustrous fabrics such as **satin sateen.**

Twill. The weft thread passes over and then under two or more warp threads and in so doing diagonal ribs are produced from left to right in fabrics such as **barathea, denim foulard, garbardine,** or variations as in **herringbone** and **dogtooth** patterns.

Textile Finishes and End Treatments

These are basically divided into three groups:

1. **Permanent.** Should last throughout the life of the fabric.
2. **Durable.** Should last through several times of washing or dry-cleaning.
3. **Nondurable.** Lasts only until first time of washing or cleaning.

Anti-static. A finish to reduce the effects of static electricity, slight shocks, and the tendency of the fabric to cling to the body (caused by friction of a fabric rubbing against itself or other objects).

Bleaching. The cleaning and whitening of "grey" fabrics. Natural fibers are off-white because of the impurities they contain. Cotton fabrics can easily be bleached, woolen ones less easily.

Bonding. The pressing of fibers or layers of fabric together with chemical substances.

Brushed. Fabrics in which loose fibers are raised to the surface.

Bulking. Fluffing up the surface of synthetic, mainly acrylic, fibers.

Colorfast. Refers to colors that do not change during the life of the fabric. They should not rub off, fade through washing, dry-cleaning, exposure to sunlight, perspiration, temperature, or ironing.

Crease-resistance. Treatment of fabrics, by the application of resin finish, reducing the tendency to crease, and allowing recovery from creasing when clothes are left to hang.

Drip-dry. Describes garments which, after washing, shed wrinkles and thus require little or no ironing.

Dyeing. The coloring of yarns or fabrics.

Embossing. The transfer of designs from heavy engraved rollers onto cloth.

Embroidery. Decorative needlework, of which there are many different types.

Flameproofing. Enables fabrics to resist fast burning if they catch fire.

Flocking. Application of patterns and designs to fabrics by adhesives.

Glazing. Produces high gloss and firm finish of fabrics.

Laminating. The joining of a fabric to a synthetic foam backing.

Mercerizing. A process that adds strength, produces lustrous sheen finish on some fabrics—e.g., cotton, sateen, chintz.

Mildew resistance. Achieved by a treatment that discourages the growth of bacteria. Mildew grows on and damages fabrics (not thermoplastic fibers), especially in periods of high humidity. Cotton, linen, and rayon fabrics without this finish should be kept particularly dry and clean.

Permanent press. The ability of garments to retain their shape through wear and washing, including pleats and creases deliberately put in during manufacture for fashion interest. Simultaneously, these garments have the ability to shed creases and wrinkles appearing in the course of wear. Fabrics before construction are **pre-cured,** a term that describes a chemical process at the finishing stage, which is similar to crease-resistance. Materials so treated are called **durable press. Post-cured** describes the pressing in of pleats or creases after the garment has been made and then called permanent press. Polyester is the most suitable fiber used for these processes.

Preshrunk. Refers to a process that keeps fabrics from shrinking more than 3 percent.

Sanforizing. A registered trade name of a controlled preshrinking process for cotton and color blends.

Shrinking. Obtaining a permanent contraction of fabrics by heat treatment.

Sizing. Producing a stiff effect by the use of starch. (This is not always permanent.)

Stain/Spot resistant.   A process that allows some spots or stains to be wiped off material.

Wash and wear.   A term to describe a number of treatments developed from crease-resistance processes. Wash and wear fabrics need little or no ironing after laundering, depending on the fibers used to make them, their construction, and the finish applied.

Waterproofing.   This is usually a process of applying a coating of rubber or plastic, such as Vinyl, to close all open spaces between yarns. Implies complete water-resistance.

Water repellent.   Not fully waterproofed, but penetration of water is reduced.

General Textile Terms

Abrasion.   The ability of a fiber to withstand rubbing or abrasion in everyday use. Nylon is most resistant to abrasion but wool, cotton, rayon, and acetate are less so.

Blending.   Natural or synthetic fibers or yarns mixed to combine their desirable qualities.

Carding.   The process of cleaning fibers in their raw state and separating them from one another.

Combing.   A continuation of the carding process which produces smoother and finer yarn.

Converting.   Any finishing process carried out after the basic fabric is made.

Cords/Ribs.   A distinct raised surface with pronounced sunken lines in between ribs. This is formed by heavier thread running lengthwise, crosswise, or diagonally (as in bedford cord—lengthwise; in broadcloth, poplin, ottoman—crosswise).

Color bleeding.   The running of color in water.

Crimping.   To "curl" synthetic fibers for elasticity by the use of chemicals and heat setting, or the shrinking of sections of the fabric.

Denier/Gauge.   The fineness of a synthetic yarn affected by weight. The lower the denier, the finer the yarn.

Elasticity.   The amount of "give" in a fabric when stretched, recovering to its original shape when released.

Fiber.   Basic substances of natural or synthetic origin used to make yarns. Staple ones are short, continuous filament and as the name implies, can be very long, as in silk or manufactured fibers.

Grey goods.   Fabrics before any processing takes place.

Handle.   The feel and touch of fabric.

Milling.   A shrinking process to produce a firmer fabric and to obscure the weave.

Nap.   Hairy fibers brought to the surface and either brushed or pressed flat to give a sheen. Napped fabrics reflect a different light in each direction, so all garment pieces must be cut with the nap in one direction only.

Piece dye.   Fabrics dyed after weaving or knitting.

Pile.   Fabrics woven with sets of looped yarns raised onto the surface.

Pilling.   The fluffing of wool and wool-like fabrics in wear.

Reversibles.   Refers to fabrics that can be used on either side. This is achieved by the bonding of two fabrics for extra weight and stability, or as an alternative to a lining. Contrasting woven or knitted sides can also be bonded for variety in color and/or texture for added interest.

Sheer fabrics.   The transparent quality, ranging from soft and light-weight chiffon, to semi-soft, voile, lawn, batiste, to crisper, organza, organdy, dimity.

Slubbed.   Use of uneven yarns (think or thick areas) in weaving, producing a rough effect on surfaces often found in fabrics such as dupion, shantung, or linen.

Teazling.   To raise the nap of a cloth by scrubbing it with the heads of the teazel plant, or with wire hooks.

Tensile strength.   The ability of yarn or fabric to withstand breakage by tension.

Thermoplastic.   Refers to fibers that can be softened by heat, and permanently shaped by heat-setting.

Texture.   The surface effect of cloth.

Warp.   Yarns running lengthwise in fabrics.

Weft.   Yarns running crosswise in fabrics.

Yarn.   Strands of spun fibers for weaving and knitting.

Yarn dye.   Yarns dyed before weaving or knitting.

Index